The Southwest Center Series

Ignaz Pfefferkorn, *Sonora: A Description of the Province*

Carl Lumholtz, *New Trails in Mexico*

Buford Pickens, *The Missions of Northern Sonora: A 1935 Field Documentation*

Gary Paul Nabhan, editor, *Counting Sheep: Twenty Ways of Seeing Desert Bighorn*

Eileen Oktavec, *Answered Prayers: Miracles and Milagros along the Border*

Curtis M. Hinsley and David R. Wilcox, editors, *Frank Hamilton Cushing and the Hemenway Southwestern Archaeological Expedition, 1886–1889*

VOLUME I: *The Southwest in the American Imagination: The Writings of Sylvester Baxter, 1881–1889*

VOLUME I

of the multivolume work

Frank Hamilton Cushing and the Hemenway Southwestern Archaeological Expedition, 1886–1889

The Southwest in the American Imagination

The Writings of Sylvester Baxter, 1881–1889

Edited by Curtis M. Hinsley
and David R. Wilcox

▼

The University of Arizona Press
Tucson

To Victoria and Susan

The University of Arizona Press

This book is printed on acid-free,
archival-quality paper.
Manufactured in the United States of America

01 00 99 98 97 96 6 5 4 3 2 1

Library of Congress Cataloging-in-Publication Data
appear on the last printed page of this book.

British Cataloguing-in-Publication Data
A catalogue record for this book is available from the
British Library.

Publication of this book was made possible in part
by a grant from the Southwest Center of the
University of Arizona.

Contents

Illustrations

Map

Figures

Foreword to the Multivolume Work

The Southwest Center is proud to include in its University of Arizona Press series Curtis Hinsley and David Wilcox's multivolume study *Frank Hamilton Cushing and the Hemenway Southwestern Archaeological Expedition, 1886–1889*. With this work, Hinsley and Wilcox have established—through ingenious documentary recovery, discerning textual selection, and trenchant interpretation—the history of the first major archaeological expedition into the Southwest. In doing so, they also lay the basis for a provocative new historiography of the region. This project of documentation and analysis by an archaeologist and an historian is a classic in the critical study of the Southwest, a monumental work that will serve as the foundation for a fresh understanding of the development of this region. It is, too, a model for the interdisciplinary scholarship that the field of regional studies, at its very best, can produce.

Hinsley and Wilcox have performed a signal service with their work in tracing the rise and fall of the Hemenway Expedition, the role of New England philanthropy in southwestern developments, the details of daily "archaeological camping" in the deserts of Arizona and New Mexico a century ago, and the social bases and cultural consequences of nineteenth-century archaeology. Above all, these are volumes of voices, recalling for us the drama of scientific and aesthetic discovery from a nearly forgotten time. *Frank Hamilton Cushing and the Hemenway Southwestern Archaeological Expedition* combines expedition documents long unavailable; carefully selected personal correspondence and diaries of expedition members and sponsors; a rich visual record of drawings, paintings, and photographs; and the editors' own searching interpretations—weaving all into a tapestry of narrative and commentary. The result is a social history of archaeology and anthropology in the Southwest that draws on contemporary cultural theory to paint a moving personal picture of southwestern pioneers, men and women who contributed to a new concept of the land and its human lineage.

Joseph C. Wilder, Director
The Southwest Center

Introduction to the Multivolume Work

In the fall of 1886, Mary Tileston Hemenway, reputedly the most munificent lady in Boston, agreed to sponsor the Hemenway Southwestern Archaeological Expedition under the direction of anthropologist Frank Hamilton Cushing.[1] Hemenway quietly supported many worthy causes, most of them concerned with education and American history, and she was intrigued by Cushing, his Zuñi experiences, and his vision for the future of American ethnology and archaeology. Together they dreamed of founding a private institution in Salem, Massachusetts, a Pueblo Museum for the study of American Indians. The artifact collections of the Hemenway Expedition were to form the nucleus of the museum. Accordingly, in late 1886 Hemenway appointed a board to oversee the project, and early the following year Cushing outfitted the expedition and took to the field in Arizona in high hopes of tracing the ancestors of the Zuñis and perhaps even solving larger puzzles of aboriginal migration through the Americas.

By the third year of fieldwork, Cushing's persistent illnesses; growing doubts among board members about his integrity, ideas, and even sanity; and Hemenway's own declining health led her son Augustus and the board of the expedition to act. In mid-1889 they fired Cushing and appointed Jesse Walter Fewkes to succeed him as director.[2] For two years Cushing withdrew into serious illness and depression. Without access to his records, in 1891 he nevertheless began a report, a retrospective daily "itinerary" of the expedition. Then, after two years of intermittent effort, in frustration and disappointment he turned wholly to other interests. He never returned to the Hemenway project or the Southwest, and he never again saw the artifact collections, field maps, catalogues, and other materials—or Mary Hemenway. The Pueblo Museum never materialized, and at her death in 1894 Hemenway willed the collections (most of which were in storage in Salem) to the Peabody Museum of Harvard University. Several fragmentary studies from the expedition found their way into print, but Cushing's notes and partial reports were still in manuscript form at his own sudden death at age forty-three in 1900.

Frederick Webb Hodge began his long anthropological career as Cushing's personal secretary on the expedition, and when he married Margaret Magill in 1891 he became Cushing's brother-in-law as well. By the mid-1890s Hodge had become a central figure in both the Smithsonian Institution and its Bureau of American Ethnology, rising to be the head of the BAE from 1910 to 1918. He then moved to George Heye's Museum of the American Indian in New York City (1918–1930) as editor and assistant to Heye and from there to the Southwest Museum in Los Angeles, which he directed until the year before his death, at age ninety-two, in 1956. Because of his institutional prominence and long life (he outlived all other expedition participants by at least two decades and Cushing by more than half a century) Hodge had a profound influence on the reputation of the Hemenway Expedition in the twentieth century.

In the 1930s Alfred Tozzer suggested to Emil W. Haury that he write his dissertation at Harvard on the Peabody Museum's Hemenway collections, and Haury produced a classic study of late Hohokam ceramics and material culture.[3] The only archival materials he had at hand, though, were those he found at Harvard and a few illustrations at the Brooklyn Museum. In the course of his research he wrote to Hodge at the Southwest Museum. Hodge responded that he had a "considerable body of Cushing's notes" but that they were "in much of a jumble."[4] He then proceeded, at some epistolary length, to accuse Cushing, his former brother-in-law, of faking an artifact, a turquoise-encrusted toad. Later, in his foreword to Haury's book *The Excavations of Los Muertos and Neighboring Ruins in the Salt River Valley, Southern Arizona* (1945), Hodge recounted more stories about Cushing that made light of him and his ideas, creating a strongly negative image. In Hodge's view, Cushing was "a visionary" who kept few notes, did not hesitate to exaggerate to gain a point, was a slacker, and suffered from "an overwrought imagination and a species of egotism that brooked no opinion adverse to his own."[5] Cushing, he further recalled, had "fiddled away his time in making flags for the tents and other useless trifles" at the expedition's campsites, leaving his field-workers without supervision for weeks at a time.[6] He further implied that if there were few archival remains of the Hemenway Expedition it was Cushing's fault. Haury understandably believed Hodge, and so have several generations of anthropologists, archaeologists, and historians.

Today's evidence about the expedition—its roots, practices, results, and reputation—suggests a complex and quite different story. A remarkably large unpublished record of the Hemenway Expedition did in fact survive—and Hodge, ironically, did much to preserve it. Soon after Cushing's death, his close friend Stewart Culin, curator at the Brooklyn Museum, obtained Cushing's personal library and manuscripts from his widow, Emily.[7] In 1921, at a time when his own interests were changing, Culin sent Hodge three crates of Cushing manuscripts, letter books, and related material.[8] Hodge apparently culled through this material, selecting what he thought was most interesting and depositing it at the library of the Heye Foundation at the Huntington Free Library in the Bronx. The rest of Cushing's material ("in much of a jumble") he took with him to California in 1930, where it eventually became part of the Southwest Museum's Hodge and Cushing collections.[9] In this way the major records of the Hemenway Expedition came to be distributed among the Peabody Museum of Harvard, the Huntington Free Library, the Brooklyn Museum, the Smithsonian Institution, and the Southwest Museum.

After Hodge's death, the Hemenway records that he had kept in his possession for thirty-five years were opened to scholars at the Southwest Museum. Ray Brandes constructed a pioneering 1965 dissertation on Cushing partly from these materials, and Charles Lange and his colleagues, in their multivolume study of Adolph F. Bandelier's years in the Southwest, drew significantly on them as well.[10] Joan Mark, in proposing Cushing as one of the critical figures in the history of American anthropology, recalled Claude Lévi-Strauss's praise for Cushing as a precursor of structuralism; and Jesse Green's annotated edition of Cushing's Zuñi writings, published in 1979, also brought his ethnographic work renewed professional and public attention.[11]

In short, with the increased interest in Cushing's place in the history of

American anthropology, students of anthropology and the nineteenth-century Southwest turned to the Hodge-Cushing materials and began to recognize their value and depth.[12] At the same time, other relevant documents surfaced, such as the Hemenway family archives at the Peabody/Essex Museum in Salem[13] and Cushing's personal diaries.[14] Still, the Hemenway Expedition remained obscure and puzzling, its meaning lost in the fragments.

Wilcox, an archaeologist, had had the opportunity in 1979 to excavate a large portion of a site in Tempe that Cushing, in 1887, had named La Ciudad de los Hornos (City of the Ovens).[15] Curious to learn what Cushing and his party had seen before the Salt River Valley was plowed or covered over by urban landscape, he, too, soon discovered the wealth of archival materials. At the Hayden Library of Arizona State University he discovered a copy of one installment of Cushing's Hemenway "itinerary," the original of which was at Harvard's Peabody Museum.[16] A friend told him of the Southwest Museum's holdings, and another, Gina Laczko, knew of the Hemenway materials archived at the Huntington Free Library in the Bronx. The richness of the Hodge-Cushing collection in Los Angeles astonished him, and he soon employed it for a report on the Casa Grande ruins, which Hemenway and Cushing had been instrumental in preserving.

After visiting other collections, by 1983 Wilcox could foresee the need for a multivolume work, and he began circulating a proposal. A few months later Raymond H. Thompson, director of the Arizona State Museum, in discussion with Lea S. McChesney of the Peabody Museum, discovered that Edwin L. Wade, Hinsley, and she were thinking along similar lines.[17]

A collaboration seemed natural, and in 1983 Wilcox, Hinsley, and McChesney met at the Peabody Museum. Over the next several years they continued to assemble and transcribe materials, with Wilcox being aided in part by a grant from the Agnese N. Lindley Foundation. Progress was slow, however. In 1988 Hinsley moved from upstate New York to Northern Arizona University in Flagstaff, while Wilcox became head of Anthropology at the Museum of Northern Arizona, also in Flagstaff. Soon thereafter, McChesney decided to pursue further graduate work in anthropology at New York University, examining the production and marketing of Hopi ceramics.

Our initial goal was to publish only Cushing's unfinished "itinerary," written in the early 1890s—his largest and most unusual unpublished work. In addition to its literary qualities, Cushing's narrative contains valuable and unique archaeological data of relevance to contemporary Hohokam studies.[18] But chance changed these plans. In 1991 Mary B. Davis, librarian at the Huntington Free Library, was inventorying the library's vault. Upon pulling down several books from a high, dusty shelf, she opened them to find, to her amazement, Cushing's distinctive handwriting. Closer inspection revealed that she had found nine letter books totaling more than 4,000 pages—virtually the entire official correspondence of the Hemenway Expedition, stored away by Hodge and forgotten for sixty years. Included were all of Cushing's letters to Mrs. Hemenway, correspondence with Sylvester Baxter, the secretary-treasurer of the expedition's board, communications with merchants in Phoenix, Tempe, and Albuquerque, and a wide assortment of other records, including Cushing's instructions to Hodge during the director's long periods of recuperation in California.

Wilcox inventoried the letter books, as well as Hemenway collections at other institutions, and began the enormous task of transcribing selected materials into a computer database. Before the letter books came to light, the Hemenway Expedition existed for us only through fascinating but widely scattered fragments. Now, with the correspondence as a core, the pieces formed a more coherent if still incomplete picture. The Hemenway Expedition puzzle began to make sense, but a larger number of volumes seemed necessary in order to tell the story in all its complexity. The projected multivolume work is the result: a cultural history of the Hemenway Expedition and early anthropology in the American Southwest, told in the voices of the participants and interpreted by us.

The Hemenway Expedition occupies several critical points in the history of North American anthropology and archaeology. Cushing hoped it would stand as a "rock of ages" for the study of New World prehistory. Despite the largely unpublished nature of its work, the expedition is widely recognized as the foundation of Hohokam studies and a critical base for research into Zuñi prehistory as well. Additionally, Cushing brilliantly anticipated modern strategies of multidisciplinary teamwork, with Bandelier as historian; Matthews, ten Kate, and Wortman as physical anthropologists; Margaret Magill as artist; Baxter as publicist; Hodge as secretary/amanuensis; and Cushing himself as linguist, ethnographer, and archaeologist. Most important, perhaps, Cushing's struggle to find a language—a scientific poetics—suitable to his experiential and observational methods reflected a wider struggle between intuitive understanding and disciplined knowledge that continued throughout the twentieth century.[19]

Critically positioned historically, the Hemenway Expedition promises to enlighten current debates over the development of touristic rhetoric and sensibilities in the Southwest, a region that by the 1930s—when Aldous Huxley identified it as the "rest-cure reservation" of his "brave new world"—was already among the most heavily encoded spaces in the global economy and imagination. Frank Cushing's expedition entered the Salt River Valley of central Arizona Territory only a few years after the Atlantic and Pacific Railroad (a subsidiary of the Atchison, Topeka and Santa Fe) completed its main line across northern New Mexico and Arizona en route to Los Angeles. During 1886, too, the last serious Native American armed resistance in the region ended, and local boosters and land speculators were already hastening to alter the territory's image from one of miners, deserts, and wild Indians to a vision of farmers, green orchards, and peaceful pueblos. These were the crucial early years of the dreaming and inventing of the Southwest and of its incorporation into the national imagination.

Through this process, a distinctive regional entity eventually emerged, based on its landscapes, natural resources, and human inhabitants, and appealing strongly to the wishes and projected desires of outsiders. Because the Southwest is an astoundingly rich archaeological field, but also because the acts of digging, removing, and displaying buried artifacts provide ready signs and objects of belonging and proprietary relationship to the land, archaeological exploration and collection came to be central in this cultural exercise of incorporating the Southwest.

Each of these considerations has its place in our project of reconstruction and interpretation. But we return always to the documents, the multilayered and multivocal testimony of a complex endeavor, an enterprise that was at once a scientific exploration, a poetic experience, a financial investment, and a set of convoluted human relationships. The stories and texts come to us on many levels: from Hodge's personal shorthand diary notations of his quiet "portrait" meetings with Margaret Magill under the mesquite trees to Cushing's 40-page letter to Mary Hemenway on the proposed museum; from quartermaster Charles Garlick's invoices for hay and beans to Cushing's stunning, visionary report to the Congress of Americanists in Berlin; from intimate accounts of nausea and delirium to soaring speeches about prehistoric hemispheric connections; and finally from the dreams of 1886 to the misery of sickness and a sense of failure less than three years later. Mistakes, misjudgments, and misunderstandings all played their roles in Mary Hemenway's expedition, to be sure; but so did love, jealousy, and pride. In the end, we argue, a deep conflict of values and aesthetics doomed the expedition in its own time. It is this conflict which must be fully explored and understood if the rich legacy of Mary Hemenway and Frank Cushing is finally to be realized today.

David R. Wilcox
Curtis M. Hinsley

Chronology of the Hemenway Expedition

Entries with an asterisk are for events discussed in this volume.

22 July 1857	Frank Hamilton Cushing is born in Erie County, Pennsylvania.
1875	Cushing joins the National Museum of the Smithsonian Institution under the tutelage of Assistant Secretary Spencer F. Baird.
July 1879	John Wesley Powell establishes the Bureau of Ethnology as a branch of the Smithsonian.
5 August 1879	Upon Secretary Baird's recommendation, and as a representative of the National Museum, Cushing leaves Washington, D.C., with Col. James Stevenson, Matilda Coxe Stevenson, and Jack Hillers for the Southwest.
19 September 1879	Cushing reaches Zuñi for the first time.
28 May 1881*	Sylvester Baxter and Willard Metcalf meet Cushing at Fort Wingate, N.M.
16 June 1881*	"Solved at Last" is published in the *Boston Herald*.

June 1882*	"Father of the Pueblos" is published in *Harper's Magazine.*
July 1882	Cushing is transferred to the Bureau of Ethnology payroll.
August 1882*	"An Aboriginal Pilgrimage" is published in *Century Magazine.*
11 December 1882*	"Logan's Land" is published in the *Boston Herald.*
17 March 1883*	"Zuñi Revisited" is published in the *American Architect and Building News.*
24 March 1884	Powell recalls Cushing to Washington due to political pressure from Senator John Logan, Republican candidate for vice president.
26 April 1884	Cushing leaves Zuñi, arriving in Washington on April 29.
13 January 1885	Cushing addresses the American Geographical Society on the Seven Cities of Cibola.
April 1885*	"Along the Rio Grande" is published in *Harper's Magazine.*
June 1885	Cushing goes home to Barre Center, N.Y., for recuperation.
September–November 1885	Cushing lives at Eben Horsford's summer place on Shelter Island.
ca. 9 November 1885	Cushing arrives at the home of Eben Horsford in Boston.
spring 1886	At Old Farm, Milford, Mass., Mary Hemenway suggests to Cushing that Zuñi priests come east during the summer to work with him.
June 1886	Herman ten Kate visits Cushing and Hemenway at Old Farm.
13 August 1886	Palowatiwa, Waihusiwa, and Heluta arrive at Manchester-by-the-Sea in Massachusetts, having left Zuñi 20 days before (July 25).
September 1886*	The idea of the Hemenway Expedition is proposed

	by Mary Hemenway. Sylvester Baxter is appointed secretary-treasurer of the expedition.
12 September 1886	Adolph Bandelier is invited to join the expedition as historian; he accepts on September 18.
12 November 1886	Cushing writes a "research design" for the expedition.
22 November 1886	Cushing meets with Major John Wesley Powell, who suggests he begin with a reconnaissance.
4 December 1886	Frederick Webb Hodge, newly engaged as field secretary (on 1 December) begins his Hemenway diary.
13 December 1886	Cushing, his wife Emily, his sister-in-law Margaret Magill, Hodge, and the three Zuñis leave Albion, N.Y., by train for the Southwest.
17 December 1886	Bandelier joins the Cushing party on the train at Lamy, N.M., and accompanies them to Albuquerque.
21 December 1886	Cushing and Hodge visit Zuñi in time for the winter solstice ceremonies.
14 January 1887	On her way to California, Mary Hemenway arrives in Albuquerque in her private railroad car and is met by Cushing, who accompanies her to Flagstaff.
January 1887	Charles A. Garlick joins the expedition as foreman.
20 January 1887	The Cushing party, joined by the Zuñi Indians Weta and Siwatitsailu, begins their reconnaissance, traveling by train to Prescott Junction, then south by wagon.
6 February 1887	Margaret Magill begins her Hemenway diary.
12 February 1887	Cushing party establishes Camp Augustus opposite Tempe in Arizona Territory.
21 February 1887	Excavations commence in Ciudad de los Pueblitos (Pueblo Grande), and they first visit Ciudad de los Hornos the next day.
27 February 1887	Cushing first visits Ciudad de los Muertos.
22 March 1887	A side camp is established at Los Muertos.
29 March 1887	At Cushing's request, Hodge begins a "synopsis of events" of the expedition.

1 April 1887	Hotel del Monte, near Monterey, Calif., burns while Mary Hemenway is staying there.
3 May 1887	The Great Sonora earthquake is felt at Camp Hemenway. Hodge and Garlick begin a reconnaissance trip west to the Gila River.
13 May 1887	Cushing party transfers to Camp Hemenway, near Los Muertos.
5 June 1887	Mary Hemenway arrives back in Boston from California.
17 June 1887	Fred and Margaret discover their love for one another.
3 July 1887	Maricopa and Phoenix Railroad construction is completed, connecting Tempe to the Southern Pacific Railroad.
7–8 August 1887	Cushing works on restoring the turquoise inlaid shell frog (or toad) fetish.
15 August 1887*	Baxter and John G. Bourke meet with Mary Hemenway about Cushing's illness.
1 September 1887	Dr. Washington Matthews arrives at Camp Hemenway.
9 September 1887	Cushing, Emily, and Margaret depart for California, returning to Camp Hemenway 14 September.
23 September 1887	Mary Hemenway pays $16,000 for land on Bachelor's Point in Salem, Mass., as a site for a Pueblo Museum and school.
26 September 1887	Cushing, Emily, and Margaret again depart for California, leaving Hodge and Garlick in charge of the field operations.
late October 1887	Cushing party travels by steamer to San Francisco.
18 November 1887	Dr. Herman ten Kate arrives in Tempe after passing through Boston on November 1.
25 November 1887	Dr. Jacob L. Wortman arrives in Camp Hemenway.
8 December 1887	Henry B. McDowell, associate editor of the *San Francisco Examiner,* arrives at Camp Hemenway to write a series of articles.

16 December 1887	Cushing party returns by steamer to San Diego.
22 December 1887	Cushing party arrives back at Camp Hemenway from San Diego.
27 December 1887	Wortman and McDowell go to El Paso to check out cave sites, returning on January 5.
29 December 1887*	Baxter leaves for the Southwest, arriving in Camp Hemenway on January 11, 1888.
13 January 1888	Ten Kate takes over operations at Camp Baxter (near Las Acequias).
2 February 1888	Bandelier arrives at Camp Hemenway for a council on 3 February.
ca. 25 February 1888	Edward P. Gaston arrives at Camp Hemenway.
6 March 1888	Ten Kate leaves on his reconnaissance to the Pimas and Papagos (Tohono O'odham).
16 March 1888	The photographer Percy Yates begins work.
20 March 1888	Don Eusebio Molera, from San Francisco, arrives at Camp Hemenway.
30 March 1888	Edward S. Morse arrives in Tempe.
4 April 1888*	Baxter finishes "The Old New World" at Camp Hemenway.
4–8 April 1888	A field trip by Cushing, Baxter, Morse, Wortman, Hodge, and others to Cave Creek and Las Canopas.
11 April 1888	Professor Morse leaves Camp Hemenway for Salem.
13 April 1888*	Baxter, Wortman, and party start on Florence reconnaissance.
15 April 1888*	"The Old New World" is published in the *Boston Herald*.
20 April 1888*	Baxter leaves Camp Hemenway for California, arriving in Boston on 22 May.
28 April 1888	Daniel Walter Lord arrives at Camp Hemenway.
5 May 1888	Ten Kate returns to Camp Hemenway from his reconnaissance to the Pimas and Papagos.

10 May 1888	Wortman departs Camp Hemenway, arriving in Washington on 7 August.
12 May 1888	The Hemenway collections from the Salt River Valley leave Tempe by train for Salem, Mass.
14 May 1888	Cushing, Emily, and Margaret leave for California, arriving at Hotel del Coronado on 16 May.
17 May 1888	Ten Kate begins a field trip to the Maricopas on the Verde River.
26 May 1888*	Baxter sends a petition to the commissioner of the General Land Office to set aside the Casa Grande ruins.
29 May 1888	Mary Hemenway engages the architect L. Edwin Tobey to build a museum and school building at the Bachelor's Point land in Salem.
4 June 1888	A field party leaves Camp Hemenway for Zuñi, passing through Flagstaff on 26 June and arriving at Zuñi on 13 July.
12 June 1888	Cushing, Emily, and Margaret arrive in San Francisco.
2 August 1888	Cushing, Emily, Margaret, and the photographer E. H. Husher reach Zuñi.
mid-August 1888	Excavations at Halonawan begin.
24 August 1888	Catalogue entries for Halonawan begin.
27 August 1888	Ten Kate leaves Camp Cibola for Salem, Mass.
September 1888*	Baxter and Morse represent the expedition at the International Congress of Americanists in Berlin, presenting papers by Cushing, Bandelier, and Wortman and ten Kate.
13 October 1888	Cushing, Bandelier, and Husher go to El Morro, near Zuñi.
20 October 1888	Last entries are made in the Halowan catalogue. Cushing and Emily leave for the East, leaving Garlick and Hodge in charge, and arrive in Boston on 27 October.
24 October 1888	A camp is established to excavate Hé-sho-ta-Ú-thla.
early December 1888	An overdraft of the Hemenway account is reported by the Bank of Albuquerque.

9 December 1888	Husher and Hodge depart for central Mexico; they see Teotihuacan in late December.
14 December 1888	Last entries are made in the Hé-sho-ta-Ú-thla catalogue.
20 December 1888	Edward Gaston, who had been keeping the catalogue, resigns and returns home to Lacon, Ill.
late December 1888*	Baxter is dismissed as secretary-treasurer of the Hemenway board and is replaced by Katherine Stone.
5 January 1889*	The first installment of "Archaeological Camping in Arizona" is published in the *American Architect and Building News* (others are published 12, 19, 26 January; 31 August; and 14 September 1889).
ca. 18 January 1889	Cushing goes to Washington to lobby for preservation of the Casa Grande ruin.
late January 1889	The camp at Hé-sho-ta-Ú-thla is shut down.
mid-March 1889	E. H. Husher leaves Camp Cibola for San Francisco.
31 March 1889	Cushing replies to Hodge's letter of resignation.
ca. 10 May 1889	Jesse Walter Fewkes is appointed to the Hemenway Expedition board, replacing the recently deceased Martha LeBaron Goddard.
mid-May, 1889	Daniel Lord leaves Camp Cibola for the East.
15 June 1889	Augustus Hemenway dismisses Cushing as director of the expedition. Fewkes is appointed to replace him.
mid-June 1889	Cushing and Emily leave Garfield Hospital in Washington for Albion and later Barre Center, N.Y.
summer 1889	Fewkes visits the Zuñi region.
July 1889	Hodge joins the Bureau of Ethnology as an assistant ethnologist.
October 1889	Garlick sends Cushing a box of manuscript material and informs him that the Hemenways are trying to sell his house at Zuñi.
20 February 1890	Cushing reports to Dr. Matthews that he has finally expelled the last tapeworm, pickling it in alcohol.

ca. 15 April 1890	Mary E. Dewey is appointed to the Hemenway Expedition board.
summer 1890	Fewkes again visits the Zuñi region.
15 December 1890	Cushing delivers a lecture to the Buffalo Academy of Sciences.
January 1891	Cushing works on the Hemenway Expedition journal, a day-by-day itinerary.
May 1891	Fewkes edits the first volume of the *Journal of American Ethnology and Archaeology* on the Hemenway Expedition.
12 June 1891	Cushing sets out conditions to William T. Harris for continuing to write up his expedition work for Mary Hemenway.
31 August 1891	Fred and Margaret are married.
December 1891	Fewkes abandons the Zuñi field for Hopi.
January 1892	Cushing works intensively on the itinerary, with Hodge as his typist.
1 February 1892	Cushing accepts a position at the Bureau of Ethnology as an assistant ethnologist.
6 March 1892	Cushings rent a house in Georgetown at 1506 30th Street.
18 August 1892	Cushing turns over first installment of the itinerary to Dr. Harris and then goes to Albion, N.Y. He also attends the American Association for the Advancement of Science meetings in Rochester.
ca. 5 September 1892	Harris, Mary Hemenway, and Katherine Stone read the first installment of Cushing's "Itinerary." Harris tells Cushing it is "wonderful."
19 October 1892*	Baxter warns Cushing not to trust J. Walter Fewkes.
17 February 1893	Cushing begins dictating another installment of the itinerary to Hodge.
25 February 1893	Cushing meets Stewart Culin for the first time.
18 March 1893	Hodge claims proprietary rights to his diary and his "synopsis of events."

5 April 1893	Hodge gives Cushing a copy of his irrigation paper, published in the *American Anthropologist* later in 1893.
13 May 1893	Cushing is informed by Dr. Harris that Augustus Hemenway, as his mother's trustee, refuses to pay him for his work on the itinerary.
26 June 1893	Cushing and Emily leave Washington for the Chicago World's Fair. Emily returns on 26 August, Cushing on 11 September, to a rented home at 1610 13th Street.
6 March 1894	Mary Hemenway dies from diabetes in Boston.
6 April 1897	Frederick Putnam, in cooperation with Major Powell, proposes a method of completing the report on the Hemenway Expedition. Augustus Hemenway rejects it.
10 April 1900	Cushing dies from complications three days after swallowing a fish bone.

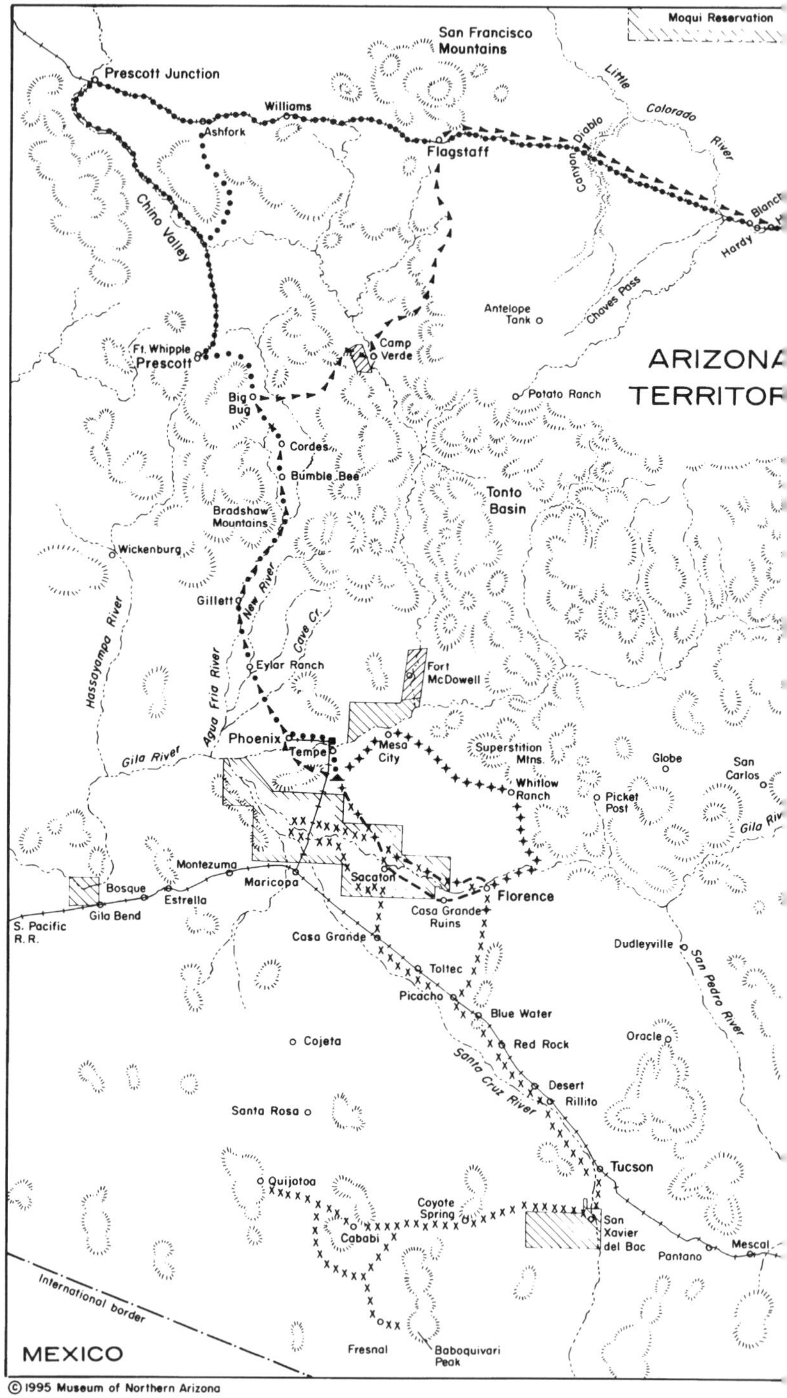

Routes of principal reconnaissances conducted during the Hemenway Expedition in the Southwest, 1886–1889. *(Map by Jody Griffith, Museum of Northern Arizona)*

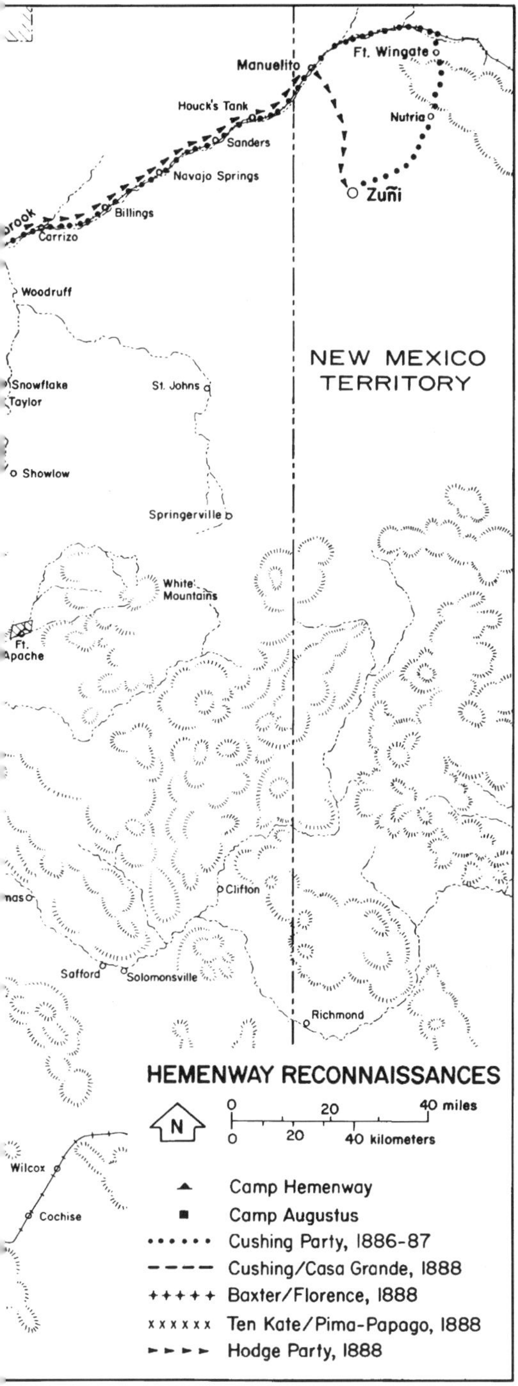

Manuelito
Ft. Wingate
Houck's Tank
Nutria
Sanders
Navajo Springs
Zuñi
Billings
Carrizo
Woodruff
NEW MEXICO TERRITORY
Snowflake
Taylor
St. Johns
Showlow
Springerville
White Mountains
Ft. Apache
Clifton
Safford
Solomonsville
Richmond
Wilcox
Cochise
HEMENWAY RECONNAISSANCES
N
0 20 40 miles
0 20 40 kilometers
Camp Hemenway
Camp Augustus
Cushing Party, 1886-87
Cushing/Casa Grande, 1888
Baxter/Florence, 1888
Ten Kate/Pima-Papago, 1888
Hodge Party, 1888

Preface to Volume 1

This volume presents the southwestern writings of Sylvester Baxter, a journalist who became Cushing's friend and publicist in the early 1880s. As Cushing's man on the Hemenway board, Baxter acted quite effectively for more than a year, running interference for Cushing with Mary Hemenway and other members of the board. However, increasingly critical questions began to be raised about the results of the work, accelerating in late 1887 once Cushing had to go to California for his health. Hoping to quell these criticisms, at the beginning of 1888 Baxter traveled to the Southwest, where he spent several months in "archaeological camping in Arizona" with Cushing. He then wrote a serialized account of this experience for the *American Architect and Building News* and a popular introduction to the work of the expedition ("The Old New World"). Later in 1888, Baxter joined the distinguished natural scientist Edward S. Morse in representing the Hemenway Expedition at the International Congress of Americanists in Berlin. Shortly after he returned, however, he was dismissed as secretary-treasurer, with an overdraft at the Albuquerque Bank being the proximate cause. That event also marked the beginning of the worst year in Frank Cushing's life, when an infestation of tapeworm brought him near death and he was dismissed as director of the Hemenway Expedition. Through it all, Sylvester

Baxter remained his friend, providing him moral support and heartfelt advice. To the end of his life, Baxter would remember his time with Cushing as "great days."

The first essay provides an account of Sylvester Baxter's life and his relationship to Cushing. We analyze his role as Cushing's publicist to reveal the sources of resonance between them, and we examine the quality of nostalgia they both felt for the southwestern deserts at the very moment that the region was first experiencing the impact of industrial America. In the closing essay, we inquire further into the lasting implications of that feeling for the "invention of the Southwest," arguing that this aesthetic was central to the emergence and development of southwestern archaeology—and vice versa.

The original writings framed by these essays are all Baxter's. We have divided them into two parts: (1) the early writings about Cushing and the Southwest, 1881–83; and (2) his published accounts of the Hemenway Expedition and its scientific promise, 1888–89. Subsequent volumes in the work will reveal what became of that promise, suggest what might have been lost in the conflicts that destroyed it, and demonstrate, we hope, how much of it can yet be realized.

Curtis M. Hinsley
David R. Wilcox

Acknowledgments

The debts of a decade run deep. Lea S. McChesney and Raymond H. Thompson initially facilitated our collaboration and have remained supportive ever since. For financial support we are grateful to the National Science Foundation, the Colgate University Research Council, the Organized Research Council of Northern Arizona University, the Southwest Center at the University of Arizona, and especially Agnese N. Haury for a sponsoring grant to the Museum of Northern Arizona.

This project owes its fulfillment (more than most, we suspect) to the patience, persistence, and remarkable resourcefulness of directors, librarians, and archivists at numerous institutions. At the Huntington Free Library, Mary B. Davis and her staff have been unfailingly enthusiastic and cooperative. We are deeply grateful to her. At the Southwest Museum, librarians Daniela Moneta and Kim Walters responded kindly to repeated requests. At the Peabody Museum of Archaeology and Ethnology, Harvard University, the list has grown long over time: Directors C. C. Lamberg-Karlovsky, Stephen Williams, and David Pilbeam; Melissa Banta, Barbara Isaac, and Martha Labell; Vicky Swerdlow, Gloria Greis, Beth Sanager, and Kathy Skelly. At the Brooklyn Museum, Diana Fane, Deirdre

Lawrence, and Ira Jacknis (now at the Phoebe A. Hearst Museum of Anthropology at Berkeley) provided access and information about the Cushing-Culin collections. At the Peabody/Essex Museum of Salem, John Koza, director of the Stephen Philips Library, and Will Lamoy assisted our investigation of their Hemenway and Morse collections. Other institutions and individuals who aided us include Jim Gallagher at the George H. Beebe Communication Reference Library, Boston University; Denison Beach at the Houghton Library, Harvard University; Karen Kearns at the Manuscript Department of the Henry E. Huntington Library; Michael Plunkitt of Special Collections, Alderman Library, University of Virginia; Jean Condito of Sturgis Library, Barnstable, Massachusetts; Patricia W. Fisher of the Library and Learning Resource Center, Cape Cod Community College, West Barnstable, Massachusetts; Jill Triplett of Special Collections and Wilma Slate of the Wellesley College Archives, Margaret Clapp Library, Wellesley College; Ernest Emrich and James H. Hutson of the Manuscripts Division, Library of Congress; Martha Clevenger, archivist at the Missouri Historical Society; Stephen Z. Nonack and Catharina Slautterback of the Boston Athenæum; Daniel J. Linke, Mudd Manuscript Library, Princeton University; Scott Solliday and others at the Tempe Historical Society Museum, Tempe, Arizona; the staff of the Department of Archives and Public Records, State of Arizona, Phoenix; the staff of the Arizona Historical Foundation and Arizona Room, Hayden Library, Arizona State University, Tempe; and the staff of Special Collections, Cline Library, Northern Arizona University.

For help with locating, identifying, and producing illustrations, we thank Jodi Griffith, Museum of Northern Arizona Exhibits Department, who produced the map of Hemenway reconnaissances; Paula Fleming of the National Anthropological Archives, Smithsonian Institution; and Dan Boone, Bilby Research Center, Northern Arizona University. Special thanks for last-minute help to the audiovisual staff at the Oberlin College Library and to Richard Arenstrup of Hyannis, Massachusetts.

We are especially thankful for the friendship and assistance of Ellie Reichlin, Jesse Green, Pieter Hovens, Jerry B. Howard, Keith Kintigh, Lea McChesney, Judy Brunson, Roger Anyon, Bill Sturtevant, and Ed Lurie. For reading and criticizing seemingly endless drafts, thanks also to Jesse Green, Don Fowler, Edmund Ladd, Nancy Parezo, Ray Thompson, Keith Kintigh, and Richard Woodbury.

Christine Szuter at the University of Arizona Press has from the beginning been both visionary and sensible about what this work should be. Alan Schroder seemed to sense from the outset the tone and style we sought. Joe Wilder, director of the Southwest Center of the University of Arizona, has proven to be a magnificent and magnanimous supporter for both finances and morale. His faith in our ability has meant a great deal.

A Selected Bibliography of Sylvester Baxter's Southwestern Writings, 1881–1901

1881

"Solved at Last: Mysteries of Ancient Aztec History Unveiled by an Explorer from the Smithsonian Institution; Wonderful Achievements of Frank H. Cushing." *Boston Herald,* June 16.

"Indian Questions: Some More Facts about Agency Corruptions; Official Misdeeds the Cause of Great Wrongs; The Management Needed for the Indians." *Boston Herald,* June 26.

"Around Santa Fe: The Natural Attractions as a Summer Resort; A Visit to the San Pedro Mines; The Largest Mining Operations in New Mexico." *Boston Herald,* June 29.

"Rambles in the Rockies: A Picturesque Trip from Cimarron to Taos; A Gold-Mining Town in Its Decay; Some Romantic Scraps of New Mexican History." *Boston Herald,* July 10.

"Our Neighbor's Portal: El Paso as a Juvenile Great Railroad Centre; The Mexican Central's Northern Beginning; Progress of the Trans-continental Railroads." *Boston Herald,* July 17.

1882

"The Father of the Pueblos." *Harper's New Monthly Magazine* 65:72–91.

"An Aboriginal Pilgrimage." *Century Illustrated Monthly Magazine* 24 (n.s. 2) (August): 526–36.

"F. H. Cushing at Zuni." *American Architect and Building News* 11 (February 4): 56–57.

"Some Results of Mr. Cushing's Visit." *American Architect and Building News* 11 (April 29): 195–96.

"The Tenacity of Indian Customs." *American Architect and Building News* 12 (October 21): 195–97.

"Logan's Land?" *Boston Herald,* 11 December.

1883

"Zuñi Revisited." *American Architect and Building News* 13 (March 17): 124–26.

1885

"A Winter in Sonora." *Outing and the Wheelman Magazine* 5 (March): 403–13.

"Along the Rio Grande." *Harper's New Monthly Magazine* 70 (April): 687–700.

"The Eucalyptus Tree." *Mexican Financier and Weekly Herald,* pp. 221–23, 235–37, 244–45.

1888

The Old New World: An Account of the Explorations of the Hemenway Southwestern Archaeological Expedition in 1887–88, under the Direction of Frank Hamilton Cushing. Salem, Mass: Salem Press. Reprinted from the *Boston Herald,* April 15, 1888.

"Mr. Cushing's Discovery of Buried Cities in the Gila River Valley." *American Architect and Building News* 23 (January 7): 1.

Review of the *Fourth Annual Report of the Bureau of Ethnology—III: Frank Hamilton Cushing on Pueblo Pottery and Zuni Cultural Growth*. *American Architect and Building News* 23 (February 11): 66–68.

1889

"Archaeological Camping in Arizona." *American Architect and Building News* 25 (January 5, 12, 19, 26): 8–10, 15–16, 32–34, 43–44; 26 (August 31, September 14): 101–2, 120–22.

1891

"An Indian Fair in the Mexican Hot Country." *Harper's New Monthly Magazine* 84 (October): 757–71.

The Cruise of a Land-Yacht. Boston: Authors' Mutual Publishing Company.

1900

"Obituary Notice of Frank H. Cushing." *American Architect and Building News* 18 (28 April): 26.

1901

Spanish-Colonial Architecture in Mexico. 10 vols. Boston: J. B. Millett.

PART I

Introduction

Boston Meets the Southwest

The World of Frank Hamilton Cushing and Sylvester Baxter

Curtis M. Hinsley

On 5 March 1887, Frank Hamilton Cushing wrote in a confident mood from Camp Augustus, near Tempe, Arizona, to his friend Sylvester Baxter in Boston that the fieldwork then getting underway for the Hemenway Southwestern Archaeological Expedition would serve as the basis of future work in southwestern archaeology. "Given such a solid foundation," Cushing exulted, "it is the rock of ages, and even if left exposed to the storms of neglect and to the changeful seasons of interest, must always prove of value as the foundation of something good and great."[1] Cushing's hopes and fears proved prophetic. Two years later, disgusted with the collapse of the expedition, Adolph Bandelier expostulated to Charles Eliot Norton: "The Lord preserve me from scientific enterprises patronized by old women."[2] Mary Hemenway died in 1894; Cushing, six years later. By the turn of the century, their enterprise had generally come to be considered a scientific failure—"a cruel disappointment to Mrs. Hemenway," the "crash of doom" to Cushing, "a scattered and uncoordinated wreckage" for anthropology.[3] Frederick Webb Hodge, the expedition's secretary and Cushing's brother-in-law, sealed the general interpretation at various points in his long and influential life, giving the impression to archaeologist Emil Haury, among others, that Cushing kept minimal field notes and produced largely "bunk."[4]

Now, a century later, we are experiencing a renewed interest in and a clearer understanding of Mary Hemenway's intentions and Frank Cushing's visionary efforts. Having reconstructed the dispersed archival and artifactual record of the Hemenway Expedition, our concern is not to judge success or failure but to inquire into those categories; to embed this remarkable enterprise in its multiple personal and historical contexts; to permit its many narrative voices to speak as fully as possible; and to reach beyond the "storms of neglect" for an understanding of the expedition's significance for the history of archaeology and American culture. As Charles F. Lummis editorialized in 1900, the Hemenway Expedition was "an affair which may invite scientific criticism, but certainly merits comprehension."[5]

The story, a dialogue between regions, begins properly in Boston. In the spring of 1882, Cushing brought a group of Zuñi Indians to the city. The visit was effectively publicized by Sylvester Baxter (a journalist for the *Boston Herald* who had met Cushing in New Mexico the preceding year), and it aroused considerable interest in the Indian Southwest and Cushing's work at Zuñi pueblo—particularly among a prominent circle of reform-minded citizens that revolved around Reverend Edward Everett Hale and that included Mary Tileston Hemenway. Personally fascinated by the region, the Indians, and Cushing himself, Baxter kept all of them in the local public eye over the next several years through articles in the *Herald,* the *American Architect and Building News, Harper's, Scribner's,* and elsewhere. It would be too much to claim that Baxter single-handedly shaped the public's image of the American Southwest beginning to form in the 1880s. Most of his writing had relatively limited circulation, and many other voices, from land speculators to politicians, vied for attention. Still, his remarkable writings did serve to introduce the region to a national audience from aesthetic perspectives that would ultimately bear directly on the social and economic development of the Southwest. Furthermore, Baxter's concern, through Cushing, with ethnography and prehistory as central elements in the meaning of the Southwest for the nation permanently contributed to the cultural construction of the region.

Baxter's Southwest was in many respects the region as seen through Cushing's eyes and purposes—but not entirely. As explained below, Baxter came to New Mexico and Arizona with purposes and projections of his own, and between the two young men the influence was mutual. Over a decade their relationship changed, and so did the southwestern world they loved, in ways that alternately excited and saddened them both. The representations they created were eventually elaborated by the following generation—Edgar Lee Hewett, Mary Austin, and Willa Cather among them—just as theirs was, in turn, by the next. But the 1880s were the years of initial shaping. Baxter stood with Cushing and the Zuñis in the midst of that process.

Sylvester Baxter: Boston Journalist

Although he lived most of his long life (1850–1927) in the North Boston suburb of Malden, Sylvester Baxter always considered himself a "son of the Cape." Cape Cod—"everything southeast of Boston," as far as Baxter's ancestors were concerned[6]—had been the home of six generations of Baxters. Thomas Baxter (1653–1713) arrived in Yarmouth, a fishing port on Nantucket Sound, from Scotland sometime in the middle years of the seventeenth century and married the widow Temperance Gorham Sturges in 1679. Their son John and his wife, Desire Gorham, produced twelve children, thereby solidly establishing the Baxter clan of Cape Cod. Succeeding generations proved equally prolific, and through colony, revolution, and early nationhood the seafaring Baxters of Yarmouth prospered.

The elder Sylvester (Baker) Baxter, born in 1799, was the fourth of eleven children. "Captain Baxter" was, according to his son, an "old deep-sea shipmaster" who along with several brothers was a "considerable ship-owner." "Their properties," Sylvester recalled, "were usually square-riggers, ships and barks, in foreign trade." Looking back from 1920 he remembered little of his father, but he did emphasize the captain's devotion to Freemasonry in the 1850s: "He was the first master of Fraternal Lodge when it was reorganized after long inactivity in consequence of the anti-Masonic agitation, and transferred from Barnstable Village across the Cape to Hyannis. He was the first high priest of Orient Chapter of Hyannis. Sylvester Baxter Chapter of West Harwich was named in his honor. He was a prominent member of Boston Encampment (now Commandery) of Knight Templars."[7]

Captain Baxter married three times, the final marriage occurring in 1841 to Rosella Ford of Hyannis, who traced her lineage directly to the Mayflower. The younger Sylvester was born of this marriage in 1850. The following year his father undertook his final voyage, and in 1861 he died, leaving his wife, eleven-year-old Sylvester, and two younger sisters.[8] Rosella Ford Baxter (1815–1905) survived her husband by more than four decades, raised their three children, moved from the Cape to Malden, and lived to be ninety. The daughter of Oliver Ford, a Yarmouth physician,[9] she had been born in Barnstable, where she taught school and raised the children until moving to Boston in 1871. There she set up house on Murray Hill Road in Malden. The Murray Hill home became the Baxter homestead. From here she pursued an active civic career in Boston women's literary and cultural circles as a founder of the Writing Club of Malden. On the centennial of her birth, Sylvester honored the memory of his mother with a literary get-together at the Murray Hill home.[10] On his own death he established a book fund in her name at the Hyannis Free Library, of which she had been the founder and first president.[11]

Baxter attended a variety of public and private schools on the Cape until he was seventeen. In 1871 he moved to Chelsea, a northern suburb of metropolitan Boston adjacent to Malden (and close to his mother and sisters). After brief experiments with various jobs, Baxter began a career in the exciting new post–Civil War world of American journalism as a "suburban reporter," along with his lifelong friend, Edward Page Mitchell (later the editor of the *New York Sun*).[12] In 1871, Baxter remembered, "Mitchell and I had started almost together as reporters on the [Boston] Advertiser. We shared the same bed in a hall bedroom on Bullfinch Street."[13]

Boston in the Gilded Age was a city undergoing rapid demographic and political change, with rampant political corruption and seemingly chaotic, unmanageable expansion. Historians and literary critics have not been kind to this period of American history, especially its ugly urban aspects. "By the time the war was over," Lewis Mumford wrote of American aesthetics of the period, "browns had spread everywhere: mediocre drabs, dingy chocolate browns, sooty browns that merged into black. Autumn had come."[14] Edwin D. Mead, remembering fifty years in Boston in 1932, placed the break between a "period of great distinction and a period of mediocrity" at around 1868.[15] Whatever these decades may have seemed like through the eyes of intellectuals looking back from the early twentieth century, Baxter and his contemporaries on the competitive daily newspapers of Boston experienced life differently. Like a subsequent generation of city newspaper reporters who became the muckrakers of the Progressive era—Lincoln Steffens, Ida Tarbell, Ray Stannard Baker, Charles Edward

Russell—they experienced the cities of their youth as exciting sources of raw material for an increasingly realistic journalism.

Mitchell, recalling his early days as a cub reporter with Baxter on the *Advertiser,* described the urban excitement: "The bells clanged the alarm and indicated for all who cared to listen the locality of the conflagration. A second alarm signified a disaster requiring the personal attendance of one or other of us, and sent him plunging down the stairs into the alleyway between Court Street and Cornhill, in the footsteps of Benjamin Franklin—for it was exactly here that Franklin learned the printer's trade—and scurrying thence by the best available means of transportation to the scene of combustion, whether it was right around the corner or in East Boston or South."[16] For his part, Baxter recalled those years in the third person and with evident fondness: "Here he remained from early 1871 till 1875, engaged in general reporting together with occasional editorial activities. Under Delano A. Goddard the 'Daily', as it was called on the street in those days, maintained the traditions established by Nathan Hale in its rigid insistence upon good English in its columns. So for the young reporter, with the associations acquired in the course of his duties, life was almost the equivalent of a liberal education."[17]

In 1875, when he was twenty-five, Baxter joined the flow of young American men going to Germany for higher education. Like the Grand Tour of an earlier time, it seemed obligatory, given the lack of systematic graduate study in the American university system. Consequently, in the 1870s Americans at the universities of Berlin and Leipzig—where Baxter enrolled for two years—"outnumbered all other foreigners put together."[18] During his *Wanderjahre,* Baxter attended concerts and operas, including the Wagner festival at Beyreuth, and traveled widely and cheaply while serving as special correspondent to the *Advertiser.*[19] It also appears that in Leipzig he made the acquaintance of Edwin Mead, who later guided Mary Hemenway's philanthropic activities regarding the Old South Meeting House, citizenship, and the Boston public schools.[20]

Baxter returned to Boston in the summer of 1878, "feeling himself a better and more devoted American than ever," he later wrote.[21] Four decades later, in the tense months surrounding the Treaty of Versailles at the close of World War I—when American attitudes toward German thought and culture were far less positive—Baxter publicly defended his call for generosity toward Germany by recalling: "Many years ago, when I returned from student days in Germany, I felt myself more an American than ever, glad to be among my own people and

1875

1885

1889

1887

Photographic portraits of Sylvester Baxter. (Courtesy of Richard Arenstrop, Hyannis, Massachusetts)

desiring to apply whatever of good I had learned to the betterment of my native land, so far as one individual might do. I think that in certain ways that desire has been of account."[22]

By the time Baxter had returned to Boston and begun his twenty-five-year career with the *Herald,* he had received, through his early years with the *Advertiser* and his European travels, a liberal education in the condition of modern civilization and a sense of personal obligation for its maintenance and improvement. That education, and the principles he carried through the rest of his journalistic and civic life, were deeply influenced by the models of social reform to which he was exposed in Boston. Already displaying signs of serious commitment to municipal reform and regional development, Baxter now returned to a city in which the gap between gentility and real political power was felt with increasing concern.[23] The situation spawned numerous attempts to assert moral rather than directly political guidance in an increasingly pluralistic, democratic, and seemingly unmanageable city. From the viewpoint of some Boston social and intellectual circles, the fabric of New England culture seemed to be visibly fraying, and only men and women of courage and energy might prevent further shredding. In their efforts to hold society together, education seemed central: the education of leaders, preferably at Harvard, and the improvement of the general public through schools, museums, and other institutions. Theodore Lyman provided one Brahmanic expression of concern to his brother-in-law, Alexander Agassiz, in 1873: "Just now there is a tidal stream of commercial life which sweeps into itself all the energy and talent of the United States—only here and there is it resisted by men of peculiar temperament or peculiar genius. The state of mind thus induced is so incompatible with that of scientific thought that, when men of success, or through exhaustion, leave commercial enterprise, they are incapable even of conceiving what science is and mistake it—when they try to understand it—for something that will lead to preserved beef, or patent washing fluids."[24]

Whether the immediate subject was science or art, the ultimate concern of such observers lay with the moral state of society. As Neil Harris has noted about the board of directors of the Boston Museum of Fine Arts of the period, "this was not a group of idle aristocrats or newly rich entrepreneurs intent on raising their social status through a connection with the fine arts."[25] Rather, they were earnest and concerned groups for whom Western civilization was a product of hard work and inspired genius, and for whom the burden of public enlightenment was tangible and serious. It was an obligation that offered the surest route to peaceful, gradual improvement in community and nation. Arguing to Harvard president Charles W. Eliot in 1874 for the creation of a Harvard professorship in the history and literature of the fine arts, Charles Eliot Norton expressed the educational vision of his influential circle:

> Deprived as we are of the high & constant source of cultivation found in the presence of the great works of past ages, there is the greater need that we should use every means in our power to make up for the loss of this influence upon our youth, and give to them so far as possible some knowledge of the place these works hold in history, and of the principles of life & character which they illustrate. We need to quicken the sense of connection between the present generation and the past; to develop the conviction that culture is but the name for that inheritance, alike material and moral, that we have received from our predecessors, and which we are to transmit, with such additions as we can make to it, to our successors.[26]

Or, as Theodore Lyman also advised Eliot somewhat less loftily: "A young and learned man, who yet has . . . no belief that one thing is really *better* than another, is one of the most dismal spectacles conceivable." Such a generation, he advised, would drift the country "Devilward." [27]

On spiritual and social matters, Baxter's own reform circle revolved around Edward Everett Hale. Hale's family had founded and still owned the *Advertiser,* he regularly appeared in its offices during Baxter's tenure there, and he advocated a genteel gospel of self-improvement, literacy, and uplift, speaking from his various pulpits: the Old South Congregational Church, his *Old and New* magazine (1870–75), his "Ten Times One Is Ten" clubs, and the meetings of the Twentieth Century Club, founded "to promote a finer public spirit and better social order."[28] Indeed, Hale seemed to his acquaintances to be a veritable dynamo of optimism and human possibility. Under the Hale family's editorship, the *Advertiser* enjoyed a clear, respectable profile: "Not only of the culture of Harvard, but also of Boston's commercial greatness, Boston's political conservatism, and Boston's social propriety was the old *Advertiser* considered to be the leading newspaper exponent," recalled Edward Page Mitchell. "The magnates of State and Devonshire Streets and the chosen of Beacon Hill and the Back Bay were visitors to the room of its chief editor, Mr. D. A. Goddard."[29]

Hale was, by 1880, America's premier preacher of optimism and uplift. Like

Baxter, the minister of Old South was a genealogical and spiritual descendant of the original Massachusetts migration. Not surprisingly, he saw American history as a vast pageant, a divine plan for the redemptive transfer of the North American continent from savage and Catholic hands to the stewardship of civilized Protestantism. As a young man he had read documents for the nearly blind William Hickling Prescott and hoped to follow the historian's model by devoting his life to demonstrating the manifest purposes of American history. But Hale's path took him instead to Harvard, newspaper work, the ministry, civic affairs, and aphoristic literature.[30] After a decade in the pulpit at Worcester, in 1856 he came home to Boston and Old South. There he remained into the twentieth century, revered as a guardian of American morals and in some eyes the "dean of literary Boston."[31] By the time of Baxter's return from Germany in the late seventies, as Hale was approaching his sixtieth year and the end of active preaching, the minister was also returning to the interests of his youth: the history of New Spain and the meaning of the conquest of Mexico and the American Southwest.

Boston financial interests became increasingly conscious of railroad developments beyond the Mississippi as, in the decade after the Civil War, the course of the American commercial empire pointed southwesterly: to Arizona, New Mexico, and across the border to Mexico.[32] Accordingly, in this period the image of Arizona Territory changed from one of barbarism and crudeness to visions of peaceful agricultural settlement. "We have in the history of Arizona, a series of questions of the first interest and importance," Hale exhorted an audience in 1878. Silver, the railroad, and firm democratic government, he predicted, would soon release the great wealth of the Southwest for national economic purposes: "with the introduction of the Railway . . . and with that firm government which belongs to the same order of civilization as the Railway," silver would be so abundant that it would arrive in the East as third-class mail. In other words, natural resources, technology, and enlightened political structures, undergirded by divine providence, would assure America's destiny in the Southwest. The future prominence of the region would repay study and attention, even the effort of a personal visit by investors: "Gentlemen who have a few weeks of leisure, may well remember that in a fort-night a traveller may now go from Worcester and see the fires of the Aztecs still burning"—but only for men of intelligence and training, Hale added.[33]

As if following Hale's exhortation, during 1881 and 1882 Baxter and Willard Metcalf, an aspiring Boston artist, followed the new rail lines through Kansas, New Mexico, Arizona, and northern Mexico in search of literary and artistic material. More specifically, they intended to collaborate on an article on Zuñi for *Harper's New Monthly Magazine.* Baxter later recalled: "Before that, he [Baxter] and his colleague of the Herald, Frederic R. Guernsey, had interested themselves greatly in the study of Spanish, holding that there lay a great future in the development of our relations with Latin America, then just in their beginnings. Boston-built railways were not only opening up New Mexico and Arizona, but the Sonora had just been completed to Guaymas on the Pacific coast of Mexico and the Mexican Central had in 1882 penetrated beyond Chihuahua."[34]

His Southwest excursion of the early eighties opened new vistas, and a new stage, in Baxter's life—not only because of his meeting with Cushing at Fort Wingate in the spring of 1881 but also because the people and landscapes of the region seemed to arouse in him a new poetic voice. Just prior to his departure from Boston, Baxter had met and interviewed Walt Whitman, who deeply influenced Baxter's style and, over the next decade, affected him as a personal friend as well.[35] The consequence was that a decade before Charles Lummis began advertising the Southwest as the "land of poco tiempo" (1891), Baxter was describing a Southwest of heat, drowsiness, and stasis, and verbally painting scenes of peaceful, rhythmic pueblo life. He spent the next decade—including the years of the Hemenway Expedition—traveling between extremes of cold and heat, cloud and sun, urban and provincial life.

Following Cushing's 1882 visit to Boston with the Zuñi chiefs—the "aboriginal pilgrimage" to the "ocean of sunrise," which he widely publicized in the *Herald* and elsewhere—Baxter moved for a year to Mexico to edit the *Mexican Financier,* a Spanish and English weekly newspaper, and to serve as a correspondent for both the *Herald* and the *New York Sun.*[36] In Mexico he promoted railroad development and municipal improvements in Mexico City. After his return in 1884, he briefly edited *Outing Magazine,* a publication devoted to bicycling and outdoor activities (figure 1 records Baxter's own experience as a wheelman).[37] By the time of his engagement as secretary-treasurer of the Hemenway Expedition in late 1886, Baxter had returned to full-time work with the *Herald.* Following his visit to the expedition's southwestern sites in the first half of 1888, Baxter publicized Cushing's operations with a series of articles, "Archaeological

Camping in Arizona," in the *American Architect and Building News* (1889), and a pamphlet entitled *The Old New World,* which also appeared as an article in the *Herald*. In the fall of 1888 he traveled to Berlin with Edward S. Morse to deliver Cushing's programmatic progress report to the International Congress of Americanists.[38] By the time of the Berlin trip, however, Cushing's expedition was already beginning to show signs of unraveling, and Baxter's own attentions were turning elsewhere. While he continued to support Cushing personally, his role in the Hemenway Expedition diminished noticeably, and by early 1889 he was no longer secretary-treasurer.

From Berlin, Baxter had enthusiastically reported to the *Herald* on that city's model government, and on his return to Boston he was invited to lecture on municipal management at Old South Meeting House.[39] Baxter's strong turn to urban politics and utopian reform coincided with the publication by his friend and fellow journalist Edward Bellamy of *Looking Backward: 2000–1887*. Bellamy called his book a "mere literary fantasy, a fairy tale of social felicity. There was no thought," he said, "of contriving a house which practical men might live in, but merely of hanging in midair, far out of reach of the sordid and material world of the present, a cloud palace for ideal humanity." Whatever his intentions, Bellamy provided, in the words of cultural critic Lewis Mumford, "one of the most important political pamphlets" of the time, "one of the first attempts to think out a logical conclusion for the processes of mechanical organization and monopoly, for the national expansion of great industries like steel and the stockyards, that were taking place under men's noses."[40]

As Bellamy's vision of a technological utopia in Boston of the year 2000 caught fire across the country, Baxter threw himself vigorously into Bellamyite nationalism.[41] Indeed, his subsequent civic career, centering on the metropolitan parks movement, was essentially an attempt to put into practice the democratic visions of Whitman and the technological utopia of Bellamy, relying on a strong, shared faith in the power of communication and transportation to centralize, coordinate, and ameliorate urban life. Between Bellamy's death in 1898 and his own nearly thirty years later, Baxter provided introductions for many editions of *Looking Backward*. Similarly, until Whitman's death in 1892, Baxter continued to write enthusiastic reviews of the poet's work in the *Herald* and raised funds to support him in his old age in Camden, New Jersey. For his part, Whitman came increasingly to appreciate Baxter's quiet steadiness: "Sylvester is on several sides my friend—my friend, I think, for general reasons[,] not one reason alone.

You see, some people like this or that in me—like nothing else: as a man might like your leg or arm and forget the body of which they form a part: Baxter is of the other, the large, sort—he sees me whole. Sylvester is a quiet, sane, agreeable make of man—don't get into flusters, don't indulge in bad tempers about humanity—yet is radical, too, if not revolutionary, and looks for some shake-up in the social order before long."[42]

Over the next twenty years, Baxter worked assiduously for civic improvement and the development of Boston. The boy from the Cape and the Malden suburbs promoted the concept of a Greater Boston, coordinated through efficient rail and road networks. At the same time, he worked closely with Frederick Law Olmsted, Olmsted Associates, and Charles Eliot, Jr., in developing Boston Common and a system of urban parks throughout the metropolitan Boston area.[43] In understanding the larger coherence of Baxter's wide-ranging program of civic reform, it is helpful to recall Mumford's description of the "Renewal of the Landscape"—a vision that Baxter fully shared:

> Now, there are three main ways of modifying and humanizing the visible landscape. One of them is by agriculture and horticulture; it involves the orderly arrangement of the ploughed field and the wood lot, the meadow and the pasture, the road and the enclosure. When these functions are undertaken consciously and intelligently, as they were by the country gentlemen of England in the eighteenth century, for example, they lead to landscape design. The second method is by city development and architecture; and the third is by works of engineering—bridges, viaducts, canals, highroads, docks, harbours, dams. These three modes intermingle, and it is impossible to neglect one without spoiling the effect of the others. What is a beautiful city with bad drains, or a fine concrete highway in a barren landscape?[44]

In accord with this vision, Baxter publicized tirelessly, arguing for beautification of railroad stations, public ownership of water utilities, the placement of civic art in the public squares of New England villages, and the preservation of historic buildings.[45]

Baxter's marriage in 1893, at age forty-three, to Lucia Millett, sister of the popular Boston artist and critic Francis (Frank) Millett, probably solidified his position in local literary and artistic circles. Lucia Millett came from a prominent East Bridgewater family and, like Baxter's mother, taught school and participated actively in women's clubs. She also wrote a small volume entitled *House-*

keepers' Handy Book. Forty-one years old at the time of her marriage, she and Baxter had no children. At her death in 1917 (shortly after her brother Francis drowned on the *Titanic*) Baxter's eulogy to her, a poem entitled "Homeward Laden," spoke of

The weight of the load
You had borne through the years in sweet patience
While steep ran the ways of the road
That for love and in duty you followed.[46]

From all indications—poetic at least—theirs was a marriage more of convenience and appearance than of passion. But from their base in Malden the Baxters came to assume a respectable place in civic and literary affairs. Sylvester, in addition to his prominence in the metropolitan parks movement, enjoyed a local reputation as a journalist, a poet, and a yachting enthusiast. He counted among his literary acquaintances William Dean Howells, Amy Lowell, and in later years Robert Frost.[47]

Through his position at the *Herald,* Baxter also maintained his contacts with Boston railroad interests, both locally and in the Southwest and Mexico. His enthusiasm for suburban and regional railways as a means of economic development never flagged. For example, in 1910 he emphasized the connection between local rail transportation, recreational tourism, and the economic growth of eastern Massachusetts. The new Boston and Maine Railroad construction, he wrote, "enormously enhances the accessibility of the entire North Shore pleasure region, both from Boston and the country at large. With opportunities for through trains, special and regular, and for private cars from New York and beyond, the national popularity of the Cape Ann region will immensely increase. This means much, both for Massachusetts and for Boston. Think of what swift daily journeys between Boston and Rockport mean in the change from discomfort to pleasure under the smokeless, cinderless and dustless conditions of electrified transit! How much oftener will people want to come to Boston!"[48]

In 1899, supported by a set of wealthy Boston investors, his old friend and traveling companion Frederic Guernsey, and (according to his acknowledgments) the "Mexican, Mexican Central, Mexican National, Mexican Southern, Interoceanic Railway Companies, and the New York and Cuba Steamship Company," Baxter made a final trip to Mexico to undertake a survey of Spanish colonial architecture.[49] The enterprise was an aesthetic salvage operation—"So much had already disappeared, and so much seemed doomed to early destruction"—which brought forth from Baxter a renewed power of language and romantic vision:

> The qualities [of Spanish colonial architecture] reside largely in strongly impressive effects,—such as monumental domination of environment, a union with an accentuation of the fascinating elements of landscape and climate, inexhaustibly picturesque and enchantingly spectacular. Classic in fundamental derivation, and possessing markedly Oriental attributes, this architecture is freely romantic in its development—often most waywardly so. In these traits, of course, it is thoroughly Spanish; as, indeed, it is Spanish practically throughout. But the foreign flavorings imparted to home-derived essentials in the colonial parts of an imperial domain are customarily distinctive; as in the present instance.

Thoroughly enchanted and imaginatively engaged, Baxter in turn-of-the-century Mexico—as he had fifteen years previously at Camp Hemenway—painted a loving, Ruskinesque picture of artisans ("stone-cutters, wood-carvers, metal-workers, tile-makers, potters, and the like") at work in colonial Mexico:

> Their traditions survive to this day, and one is often struck by the skill and taste displayed by humble native workmen when proceeding unhampered along their own lines. The fine old spirit is now no longer dominant in the art of the country. The controlling impulse has ceased to be exerted by master-minds, and has largely passed into the feeble hold of philistine hands to whom artistic motives are as sealed books. Yet there still survive the intelligence and the fine feeling with which so many workmen give themselves to their tasks, in spite of scanty hire and slight appreciation—animated solely by the pleasure of producing something beautiful, even though of lowly utility. This indicates that when a new Renaissance at last dawns in Mexico . . . there will be ready at hand a fine body of skilled and tasteful workers.[50]

But it was in his appreciative description of the colonial "Churrigueresque" style that Baxter finally released himself completely through his language. The early colonial style, he wrote, "appealing as it did, so strongly to the native temperament in the riotous luxuriance of its imaginative quality—akin to the entangled profusion of a tropical forest where the interlaced vegetation is starred with vivid blossomings, fantastically adorned with clinging orchids, and the air is heavy with rich perfumes—was followed early in the present century by what seems to have been almost a fanatical rage for its extermination."[51] Baxter's powerfully evocative language, seemingly called forth again by the subtropical heat and fecundity, could not have been farther from the common speech of Boston suburbia. Baxter lived another quarter-century and produced two volumes of verse, but he never returned to Mexico, the American Southwest, or his luxuriantly tangled poetic voice.[52]

Baxter and Cushing: The Fraternal Bond

Cushing and Baxter, born eight years apart, had very different boyhoods. By all accounts an unusual child, Cushing grew up in the farm country of western New York surrounded by two brothers, at least one sister, his mother, and a very powerful father figure: a surgeon who served in the Civil War.[53] Cushing outlived his father by only two years. Born prematurely and frail throughout his early years, as a boy Cushing received special attention due to his health and his precocity. Throughout his adult life he displayed a pattern of strong filial relationships and needs, forming meaningful but ambivalent bonds with both paternal superiors and maternal patrons. He evoked, it seems, parental feelings. He also enjoyed lasting and important bonds with a circle of male cohorts, a fraternity in which Baxter was a central figure.

In contrast to Cushing, Sylvester Baxter barely knew his seaman father, and he grew up in a female household: two sisters and a beloved mother. He remained deeply attached to them all of his life. It appears that, both before and after his late marriage, all of Baxter's significant professional and personal friendships were with other men, as were his travels. In his recent insightful study of American manhood, E. Anthony Rotundo argues that in the transition from a boyhood domestic environment in which women "set the tone" to the male adult world defined by "independent action, cool detachment, and sober responsibility," American middle-class men of the nineteenth century constantly created and left behind networks of male friends as they moved from boy culture to youthful friendships to young manhood. These relationships were in effect "rehearsals for marriage" and involved varied, somewhat experimental degrees of intimacy, dependence, and tenderness. The external signs of commitment to male adulthood were marriage, a settled career, and a home of one's own. "Once these commitments were made," Rotundo observes, "a male became a man, and the romance and carefree play of boyhood and youth were set aside."[54]

For Baxter as for Cushing, then, the confrontation with southwestern environments and experiences was associated with, indeed was a function of, the period of male transition from boyhood to manhood—a stage of androgynous negotiation between a world to be left and another to be attained. It should not be surprising, then, to see elements of both in their representations of the region and their accounts of their adventures in it. The two men met when both were still relatively young (Baxter was thirty-one, Cushing twenty-three) and unmarried; a year later, however, Cushing married Emily and established a household at Zuñi pueblo—clear signs of adult male status. While based in Boston, Baxter moved for a year or so (1884–85) to Mexico, then back to Boston but did not marry for another decade. For him, then, the 1880s, when he was in his thirties, were a period of considerable mobility and prolonged youth, while Cushing was making adult commitments. Their correspondence over these years displays their strategies to maintain balance in the relationship as a means of weathering these and associated changes. For years they addressed each other in terms of equivalence: either "My Dear Baxter" and "My Dear Cushing" or by their Zuñi adoptive names, Tenatsali and Thli a kwa.[55] Cushing almost never used Baxter's first name in writing; Baxter began calling him "Frank" only in 1893, after both were married, the expedition was long over, and they were in only distant, sporadic contact.

On the face of it, the friendship was markedly asymmetrical. As a reporter and an enthusiast for Cushing's adventures and theories, Baxter found considerable appreciation. But his few efforts to offer suggestions or engage Cushing in dialogue about southwestern ethnology or archaeology were largely ignored by his friend. In moments of enthusiasm or exhortation, Cushing interspersed sentences with "my dear boy," but during the frequent times of despair and sickness, Baxter became "my dear old Baxter," "my dear faithful *Thli' a ḳwa* my good secretary" or "My dear Good Steady Baxter." To the last he added, "What would I do without your friendship and association. I fully love them both."[56] Baxter, then, served as a vital support and outlet for Cushing's psychological state.

Central to the pattern was Baxter's sincere solicitude for Cushing's ever-precarious health. Male sickness in the late nineteenth century was not easily accepted or well understood, especially incapacitating illnesses (often simply lumped together as "neurasthenia"), and they carried the stigma of weakness of will, laziness, and a shirking of proper duties. At the same time, neurasthenia in men (and in women) was thought to be the result of the breakdown of the human body (a closed energy system) from overwork, especially mental overwork, and emotional strain, and was widely viewed as a sign or cost of civilized progress. As Rotundo summarizes the view, this "self-congratulatory theory" argued that "some men who worked at the pinnacle of social evolution . . . broke down from the strain."[57] In Cushing's case, there was a very real, prolonged illness: he suffered from a form of diverticulitis in his stomach, which required periodic pumping and special diets. More gravely, for years he was infested with *taenia,* a virulent, persistent tapeworm that he seems to have finally expelled in 1890. The pattern of Baxter's advice and solicitude for Cushing's health, treatment, and diet through the years reflects the assumption that he was a brilliant man of delicate constitution, with great gifts and great vulnerabilities, who required gentle handling. Baxter attempted, consistently and sincerely, to provide it.[58]

It was not always easy. When he accepted the position as secretary-treasurer of the Hemenway Expedition in late 1886, Baxter assumed a delicate mediating role between Cushing and Mary Hemenway. She apparently relied on him to relay her desires to Cushing (and buffer her as well), while Cushing expected Baxter to explain his plans, discoveries, and other matters to the patroness and, in effect, to act as his advocate to the Hemenway board in Boston. All things considered, Baxter functioned remarkably well, gently prodding Cushing and deflecting, it seems, the growing consternation among the board members when the expedition did not seem to be producing the expected results. In the last days of 1888, just as Cushing's enterprise (along with his health) was about to collapse, Baxter—by now associated with Cushing as his advocate—was removed from the circle of Hemenway intimates. There is no evidence that Cushing ever recognized what the failure of the expedition may have cost Baxter, nor is there evidence that Baxter ever intimated such feelings. On the contrary, in his lowest depths of self-pity, Cushing was capable of including Baxter among his detractors and betrayers.[59] For his part, Baxter came to focus on Cushing's successor, Jesse Walter Fewkes, as an incompetent scoundrel and William Torrey Harris as the innocently ignorant adviser to the Hemenways in the whole sad affair. He re-established camaraderie with Cushing largely on these grounds.[60] Both men exempted Mary Hemenway from fault. The enmities aroused by the expedition abated slowly, however. Many years later, when Baxter and Edward S. Morse were among the few principals (other than Hodge) who were still alive, Baxter sent his old friend a birthday greeting: "Those were great days with Cushing.... What has become of Hodge? I am told that Fewkes is now head of the Bureau of Ethnology. He does not deserve it."[61]

Pullmans and Pueblos: Baxter's Southwest

After dinner on Sunday evening, 29 May 1881, a group of men and women gathered together in the home of General Luther Bradley, commandant of Fort Wingate in New Mexico, to hear Frank Cushing read and explain the poetic qualities of a Zuñi song, after which Palowahtiwa, governor of the pueblo, sang the same song—a song to the antelope—in Zuñi. "He sang in a sweet voice," wrote John Gregory Bourke, "a little bit tremulous from nervousness, the invocation or chant beginning: 'May-a-wee, May-a-wee!' (Spirit of the antelope, Spirit of the antelope!)." The circle of listeners included Dr. Washington Matthews, Willard Metcalf, and Sylvester Baxter, who had arrived and had met Cushing the previous day and now "took down notes of all that occurred."[62]

Meeting Cushing and sitting in the circle of listeners that summer weekend profoundly affected the young Boston men, and they wrestled to turn the new experiences into images for personal understanding and public consumption. In the coming months, Metcalf twice drew Cushing in full-length portrait, while within ten days Baxter was introducing the "remarkable young ethnologist" to Boston readers: "Hence we see him, a slender, light complexioned young man—he is not yet 24 years old—with long, flowing blonde hair, confined by the Indian head band, and dressed in the picturesque costume of the tribe—every article of native manufacture, from the cloth of the dark blue woolen serape-shirt, the buckskin knee breeches, long dark blue stockings, leather mocassins, and artistically embroidered sash, to the rows of silver buttons and other richly-worked silver ornaments that adorn his dress, and the precious ancient necklace from a mysterious cave of relics up in the mountains."[63]

Already apparent in Baxter's first report from New Mexico are the painterly penstrokes and the reach for tones of color that would soon mark his southwestern writing of the 1880s. "It is a striking and refreshing contrast," began his first report from Wingate, and he went on to contrast the "range of wilderness" with "an oasis of cultivation and refinement," nearby Navajo campfires with Fort Wingate's "intramural spaces," which he found to be "as tastefully furnished and decorated as the aesthetic homes of the East."[64] Baxter's Southwest immediately emerged as a land of contrasts strongly heightened by the propinquity of opposites. Because Cushing both literally embodied those opposites (blonde hair/Indian headband) and straddled the worlds of savagery and cultivation, he became the mediating and liminal figure in Baxter's literary constructions—a personal focus, a crossroads of differences, a bodyscape for his own and others' creative imaginings.

The central theme in Baxter's representation of the Southwest was change. This should occasion no surprise: he arrived in the region on the cusp of revolutionary and astoundingly sudden changes in economics, politics, and demography. Sensing the magnitude if not the severity of the changes taking place around him, Baxter was also enamored of the chief agents of change—the expansive, intrusive transcontinental railroad systems—and deeply committed to the ideology of progress and teleological projections they embodied.[65] At the same time, however—and here began his dilemma—like many others of his generation Baxter sought aesthetic sources for social stability and personal freedom, and these lay not in disruption but in continuity. For these vital personal and public purposes he turned to the pueblos and the pastel landscapes of the Southwest. The result was a strong tension and sense of counterpoint between change and stasis, discontinuity and continuity, linearity and cyclicity in his southwestern writing.

Baxter and Metcalf's "Along the Rio Grande," although not published in *Harper's* until 1885, recounts their original 1881 railroad trip, supplemented by Baxter's observations from his second southwestern trip in the fall of 1882. Metcalf's sketches are of sleepy streets, riverscapes, and Indian-Hispanic women carrying ollas and baskets.[66] Baxter's text, however, sets up two themes of contrast: the moving train against placid scenery, and the present against the recent past—an authorial position made possible by virtue of his repeated visits. The effect is that Baxter's changing Southwest comes to be autobiographically "known" and attested, seemingly altering before his and our eyes. The function is akin to the tour guide's claim of authority through previous familiarity, or to the older settler's authority over the newcomer by virtue of prior knowledge. Thus, writing in 1885, Baxter introduces the region as he remembers having seen it only four years before:

> This country seemed very remote and foreign four years ago, but now the tourist dashes through it on the Pacific express, marvelling at all the un-American-

> looking things to be seen from the car window, everything so different from the sights of the accustomed Western regions bordering the old transcontinental railroad line. Where, only a few months before, the complaining "tenderfoot" was cursing the miserable fare of the country, the tourist breakfasts, dines, and sups leisurely at a succession of cheerful railway hotels, for whose well-spread tables daily levy is made upon the fat prairie-lands of Kansas and the perennial orchards of southern California. . . . Everywhere are signs of an awakened, stirring life, which has changed the country as in the twinkling of an eye.[67]

In these lines Baxter, first, establishes the railroad as the national artery and places New Mexico and Arizona on that lifeline between the Middle West and the West Coast. Second, he presents the region as awakening, as "stirring with life" after a long slumber—inspiring various images of life-giving energy (the end of hibernation, for example, or the blossoming of flowers). Third, he introduces the imaginary tourist and frames the scenery for his gaze. The remainder of the article, enhanced by Metcalf's images of indolence, presents the Rio Grande as viewed through the windows of a Pullman car, as the past that is about to be superseded approaches and recedes before the moving tourist eye. Everywhere there is the apparently timeless landscape, "parching under the hot New Mexican sun, [with] an unspeakable solemnity and an awful calmness. It stretches on and on indefinitely." Conspicuous within that scenery are the Rio Grande pueblos. Santo Domingo "has an old-world picturesqueness about it, with orchards around and the gleaming river beyond, a goodly stream winding down from the north through green meadows, and with a stately background of dusky purple mountains." San Felipe approaches Baxter's startled eyes as "a ready-made picture": "Orchards, walled gardens, shrubbery-bordered *acequias,* and a few houses whose flat roofs are standing-places for statuesque figures gazing at the passing train. . . . The buildings are dazzling with whitewash, and here and there great scales have fallen off, exposing the brown adobe. A transparent golden light fills the calm sunset air. Half the population seem to be taking an evening bath. Chubby children, like bronze cherubs, splash in the shallow ditches, while the river is alive with the frolicking Indian youth."[68]

The traveler's gaze from the moving train on the static landscape and its rhythmic pueblo lives—orchards, ollas, mules, children—activates Baxter's first strategy for resolving the contradiction of change and stasis. The key to his resolution lies in the transformation of the disparate elements of immediate experience into an aesthetic whole: observer, train, pueblo and Indians, landscape, and

General view of Zuni.

the central mechanism of the moving frame/window through which it all occurs. Taken together, these constitute the tourist aesthetic, the gazing of those who are "making history" on the ahistorical, cyclical, quotidian, and mundane.[69] From this it is but one step to the live exhibit and two steps to the museum diorama. Metcalf's illustrations serve as a confirmation not only of the romantic text but also of the very form of the reader/viewer experience: he offers framed, engraved observations, finished with the authenticity of an artist's hand and sign. Together, Baxter and Metcalf represent the Indian and Hispanic Southwest as a series of dioramas, given greater value as an aesthetic production, observable from various distances, quintessentially ahistorical but teetering on the edge of historical destruction, seen, in fact, through the glass eyes of the Pullman car.[70]

Baxter's second strategy of resolution also involves movement: marking off transitional points and moments between the extremes of linear history (railroad/civilization), and cyclical stability (pueblo/primitivism). This strategy appears, for example, in the movement from the railroad depot at Gallup to Zuñi pueblo. Baxter's narrative, related in "Father of the Pueblos" (1882), his first article-length work on the Southwest, begins at Fort Wingate (which, as we have already seen, constituted an outpost of civilization and thus an initial mediating place en route to the primitive). Cushing, Baxter, Metcalf, and an army lieutenant start off from the fort early on a June morning, "with hot sunshine, but clear, invigorating air," for the 50-mile trip to the pueblo. For hours Cushing initiates them into knowledge of Zuñi history, folklore, and language until they arrive at Las Nutrias, an outlying summer settlement of Zuñi, where they lunch with an elderly Zuñi couple. Continuing on to Pescado, another outlying settlement, they meet up again with Palowahtiwa, tending his farm. Here they partake for the first time of a real Zuñi meal, complete with roasted locusts, and settle back as evening chill and moonlight envelop the adobe house:

> After supper we lay back on the sheep-skins quietly enjoying the novel scene about us. Sticks of pino [piñon] wood had been placed on end in the corner of the fireplace, and their bright crackling flame sent a ruddy light through the large room, touching up the nearer side of all objects in sharp relief against the intensity of the shadows. Gay-colored clothing and blankets, hung on poles suspended from the ceiling, caught the dancing light; curious pottery was ranged along the door by the walls; and here and there in the walls were little niches, just as we had seen them in the walls of ruined cliff dwellings. In these little niches were

Indian water-carriers.

> conveniently arranged little articles of domestic use, which had a delightfully bric-à-brac suggestiveness. The scene was just the same now as it had been within those walls hundreds of years before. We were away back in the centuries, and living the life of the remote past.[71]

From Wingate through Las Nutrias and Pescado to Zuñi pueblo the following day, Baxter thus presents himself as a traveler moving back in time as distance from the present increases with distance from the railroad. But at the final destination—Cushing's quarters in the pueblo—he finds again an oasis of civility. It is another important moment for Baxter, for it offers a third opportunity for resolution by exhibiting the "primitive" and the "cultured" in aesthetic harmony:

> Mr. Cushing's room at the house of the Governor was a picturesque mingling of culture and barbarism. A writing-table, a case of book-shelves with the books necessary to his studies, and the volumes of valuable notes that recorded his investigations, a stool, a student-lamp, and a hammock, completed the inventory of the civilized furnishings. . . . The hard earthen floor of the room was covered with Navajo and Pueblo blankets, their bright hues making them admirable for rugs . . . . The walls were also hung with some choice examples of the blankets, giving a novel tapestry effect. With the photographs of some home friends adorning the wall, the room had a charmingly bright and cozy look.[72]

In such scenes Baxter provides models for the "artistic cozy corner" that was beginning to enjoy such popularity in the parlors of late Victorian American homes: a deliberately eclectic and mildly disarranged assortment of "Oriental" (Turkish, Chinese, Japanese) and American Indian exotica intended to provide, within a larger field of decorum, a space for "repose and freedom from conventionality."[73] Whether as a locus for spiritual regeneration and moral instruction or as an expression of "personality," the parlor of the bourgeois home was coming to feature bric-à-brac displays on tables and bookcases, jumbles of exotic objects from diverse natural and cultural worlds. One popular variation of the cozy corner was the "Indian corner" in which "Native American art forms became a locus of the protest against mass production."[74] George Wharton James, the guru of this movement, exhorted his readers that "[e]very well appointed house might appropriately arrange an Indian corner. Here, baskets, pottery, blankets, arrow-points, spear-heads, wampum belts, moccasins, head-dresses, masks, pictures, spears, bows and Katchina dolls, fetishes and beadwork might be displayed with artistic . . . effect."[75]

Whether sitting in the parlor of an eastern home or reposing in an adobe outside Zuñi, there was a studied casualness in this celebration of a primitive aesthetic expressed by the distribution of artifacts within domestic space. In this connection, too, it is not insignificant that Baxter exemplified another emerging phenomenon of the 1880s: masculine domesticity. As recent historians of American masculinity have pointed out, the phrase was (or should have been) a contradiction in terms at the time,[76] but Baxter was one of an increasingly visible group of late-century American males who had a sustained interest not only in the architecture but also in the more detailed, decorative aspects of domestic space, an interest considered feminine in their time. It seems clear that the Southwest permitted him greater freedom of expression in this and other respects.[77] In response, he helped to "design" the region accordingly.

Secrecy was a central element in that design, and secret knowledge became a major theme in Baxter-Cushing representations of the Indian Southwest. Boyish in his desire to please and astound his superiors, Cushing made the discovery of "secrets" his stock-in-trade at every stage of his career but never more so than in the years at Zuñi. Accordingly, one of Baxter's major functions as his publicist was to announce Cushing's insights, theories, and recent or impending discoveries. But beneath personal style and ambition lay something more basic: a *desire* for a world of secret knowledge that appears to have been widely shared in bourgeois society. Baxter frequently compared puebloan secret male orders to the Masonic Order, which had been so important in his own father's life and which was one of the countless fraternal orders of Victorian male culture.[78] He also stressed parallels between Indian religious rites and spiritualism or séance gatherings, and he constantly announced Cushing's discovery of a "key" to or "secret knowledge" of one aspect or another of Indian life. All of these patterns reflected a shared assumption that secret knowledge indeed existed, that it was critical to explaining the observed behavior of the Indians, and that it had great potential value for the dominant culture. Its most salient characteristic—and its greatest value—was the presumed lack of change through generations, for in its pristine insight and instruction lay its profound power to regulate society and the source of its sacredness for the Indians—the source, that is, of their spiritual strength.

A bivouac in the valley of the pines.

The search for stasis—a "place of grace," in Jackson Lears' phrase—presupposed that beneath the surface of historical change lay a subterranean river of continuity, a flow of human energy and knowledge untouched by the ravages and distractions of industrial time.[79] At Zuñi, Cushing wrote of "ancient talks" or "formulas" handed down unchanged for centuries, and Baxter likened the stories and instructions to Homeric tales. In spite of appearances to the contrary, Cushing claimed that the phenomenon was pan-Indian: on the Seneca reservation in New York he said that he found that "every member of the tribe speaks perfectly the original tongue; the original Gentile, phratral and governmental institutions exist perfectly; the original folk-lore and myths are scarcely broken, although slightly modified." These were demonstrations, Baxter added, of the "inherent secretiveness of Indian character, as well as of its conservatism and tenacity of ancient institutions."[80]

Accordingly, occasions of the revelation of secret knowledge were for these men nothing less than epiphanal, the most sought-after and highly prized of southwestern experiences. These were almost invariably nighttime experiences, occasions of darkness or semidarkness. Within the pueblo, the underground kiva (*estufa,* in Spanish) became the doubly charged locus of the exchange of knowledge, at once the pueblo's most secretive space and the inquirer's most desired object of entrée.[81] At one remove from the kiva but still magnetic in their special power were those evenings around southwestern campfires with Indian companions or mediating guides (such as Cushing),[82] but such moments might be created as well at great distances outside the Southwest.[83] The cool autumn evenings on Mary Hemenway's estate at Manchester-by-the-Sea in 1886, during which the Hemenway Expedition first took shape, partook of the magic of such sharing and transference. Mary Dewey, Hemenway's close friend, remembered those occasions as special moments of cross-cultural intimacy:

> It is evening, and we have gone over to Casa Ramona, and are sitting in the great parlor, for the August evenings are chilly on the North Shore. Near the fire, in a large arm-chair sits Wai-hu-si-wa, our story-teller, his dark face half-shy, half pleased at being the centre of attention. On a low foot-stool, almost on the floor, is Mr. Cushing, his slight, active figure and his face, with its striking combination of keenness and gentleness, eager and ready for the task of interpretation. The circle forms, and Wai-hu-si-wa begins his recitation in a low voice. . . . [N]othing can give the effect that this gathering into our very ears these utterances of past centuries had upon us with Wai-hu-si-wa's dark, smiling face, and slight expressive gestures contrasting with his interpreter's highly cultivated intelligence, and both bound together by a common sympathy and appreciation which included us all, men and women, whites and Indians, in its great human clasp.[84]

In the end, the fireplace or campfire circles of "common sympathy and appreciation" and the precious moments of knowledge transfer may have provided a personally therapeutic resolution—amid spaces set aside from the harsh industrial daytime—but they offered only a small bastion against historical change. Baxter's last writings on the Hemenway Expedition—"The Old New World" (1888) and his series on "Archaeological Camping in Arizona" (1889)—returned with a new sense of immediacy to the recognition that change in the Phoenix-Tempe valley and throughout the southwestern United States was both rapid and ubiquitous. As the expedition workers dug by day in the centuries-old ruins of the Salt River Valley, on all sides of their camps the desert was being graded and irrigated for agriculture, while by night the fires of thousands of uprooted mesquite trees burned brightly in the desert air. The harsh but delicate desert was being domesticated literally before the eyes of the Hemenway workforce:

> The landscape undergoes a rapid transformation in the course of a few weeks. Here and there, the plain is dotted with the camps of laborers engaged in clearing it, consisting of Mexicans at work for some contractor who has undertaken the job for the owner. Our nights are enlivened by the brilliant brush-fires gleaming around us in all directions, near and far. The mesquite trees are cut down and burned in piles above their roots. . . .
>
> It is not long before the whole country is cleared, changing the aspect of the locality entirely. The land stretches away almost as smooth as a floor for miles, the very uniformity in contrast with the rugged mountain-chains around[,] giving it a certain attractiveness akin to beauty.[85]

"Akin to beauty"—in such words Baxter aestheticized history's trajectory of destructive progress. A few sentences later he was extolling the ease of life for newcomers in the valley: "It is an easy matter to become domiciled in this region, with its mild climate." Here, as throughout his southwestern writings, Baxter found language to express his ambivalent stance between past and future, unchanging tradition and historical disruption, boyhood innocence and adult responsibility. In the end, he found his own resolution by producing scenes of improvement within a landscape of regret.[86]

Baxter's strategy was not uncommon, but it bore a high price for American culture. In her thoughtful analysis of sentimentalism in Victorian America, Ann Douglas remarks on "the manipulation of nostalgia" that frequently became the preferred strategy of those who could neither imagine nor mount any other effective protest "in a country propelled so rapidly toward industrial capitalism with so little cultural context to slow or complicate its course." Sentimentalism, she observed, provided "a way to protest a power to which one has already in part capitulated. It is a form of dragging one's heels." However, by complying with various forms of "self-evasion," the strategy of sentimentalism becomes the aesthetic expression of a "regret calculated not to interfere with [action]." In other words, it serves as a rationalization of, rather than a challenge to, the dynamics of development.[87] Nostalgia, then, emerges as a central and revealing trope for ambivalence and powerlessness. Accordingly, Baxter's personally negotiated but culturally shared aesthetics of southwestern nostalgia, in which ethnography and archaeology already played major roles, came to enjoy strong resonance in a society struggling to come to terms with the continuing transformation of regional and national landscapes.[88]

PART II

Visiting and Revisiting Zuñi, 1881–1883

Introduction

When Sylvester Baxter arrived with Willard Metcalf in the Southwest for the first time in the spring of 1881, Frank Cushing had been living at Zuñi pueblo in northwestern New Mexico for a year and a half. Already a local celebrity, Cushing had begun to stimulate great interest (as well as some concern) among his Smithsonian superiors and other anthropologists through his participant-observer style and deepening involvement in the life of the pueblo. He was not yet, however, a public figure.[1]

In June 1881, Baxter began to report enthusiastically on Cushing's work and lifestyle at Zuñi, emphasizing both his sufferings and his "astounding revelations," calling for further support of his work, and predicting even more profound insights into Indian language, mythology, and history. In the fall Cushing began making plans to take a group of Zuñi leaders to visit the East Coast—a still-intriguing act of reciprocity and self-publicity that finally occurred in early 1882. In February Cushing left the pueblo with six Zuñi men: Palowahtiwa (Patricio Piño), the governor; Laiiuahtsaila (Pedro Piño), Patricio's father and the former governor; Naiiuhtchi, senior Bow Priest; Kiasa, junior Bow Priest; Laiiuahtsailunkia, priest of the temple; and Nanahe (Cornflower), a Hopi adopted by the Zuñi. Arriving in Washington in early March, they called on

President Chester A. Arthur, studied collections at the National Museum, climbed the Washington Monument, and performed planting ceremonies in Rock Creek Park. Pedro Piño fell sick and was left behind to recuperate while the group continued on through New York to Boston later in the month. Here the Indian group became the center of attention in churches, schools, theaters, and private homes (Edward Everett Hale and his daughter served them "prairie hens,—which they ought to like—and oysters and frozen pudding and cake").[2] They also visited Salem (where there was much comparative discussion of witches), Wellesley College and Worcester. On March 28 the "pious, aboriginal pilgrimage," as Cushing and Baxter advertised it, culminated with seaside services on Deer Island in Boston harbor, where the Zuñis and Cushing collected water from "The Ocean of Sunrise" to take back home.[3] Although there is no record of direct contact, it is likely that Mary Hemenway first encountered Cushing and became aware of his work during this visit, since he and the Indians performed twice at Old South Meeting House.

Fatigued and sick, the travelers recovered for three days in Brooklyn, then visited Zuñi children at the Carlisle Indian School in Carlisle, Pennsylvania. Pedro Piño and three others returned in early summer to Zuñi, while Palowahtiwa and Naiiutchi remained with Cushing in Washington for linguistic work. In July, Cushing married Emily Magill, eldest daughter of a Washington banker with family roots in northern Virginia. Cushing, his wife, her younger sister Margaret, a family cook, and the Indians then traveled to the Cushing family homestead in Albion, New York, stopping briefly at the Seneca reservation, on their way back to New Mexico. In late September 1882, after an absence of nearly eight months, Cushing—now with household—returned to Zuñi pueblo.[4]

Baxter covered the remarkable "pilgrimage" throughout the Boston visit, chiefly through long, colorful articles for the *Boston Herald* and in the pages of the *American Architect and Building News* (which regularly reported on transatlantic developments in archaeological explorations). The essay "Father of the Pueblos"—a compellingly romantic representation of Zuñi and New Mexico couched in terms of cultural and cosmic entropy—appeared in the June 1882 issue of *Harper's New Monthly Magazine*. Two months later Baxter's full account of the visit appeared as "An Aboriginal Pilgrimage" in the *Century Illustrated Monthly Magazine*. "Aboriginal Pilgrimage" was intended as a preface to Cush-

Portrait and autograph of Pa-lo-wah-ti-wa, Governor of Zuñi, or Head Political Chief, Clan of the Macaws.

Portrait and autograph of Nai-iu-tchi, Senior Priest, Order of the Bow, Clan of the Eagles. Sun and rattlesnake, emblems of his orders.

The reception at Wellesley College.

ing's famous three-part series, "My Adventures in Zuni," which began in the *Century* later in 1882. In this fashion between March 1882, and the following March, when Baxter described his own return (in late 1882) to the pueblo in "Zuñi Revisited," both Cushing and the Zuñis became household figures among the reading public of the Northeast.

Baxter's early literary images are heavily encoded constructions. The travel-adventure genre to which they (in part) belong emphasized verbal scene painting, a conceit that had the effect of lifting observed places and peoples out of their historical causal sequence and into a world of aestheticized experience.[5] Thus, as Baxter strolls through the dusty pueblo (in "Father of the Pueblos") he registers scenes divorced from their temporal context: "Narrow winding ways and irregular-shaped plazas, all of which have characteristic names, give the town a quaint picturesqueness. . . . Low passageways carry the thoroughfare under the buildings here and there, giving the artistic contrasts of light and shade, while the oddly costumed figures in the streets make a striking picture."

AT THE "OCEAN OF SUNRISE."

At the "Ocean of Sunrise."

His terms suggest the appeal of the irregular, curvilinear, contrasting and unexpected—the elements of "striking" art, not those of historical or anthropological understanding.

At the same time, Baxter's growing interest in evidence of the spiritual unity of humanity (which would bear different fruit a few years later in his fervid support for the Theosophy movement) attracted him to what he saw as the mysterious communal continuity of Indian life. The vision, again, could be compelling, as on a dark night's arrival after a cold, dreary drive, described in "Zuñi Revisited": "As we drove up to the town the windows gleamed with the cheery, ruddy light of hearth-fires within, and out of many of the stumpy chimney-pots leaped lurid tongues of smoky flame. Around these fires were probably many groups of old and young, listening to the wonderful tales of folk-lore as they had been handed down for centuries from generation to generation." The question arose: Whence came such aboriginal strength? The real value of anthropology, Baxter announced, lay in "the light which it throws on many secret springs and motives of human nature," shared by primitive and civilized peoples alike.

Finally—and most relevant for our purposes—Baxter discloses that by 1882 Cushing was puzzling over the Seven Cities of Cibola and the problem of Zuñi ancestry and possible migratory history.[6] Furthermore, at least as early as the Zuñi visit to Boston, Cushing had been taken by the possibility of a Zuñi cultural relationship with the Incas of Peru ("Some Results of Mr. Cushing's Visit")—long before his discovery of what appeared to be guanaco figurines in the Salado sands. In these as in other respects, as Baxter tells us, the seeds of the Hemenway Expedition were sown early.

But in 1882 they were still seeds, and Cushing was still at Zuñi, dealing with both his new notoriety and new troubles. Almost immediately upon returning

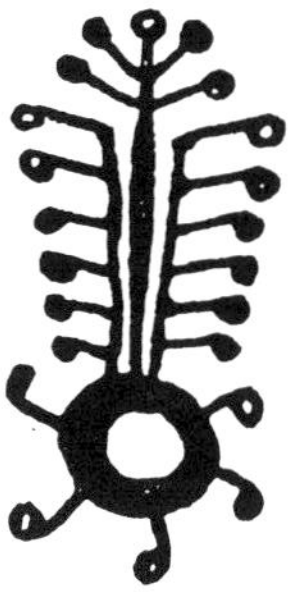

Zuñi autograph of F. H. Cushing, Té-na-tsa-li or Medicine Flower, War Chief, Order of the Bow.

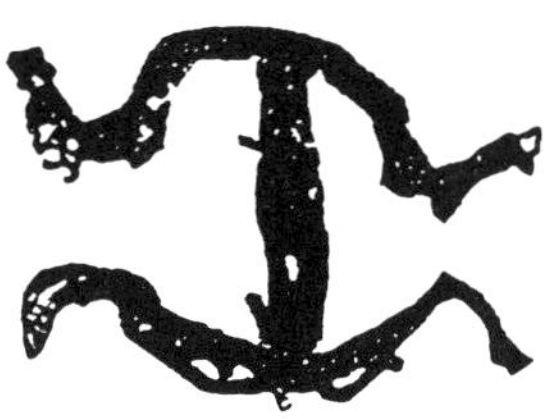

National seal of the Zuñis.

to the pueblo—in which, he now found, there were greater expectations of him as a war chief of the Zuñis—Cushing became deeply embroiled in the political controversies that would lead to his being recalled to Washington fifteen months later. Working through Baxter, Cushing leaked word of an attempt by relatives of Illinois Senator John "Black Jack" Logan—"a noisy and disagreeable man [who] ran Illinois as if it were a feudal fief"[7]—to seize the Las Nutrias lands of the Zuñi reservation. The Cushing-Baxter publicity resulted in an executive order from President Arthur blocking the "Logan land-grab," but it also created trouble for John Wesley Powell, director of the Smithsonian's Bureau of Ethnology, who recalled Cushing in early 1884. Nor was the pueblo spared other disruptions. By the time Cushing left in April, Zuñi was entering a phase of serious social disintegration brought on by external pressures and internal factionalism. Speaking in Santa Fe on Independence Day in 1883, Palowahtiwa said of his people that "if they smile not on Washington and his children, then they will pass away, or like dogs, lie hungry at the doors of strangers."[8] Baxter, for his part, moved for a season to Mexico, where he reported on financial and railroad developments and concerned himself with problems of roads and drainage in Mexico City.

Curtis M. Hinsley

SOLVED AT LAST.

Mysteries of Ancient Aztec History Unveiled By an Explorer from the Smithsonian Institution

Wonderful Achievements of Frank H. Cushing

(From Our Special Correspondent)

FORT WINGATE, N.M., JUNE 10, 1881. It is a striking and refreshing contrast to find in the midst of a range of wilderness such an oasis of cultivation and refinement as this. Fort Wingate seems to me a grandly situated post, facing from its mountain side the marvellous natural creations of sandstone architecture to the north, an architecture constantly changing its aspect with the changing light of the day, and glowing with vividly varying colors. It seems some enchanted city of the gods. Were I a painter, and wished to depict the Asgard of our northern ancestors, with its Valhalla, its frowning castle of the war god Thor, and its fairy-like palace of the beautiful Freya, here would I come for my inspiration. There is one grand rock seen across the spaciousness of the intervening valley known as "the Navajo Church," a seemingly perfect piece of early Gothic, with its massive tower, crowned by fantastic turrets, rising from the meeting of the nave and transept, as in the churches of Normandy.[9]

While just outside the gates of the fort blaze the camp-fires of the Navajos, the plaza-like parade ground is bordered by neat cottages of gray adobe—the

From the *Boston Herald,* 16 June 1881

quarters of the officers and their families—and within may be found pleasant rooms, as tastefully furnished and decorated as the aesthetic homes of the East; the adornments of Navajo blankets, Pueblo pottery, and the skins of animals shot in the mountains giving a peculiar charm of local color. Naturally even the grand impressiveness of the scene palls at last upon many, for the post must be almost a little world to itself, and there is not much to relieve the sameness of garrison life except to listen to the excellent music of the band of the 13th infantry—one of the best bands in the army—an occasional hop or an excursion into the surrounding country. One of the officers has won a considerable reputation as a successful ruin-hunter, the cañons roundabout being full of the unexplored ruins of the Aztec cliff-dwellers—ruins of unknown antiquity. There is little ennui for those who use their opportunities to study the fascinating history of the region—perhaps one of the oldest inhabited parts of the earth, and still peopled by the original folk. The commanding officer, Gen. Bradley,[10] takes an active interest in Indian affairs, and has been a careful observer of the life of the northern Indians, among whom he has, for the most part, been stationed. Dr. Washington Matthews,[11] the surgeon of the post, is one of the best scholars who have devoted themselves to the study of the Indians. While stationed at Fort Berthold, on the upper Missouri, he made most thorough studies of the Hidatsa Indians, and his grammar on their language is spoken of as a splendid philological achievement. He is now making excellent use of his advantages for similar researches among the Navajos. Lieut. Burke [Bourke[12]] of Gen. Crooke's [*sic*][13] staff was also here during the first three days of my visit. Lieut. Burke is detailed to make ethnological investigations among the Indians, and has rendered invaluable service, pursuing his purpose with rare scientific method and thorough system.

A Remarkable Young Ethnologist.

It was here at Fort Wingate, while getting ready for a trip to the famous Indian pueblo of Zuñi—the largest pueblo in America—that I had the rare good fortune to meet Mr. Frank H. Cushing, a young gentleman whose name will soon rank with those of famous scientists. Lieut. Burke said to me: "I regard Mr. Cushing as the greatest ethnologist America has yet produced." Mr. Cushing is a young man to deserve such a high title, but I think his labors will justify it.

Mr. Cushing was sent out by the Smithsonian Institution about two years ago to investigate, in the pueblos of New Mexico, the customs and history of the natives. Mr. Cushing finally selected Zuñi as the seat of his researches. The Zuñi Indians—a name probably derived by the Spaniards from Shi-iu-na, their name in their native tongue—were the principal Pueblo or town Indians with whom Coronado came in contact on his famous march, and may be regarded as the lineal descendants of the ancient Aztecs. There is a popular impression that all the Pueblo Indians of New Mexico are one people, speaking the same language, but the fact is that their tongues are widely varied. Often Pueblos widely apart, like Taoz and Isletta, will speak the same tongue with Pueblos of other languages intervening.[14] The Zuñis, being isolated from the outer world—Zuñi is in the extreme western part of New Mexico, about 40 miles south of Fort Wingate—have been little influenced by their conquerors, and live today, in all essential particulars, just as their ancestors have lived for centuries and centuries. Only a very few of them know a word or two of broken Spanish, and they have preserved their native tongue in all its purity. Like about all the other Pueblos, they have been callous to all attempts to Christianize them, whether by Catholics or Protestants, and they practice today their strange old religious rites.

As a result of Mr. Cushing's labors Aztec history will have to be rewritten. Much of what has hitherto been received as such falls to the ground, a mass of rubbish. There are no other people so distrustful of strangers as are the Indians, so reticent about everything concerning themselves. Therefore, when questioned by strangers about their religion, their past and their traditions, they have answered, to be sure, but these answers, accepted as sober truth, have been uniformly a pack of very ready and ingenious lies. Mr. Cushing, therefore, adopted the only sensible method of getting at the bottom facts; that of becoming one with the Zuñis, learning their language and living with them. Hence we see him, a slender, light complexioned young man—he is not yet 24 years old—with long, flowing blonde hair, confined by the Indian head band, and dressed in the picturesque full costume of the tribe—every article of native manufacture, from the cloth of the dark blue woolen serape-shirt, the buckskin knee breeches, long, dark blue stockings, leather moccasins, and artistically embroidered sash, to the rows of silver buttons and other richly-worked silver ornaments that adorn his dress, and the precious ancient necklace from a mysterious cave of relics up in the mountains. This dress he wears on all occasions, even when visiting Fort Wingate, for, should he be seen in citizen's garb by his adopted brethren, their confidence in his sincerity as a Zuñi, would be shaken. He has gained his cause by the use of pluck, tact and adaptability to circumstances worthy both a general and a diplomatist. In the first place he put himself at their mercy and entirely in their power. Savages, finding a stranger under such circumstances, seldom fail to be merciful. Thus, gaining their confidence by his helplessness, Mr. Cushing was made one of them and formally adopted into the tribe of the Zuñi. Gradually gaining influence among them, he has obtained into their most secret councils, and has now been made one of their chiefs, the second man of influence in their city, standing next to their governor in authority.

A Rich Reward.

Mastering their language thoroughly and scientifically, the knowledge of this has produced the key that has unlocked a treasure house, the opening of whose doors has placed in his possession a store of such wonderful facts as to justify the application of that much-abused term, "astounding revelations." The veil has been drawn from many a mystery—historical, mythological, philological, social. The work has been no holiday sport, no masquerade. Mr. Cushing has had to undergo many perils and privations. Before he could allay the suspicions of his strange fellows, he has been several times within a hair's breadth of losing his life, for the Zuñis are a warlike race. All the Pueblo Indians, though peaceable, are not, by any means, the timid lambs that many have held them to be. Their successful revolution against the Spaniards, two centuries ago, proves this. Mr. Cushing has had to endure such fare as few would submit to for the sake of science. Endless ridicule, of course, was to be expected from the "practical" Americans who are characteristic of the West—those who cannot see the good of any work that "has no money in it"—men who have no more comprehension of the purpose and use of such an undertaking than the Hottentots have of Greek roots.

Mr. Cushing has, in the study of the Zuñi religion, found for certainty that the worship and traditions of Montezuma—so long accepted in all accounts of the Aztecs—have no foundation in fact, and that Montezuma was never heard of. But he has discovered a mine of mythological lore, beliefs and superstitions, gods and spirits, that throw the full light of day on the mysteries of the Aztec religion. Among other wonderful things is the existence of 12 sacred orders, with their priests, and their secret rites as carefully guarded as the secrets of Freemasonry, an institution to which these orders have a strange resemblance. Into several of these orders he has been initiated, and has penetrated to their inmost secrets, obtaining a knowledge of ceremonials both beautiful, profound and grotesque in character. But the most marvellous thing which he has discovered in connection with their religion is the grand fact that their faith is the same thing as modern Spiritualism. The Zuñis have their circles, their mediums, their communications from the spirit world, their materializations—precisely like those of the spiritists of civilized life. Their séances are often so absorbing that they are kept up all night. Their belief in the phenomena explains many strange things about their religion which Mr. Cushing was unable to account for until he hit upon it—they had kept it carefully guarded months after he was on most intimate terms with them—by telling them about certain spiritistic phenomena he had witnessed, thus gaining their sympathy as apparently a fellow believer.

Their language has proved a most interesting study. It is thoroughly grammatical, and has a finely-arranged system of declensions and tenses. The Zuñis are most careful to teach their children to speak correctly, and drill them thoroughly. They have words for "grammatical" and "ungrammatical," "good talking" and "bad talking" literally translated. Strange to say, they have an ancient or classic language, just as English has its Anglo-Saxon. This dead language has been handed down in their religious rites, and is, for the most part, known only by the priests. Many of their sacred songs are worded in it, and these songs are of unknown antiquity. This is a striking illustration of the conservative influence of religion in preserving the institutions of the past. There is a good opportunity for an analogy between the preservation of this ancient aboriginal tongue by the Zuñi priests and the handing down of the Latin by the Catholic church. What a field for philologists here!

The Zuñi language has an extensive unwritten literature, if the term may be used. The religious ceremonials, the sacred orders and the great public festivals require the use of songs and prayers, which have been handed down for generations and generations without the changing of a single word. Then there is a wealth of tradition, fables and proverbs—the latter, many of them, strikingly like the fables and proverbs of European peoples, and particularly the fables of Æsop. For instance, their fable of the race between the turtle, the grasshopper, the sparrow hawk, the falcon and the eagle, is, in many salient points, strikingly like that of the "Hare and the Tortoise," and has a like moral. The history of the race is handed down in like way with wonderful accuracy, and the Zuñis thus have a marvellous knowledge of their past, reaching back into remote ages.[15]

Zuni Poetry.

The poetry of the Zuñis is abundant, and much of it exceedingly beautiful. In rhyme and rhythm it is as perfect as the work of our most finished lyrists. Here is an example, an incantation used by the hunter as he goes out to shoot an antelope. It is known as "A ten-thlannan awen te nan," or "The Hunting Song of the Great Dance":

Ma'a-we, ma-we,
Ma'a-we, ma-we.
Shot-si tai-ioa tai li kwá
Tai-kwan tap-te, thli-ia ni-tá
Thlu-tenon tapte thlè-pon-ne,
Ma-we, ma'a-we.

This is addressed to the antelope, in the Zuñi belief that it is possessed by the spirits of their ancestors friendly to mankind, and that, if addressed in the proper manner, it will be agreeable to the antelope to let himself be shot when it is courteously related to him how he will be prepared for eating. So they tell him: "Antelope, antelope, antelope, antelope, breast cut and skinned, then with the loin is done the same, then the fire is built, and then comes the chin." The chin is considered the daintiest tidbit by the Zuñis, and is naturally the first thing eaten. One great beauty of this little song is the plaintive, low melody to which it is sung. Some of the songs to which the dancers keep time are highly poetic. This literal rendering does not seem very poetical, but there is in the whole idea a really poetic sentiment. It is, however, as an example of form that I cite it.

Here is a part of a prayer offered by Mr. Cushing's adopted father, the second priest of the tribe, [to] the "medicine cacique" on the return of the latter from a dangerous exploring expedition, during which it was reported that he had been killed. The old priest is a man of a beautifully gentle, loving nature: "All spirits! we ask for your light. Far and in parts unknown, where the world is filled with danger, where things forbidden and the unknown are, thence ye have brought back our child. We thank ye! In spite of all danger, we now speak to each other again. We now see one another again. Thanks. Therefore, your light we ask, and we will meet ye with your own blessings." Here is the Yuni [Zuñi] harvest prayer:

"Spirits of our fathers!
Give place to the prayer-clouds which rise from my heart
From ye seeds I ask;
From ye I ask prosperity;
From ye I ask means of light,
And I will return unto ye your own blessings."

Mr. Cushing has also deciphered the secret of the inscriptions or pictographs that cover the cliffs in this part of the country. One of the most important results of this acquisition is the proof they give of the correctness with which the Zuñis had related to him the history of the ruins they mark, and of the extent of the country once covered by the race.[16]

The Cibola Controversy Settled.

An achievement of which Mr. Cushing has reason to be specially proud is the success of his effort to locate exactly the cities of Cibola, a question which has been the cause of many an archæological dispute. This he has settled beyond a shadow of a doubt, the result of his explorations corresponding exactly to the descriptions by Coronado. I myself have seen the ruins of Totentea, which was said by Coronado to be the greatest of the seven cities of Cibola. The Zuñi name of the ruins today is Topeutea, meaning the first, or head city. Coronado speaks also of the city of Ajacus as one of the seven, and Mr. Cushing finds one of the ruins named by the Zuñis as Hauiku'h. Friar Marco de Nisa, in his account, in the spring of 1839, speaks of Ajacus as the principal city, and he seems to have been right, for Hauiku'h—Ajacus was the nearest the Spanish could get to the pronunciation—was found by Mr. Cushing to have the largest ruins. At the southeast, according to Nisa, was the kingdom of Marata. Both Nisa and Coronado applied the term kingdom very vaguely, often using it for region or district. Marata is the Ma k'ia-ta of the Zuñis, and the ruins there are both extensive and of remarkably massive construction. Mr. Cushing has determined the exact sites of all the pueblos of Cibola and of those near it mentioned by Nisa and

Coronado. His proofs, which are indisputable, require too much elaboration for a newspaper article, and to attempt to give them in an abridged form would be an injustice.[17] Therefore the simple statement must answer here, placing the credit for the discovery where it belongs. His report will consider the subject in all its bearings, and will throw quite a new light on the narratives of Nisa and Coronado. I have seen the ruins of the original Cibola and the mountain from which Nisa looked off upon it—the mountain where, with the aid of the Indians, he raised a heap of stones, and erected thereon a small wooden cross, taking possession of the country in the name of the viceroy, the cross standing as a symbol of taking possession. Mr. Cushing found this stone heap still standing, and the father of Pedro Piño, formerly the Governor of Zuñi—Pedro Piño is now an aged man of something like 80 years, and his son is now Governor—saw the remains of the cross on the spot. One of the finest proofs of the location of the Cibola pueblos is the tradition which the Zuñis have of the millings [killing] of "the black Mexican with thick lips." They told this to Mr. Cushing of their own accord, and with no leading questions on his part, under circumstances most convincing that this was the negro Estevan who accompanied Coronado. Mr. Cushing knows the exact pueblo where the deed was done.[18]

From these things, which scarcely hint at the extent of his discoveries, it is easy to predict that the publication of Mr. Cushing's report will be awaited with the most intense interest in scientific circles, both in Europe and in this country. The work will be a big feather in the cap of the Smithsonian Institution, and the selection of Mr. Cushing for such an important enterprise testifies to the sagacious foresight of Prof. Baird,[19] whose confidence in the capability of his protegé for such a great task was not diminished by the thought of his extreme youth.

Personal Characteristics.

Mr. Cushing is a member of the old Cushing family, so well known and highly honored in Massachusetts. His own home is in western New York. He entered Cornell University in his 18th year, but left it while still a freshman to enter the Smithsonian Institution as assistant in the archæological department. Here he was soon promoted to take charge of the ethnological collections. He is full of energy and enthusiasm, and doubtless gains from his father's stock the valorous temper which distinguished his kinsman, Commander Cushing of the navy, who, as a young ensign, blew up the rebel ram Albemarle with his torpedo boat.

The same fearless nature is as valuable to the scientific explorer as to the warrior. Without it Mr. Cushing would have failed at the beginning.

The results of Mr. Cushing's explorations are of such great scientific importance that they ought to be given to the world as soon as possible, thus guarding against any possibility of their being lost, through accident or otherwise. To record all that he has discovered, to arrange and classify his notes and get his material into shape for publication, would, without assistance, be a work of years. Therefore, in order to satisfy the demand of the scientific world for speedy information, and to enable Mr. Cushing to turn his attention to other important work, he ought to have the assistance of a competent stenographer. Such aid would be invaluable to him in giving him the means to record with exact minuteness the notes of his daily experiences and to work up into form for publication the immense accumulation of material now on hand.

Mr. Cushing will probably stay with the Zuñis about a year longer, as there are a number of important themes which he just hit upon, and which he naturally desires to work up thoroughly. There is a vast field waiting to be worked up by a man of such powers. This summer Mr. Cushing will make a trip to Arizona to investigate an unknown tribe of Pueblo Indians, living in one of the deep "box cañons," so called, tributary to the great cañon of the Colorado.[20] In these almost inaccessible depths they are said to have beautiful peach orchards and cultivated gardens and extensive flocks of sheep. Only three or four white men have entered here, and but meagre accounts have been given of the place. Mr. Cushing, however, is famed among the southern Indians, from Texas to California—tidings spread wonderfully fast among the Indians—and, as there are constant interchanges of visits among all the Pueblos, this distant, unknown folk has extended an invitation for "the Washington Zuñi,"—as he is universally called among the Indians—to make them a visit. The place where these people live is called the cañon of Cataract creek. They are known as the Java-Supais, but the name by which they call themselves is Ku'h-ni. They are not the same people as the Koaninos, as has been supposed by some.

Mr. Cushing is confident that the mystery of the magnificent ruins of Yucatan—a mystery that has generally been supposed to be impenetrable—will some day be solved. It will be done, he says, by some one who will follow a course like that he has pursued. They must go among the Mayas, the fierce people who inhabit the mountain wilds of Yucatan, and who are the lineal descendants of the builders of those grand ruins, and let themselves be found among them some day, helpless and alone. Then, learning their language and becoming one with them, the explorer will find himself rewarded by a clear, full knowledge of their history—a knowledge that will also enable him to read the mazes of inscriptions on the stones of the ancient palaces as readily as he would read a book.[21] Perhaps it may be the mission of Mr. Cushing to do this work.

Mr. Cushing hopes to be able to bring four or five of the principal men of Zuñi East with him when he returns to Washington, and show them the homes of what they regard as the loftiest and most perfect type of man—the Eastern American, the men of the rising sun. It is to be hoped that he will, for they are a remarkable race, and have a wonderful, fascinating history that still holds the key of many grand secrets. The only Pueblo Indians who ever came East were two of the leading men of Isletta, on the Rio Grande, who once determined to see their "Great Father at Washington," and made the journey at their own expense.

S. B.

F. H. CUSHING AT ZUNI

THE ACCOUNTS OF MR. F. H. CUSHING'S remarkable ethnological work at Zuñi have been received with such deep interest that I have frequently been asked for particulars concerning his experiences. I have felt a diffidence in giving these, since being simply a layman, with a sincere interest in the development of the rich field of American archæology, in which there is room for, and need of, many earnest workers, I feared that in repeating what I have learned, there might be some inaccuracy of expression caused by a lack of preparation in these studies; but since Mr. Cushing's investigations have upset many preconceived theories concerning the Pueblo Indians of the Southwest and their institutions, all of us are, in a certain sense, unprepared: therefore, the little I have to say must necessarily be fragmentary; but I will try to be as straightforward and plain as possible. At most, it will be but a slight skimming of a small part of the surface, and we shall have to wait patiently for Mr. Cushing's report to reach the root of things. Upon parts of this report he is now hard at work. Among other things, he has in hand a monograph on the meanings of the ancient pictographic

---

From the *American Architect and Building News,* 4 February 1882

inscriptions on the rocks in the Zuñi country, and of the conventionalized decorative forms upon their pottery. It is unfortunate that one of his papers was lost in transmission to the Smithsonian Institution: it was an essay upon the numeral system of the Zuñis, and in the arrangement of data and conclusions, it showed rare scientific perception.

In fact, I was struck by the remarkable scientific quality of Mr. Cushing's mind. His rank is far above that of a gatherer of facts: he arranges and weighs his facts, and extracts from them that which is the real essence of science, making ethnology a living thing, and not a skeleton or a mummy. This, too, without romancing or tracing fancy resemblances that enable one to find what he wishes to find—a temptation too strong for many archæologists and ethnologists. It must necessarily be some time before Mr. Cushing's report is ready for the world, for he is now in the very midst of collecting his material, and feels something of a despair of grasping the whole of the rich store at his disposal. The arrangement of his notes will naturally be a long and serious task, and I wish it were possible for him to have a phonographer [stenographer] at his service, so that the work might go on more speedily and be placed beyond the danger of destruction. The life of the Zuñis, which is to-day substantially what it was before the Spanish conquest, cannot fail soon to be modified by American civilization, and it must be recorded soon or never. The scope of Mr. Cushing's researches is so extensive that it would hardly be within the power of any one man to arrange the total result, and it is his intention to place much of his material at the disposal of scientific friends. This material includes elaborate philological, mythological, and historical notes, together with studies of institutions, manners, and customs. The cloud of incongruous myths which had been gathered about the Pueblo life by the old Spanish missionaries, who were both credulous and romancing, has been dispelled, but a new array has been revealed in their stead, more marvellous because of their truth and their origin.

Mr. Cushing's scientific method is an extremely simple one, yet extremely difficult to follow, and, in fact, could not have been successfully followed except by a man of his peculiar natural aptitude. It consists simply in making himself one with the people he is studying. It required a high degree of both fortitude and adaptability to attain the confidence of these people, and of pluck, tact, and diplomatic skill to maintain his standing with them.

His success seems still more remarkable when his youth is taken into consideration, for he is but twenty-four years of age. Of course, a degree of deceit has been necessary, for his true purpose could not be made known to the Zuñis, and if known could not be comprehended. They do know, however, that he was sent to them by "the Great Father at Washington," and is under orders from him. This kind of deceit cannot be called treachery, however, for the results will not bring harm to them; on the contrary, Mr. Cushing is their truest friend, and will do his best to be their benefactor, and whatever he does is done in the cause of science. The way in which he attained admission to their ancient order of "The Bearers of the Bow" (A-pith-lan-shi-wa-ni)[22] is an illustration of the fertility of his resources and the persistency with which he follows his purpose. Admission to this order can be obtained only by one who has taken a scalp in warfare, and Mr. Cushing secured his trophy through the recent Apache outbreak. This order is the most important of the several which exist among the Zuñis, and which have a resemblance to the institution of Freemasonry. Is it not possible that the latter may be a remnant of a similar stage of culture among our own races? Mr. Cushing's membership has been of the greatest importance to his work, as may be judged by the following extract from a letter received from him recently: "I have been going through some of the pleasant (?) [*sic*] little duties incident to a membership of the A-pith-lan-shi-wa-ni, and writing night and day to keep my notes up. Four successive nights, two of them entirely sleepless, last week, and two already this week, are too much for me, or I wouldn't be writing here to-night; for all the secret orders save mine are in session, and I have, through my membership—a privilege granted by none save it—admission to all of the others. I wish I had four constitutions, and two persons; I could then keep up with my opportunities. As I have but one, however, supplied with only half a constitution, I had to content myself with going around and saying my prayers before the altars, and taking a few hungry glances—even which has required until nearly midnight." Again he writes: "I have been busy day and night with religious exercises of my order, in which I am already getting very high rank. I had to learn a prayer of more than *two thousand words,* with various shorter exercises." At latest accounts Mr. Cushing was getting material for a collection of fairy lore, which promised to be as rich, imaginative, and full of strange conceptions, as the wonderful collection of the Brothers Grimm.

While I was in Zuñi, Mr. Cushing told of a tradition about a certain man of the tribe who a long time ago, under Spanish rule, was for some reason taken down into Mexico.[23] There he was allowed to go about the country at liberty. One day he met an Indian who, to his surprise, addressed him in Zuñi. "He looked, and behold he *was* a Zuñi; in dress, speech, and everything." He learned from him that there was a nation of Zuñis there, and, if I remember rightly, he went and dwelt among them for some time, coming away with greetings for the Zuñis in the north. And this was the first that these two families of the same stock knew of each other. At last, the Zuñi returned home, escorted by Spanish soldiers, who built him a house much larger and finer than any in Zuñi at that time. The foundations of the house are still pointed out, and prove it to have been on a grander scale than its contemporary structures.

It does not seem impossible that there may be some truth in this story. The Indians of Mexico have been very little studied, and in the remote wanderings of the Zuñis this branch may have become separated, just as the Apaches and Navajos, who speak the same language, became separated. Among the Pueblos of New Mexico, Taos, on the extreme north, and Isleta, on the extreme south, are of one family, speaking the same tongue, while Pueblos speaking various other languages separate them. Therefore, it is possible that these Mexican Zuñis may still exist, and it would be interesting indeed should Mr. Cushing find them out some time.

S. B.

SOME RESULTS OF MR. CUSHING'S VISIT

THE VISIT OF MR. F. H. CUSHING to the East with his Zuñi friends, and the accounts of his adventurous, but thoroughly scientific methods of investigation, have had the natural and highly beneficial effect of quickening both a popular and a scholarly interest in the development of anthropologic studies in America. The study of the native races of North America forms one of the richest fields on the globe for ethnological investigation. We may therefore expect soon to see numbers of our young students, equipped for the task by a thorough preliminary training, and fired by Mr. Cushing's example, turn their attention in a similar direction. The opportunities are practically unbounded: there is an urgent need for an army of sincere workers in the field; the best part of the work must be done by the present generation; and Mr. Cushing says that there is not a native tribe in North America that will not richly reward a study of its institutions according to the methods he has pursued with the Zuñis. In the way of sedentary native races there is a wider opportunity for study than may appear to the casual observer. The pueblo tribes of New Mexico and Arizona are not the only original sedentary races outside of Old Mexico. Just as the Zuñis appear to be the

From *American Architect and Building News,* 29 April 1882

present representatives of the ancient Toltecs, according to Mr. Cushing's well-grounded belief—and not connected with the Aztecs, as has been supposed by many—there is reason to believe that the ancient mound-builders stock of the Mississippi valley has its living representatives in the earth-lodge building Mandans and kindred stocks of the Northwest, and also in the Natchez and Creeks of the South.[24] It is not impossible that he who goes among some of these tribes and becomes one of them for purposes of study, may discover that they have an accurate knowledge of the history of many of the famous mounds and their dwellers, just as Mr. Cushing discovered that the history of many of the ancient ruined pueblos and cliff-dwellings was accurately preserved in the traditions of the Zuñis, whose ancestors built them. Another highly interesting and finely developed class of sedentary Indians, are the Nai-das [Haidas] and other "joint-tenement-house" tribes of the Northwest coast.

A young ethnologist, however, can find for his maiden investigations good fields of work nearer home. I had the pleasure of accompanying Mr. Cushing to New York on his return to Washington from his Boston visit. At Norwich, Conn., the Zuñis were astonished and gratified at meeting a genuine native New England Indian. He was a watchman at the railway station, and he passed through the train with lantern in hand; standing in silent amazement as he came face to face with his brethren of the South-west in their native costume. He was a fine specimen of his race: over six feet in height and of stalwart proportions; he told us that he was a Narragansett. We noticed that he spoke English imperfectly, and Mr. Cushing said it was evident that he spoke the native tongue of his people. The Zuñis were told that he was one of those whose ancestors lived here at the time the white people came to this country, whereupon one of them said: "So he is one of those who the Father of the Council told us welcomed the Americans to the land" (President Bishop of the Massachusetts Senate, in his graceful speech to the Zuñis, had eloquently spoken of the welcoming of the Pilgrims by the Indians at Plymouth), and they feelingly wished the child of King Philip's race a long and prosperous life as each one grasped him warmly by the hand.

This episode led me to ask Mr. Cushing if there was not anything about the remnants of our native Indian tribes scattered here and there in the East worthy of systematic ethnological study, and he said that undoubtedly there was. The reason why they were not made the subject of such study was the prevalent belief that the field had been thoroughly worked up. Such was not the case, and there was a deal of valuable material to be obtained in this way which might perhaps throw considerable light on certain features of colonial history and the nature of the people who occupied these shores when our forefathers came. Wherever there was a remnant of an aboriginal tribe, even though its habits of life might have become radically changed and the purity of its blood destroyed by commingling with other races, there was a promising field for ethnological work, provided its language be kept alive. If the language were lost, however, there would be little opportunity for profitable labor; but the following fact should be borne in mind: a few families of Indians might live surrounded by whites, and the latter never suspect that a separate language existed among them, for a leading characteristic of the race is secretiveness and a distrust of strangers concerning such things.

Some of our college students might find it a novel and profitable manner of spending a summer vacation by instituting an investigation of this sort. Valuable suggestions for the work might be obtained by consulting the authorities of the Bureau of Ethnology at Washington, or of the American Archæological Institute at Boston. Major Powell's "Introduction to the Study of Indian Languages,"[25] and other handbooks published by the Bureau would be invaluable aids. It should be remembered, however, that a peculiar temperament is required for successful work of the kind. Sympathy and adaptability to the ways of others are needed above all. One must place himself on a thorough equality with his subjects; must share and appear to enjoy their ways of living and thinking; and must avoid giving the slightest occasion for allowing them to suppose that in any way he regards himself as socially above their level. The language, in many instances, would be a difficult thing to get hold of, but patient application and the exercise of diplomacy could hardly fail to be rewarded at last. In the investigation of these tribal remnants the acquisition of folk-lore, traditions, legends, and superstitions, together with the observation of peculiar customs and details of daily life, would probably be the most valuable results. In obtaining these the reciprocal method, as practised by Mr. Cushing, is the most practical and useful; for instance, the narration or reading of tales of folk-lore or mythology would undoubtedly be repaid in kind.

Mr. Cushing's methods are heartily approved by his principal, Major J. W. Powell, the director of the Smithsonian Institution Bureau of Ethnology, who is now recognized as one of the foremost of living scientists. Major Powell says that the days of "travelling ethnologists" have gone by. In the first annual Report of his Bureau, recently published, he has an admirable paper, "On Limitations to the Use of [Some] Anthropologic Data," in which he shows the folly of metaphysical methods in anthropologic study, and cites examples from three eminent authors—Grant Allen, Peschel, and Herbert Spencer,[26]—to illustrate the worthlessness of a vast body of anthropologic material to which even the best writers resort. "Anthropology," says Major Powell, "needs trained devotees with philosophical methods and keen observation to study every tribe and nation of the globe almost *de novo*; and from materials thus collected a science may be established.["]

Mr. Cushing's visit to Boston was marked by an ethnological discovery of great importance, being nothing less than the fact that in religion the ancient Incas of Peru were much the same as the Zuñis of to-day. In visiting the Peabody Museum at Cambridge, Mr. Cushing examined for the first time the splendid collection of Inca articles, which included certain things which have been the puzzle of archæologists, and known as the "Peruvian mysteries." These he at once saw were the religious sacrificial paraphernalia of the Incas, and in essential characteristics substantially identical with those used by the Zuñis. They were also identified by the Zuñis as corresponding to their own. It is hoped that this important subject will be worked by Mr. Cushing jointly with Professor Putnam, the latter treating it from the standpoint of Peruvian archæology, while Mr. Cushing tells of the present observances of the Zuñis.[27]

Sylvester Baxter.

THE FATHER OF THE PUEBLOS

HIGH UP ON THE WESTERN SLOPE of the Sierra Madre, in New Mexico, nearly a mile and a half above the sea-level, and but a few miles beyond the divide, where scanty waters begin their timid and uncertain way down toward the Pacific, stands ancient Zuñi, the father of the pueblos. When Coronado made his famous march into the unknown North, the Zuñis, or Shi-wi-nas, as they call themselves, were the first, and also the most numerous and powerful, of the pueblo people encountered by him. Their towns covered a great territory, almost deserving the name of "kingdom"—a term so lavishly and loosely used by Coronado and his contemporary explorers. Oppression and pestilence have so diminished their numbers, and their strict exclusiveness has so impoverished their physical condition, that the once mighty nation has now been reduced to a handful of people. These inhabit a single pueblo. But the country around is dotted with ruined towns upon whose walls is graven the symbol of the shi-wi-na, the sacred water-spider, whose figure forms the Zuñi coat of arms. Here, surrounded by the forsaken homes of their kindred and ancestry—crumbling

From *Harper's New Monthly Magazine,* June 1882

heaps which in antiquity rival the storied stones of the Old World—the Zuñis live as their fathers lived, and jealously treasure their proud history.

Zuñi is still the largest of the pueblos of New Mexico and Arizona, and is looked up to by the others, which differ entirely in language, with the veneration and homage belonging to the elder member of their family, the source whence come their religion and institutions. By the census of 1880, under an accurate count, the population of Zuñi numbered 1602, nearly 500 more than that of Isleta, the next pueblo in size. Therefore it is still a considerable town. It is only a few years since the Zuñis numbered several thousand, but an epidemic of the small-pox decimated them terribly.

With the exception of the Moquis and the Java Supais, or Ku'h-nis, in Arizona—the latter an almost unknown pueblo in Cataract Creek Cañon, one of the "box cañons" of the Colorado—the Zuñis are the most isolated of all the pueblo tribes. They have therefore been little influenced by contact either with Spanish or Anglo-American civilization, and to-day live substantially the life they led when Coronado first started out in search of the seven cities of Cibola. The river pueblos, as they are called—those ranging along the Rio Grande from Taos to Isleta—have monopolized the attention of travellers and writers, being the most convenient of access. But these, surrounded by the towns of the Mexicans on every hand, and latterly having come in contact with the more pushing American, who leaves his own indelible impress upon all whom he meets, they have naturally been materially influenced by the alien life around them, and their manners have been considerably changed thereby.

However good a copy may be, however faithful as a reproduction, the most of us have a strong preference for originals. So Zuñi, as the oldest of the pueblo families, as the father of their *Kultur,* as the Germans would say, and possessing the most distinctive characteristics, is decidedly the representative pueblo of New Mexico. For this reason, and because it had been little touched even by the pioneer tourists who have been brought to the new Southwest by the advent of railroads, we decided to visit it. It was well that we did so, for a mind of rare scientific attainments had been attracted thither for similar reasons, and the company of its possessor proved of much profit and pleasure to us.

The building of the new Atlantic and Pacific Railroad, with its strong, smooth track designed for heavy transcontinental travel, had just brought Zuñi within an easy day's wagon journey of one of the world's great highways, being about thirty miles southward from the military post of Fort Wingate, thus saving a fatiguing trip of many days across a forbidding country.

The land inhabited by the declining nation living on in the twilight of its ancient glory—worn out but not despondent, and lifting its head proudly to receive whatever fate may yet have to bestow before its life-sands run entirely out—the land also looks old and worn and weary of its prolonged battle of myriad centuries against the united elements: perhaps a foreshadowing of the time when the vital forces of all the globe shall be as spent as in this corner of it, and the great earth-ball swing its way through space as cold and dead and nakedly desolate as the lifeless, airless moon.

The hoary ruins of the other continent, draped with the verdure of vines, and embowered and crowned with aborescent beauty, impress us with the age of mankind. But here the ruined earth itself, sprinkled with the ruined dwellings of man, tells with awful eloquence of the antiquity of both the world and its dominant animal. And it tells that the youth of both is so unspeakably far away in the past! Since the ocean rolled over the land and forsook it, and mighty rivers coursed their way across it, the forces of nature have cut far down into the earth's surface, have eaten into it, hewn it away, worn it down, and skimmed it off, until now the former level only remains in gigantic detached tables, standing mountain-like thousands of feet above the arid plains of to-day. And upon the old upper plain of these mesas the ocean has left its shells, and the prehistoric rivers their bowlders and pebbles, their beds still plainly marking the surface of what is left of the structure of a continent before its geography was remodelled.

As if in sublime mockery of the insignificance of man and his works, time has wrought these ruins of a remote geological era into curious and fantastic semblances of human ruins. The most wonderful and majestically beautiful of architectural forms are here, carven in the rich sandstone which ranges through all the warm hues from brown to red and yellow, with gray and black for sober relief. Castles, halls, temples with grand gables, terraces, gateways, and porches, turrets and pinnacles, lofty towers and graceful spires, form vast Titanic cities. Though only the theatre of the dusk of a race of man, here well might be the scene of the *Götterdämmerung*.

And here the earth's ruins only are foliage-garbed and tree-crowned. Nature has kept her funeral wreaths for her own remains alone. Forests deck the roofs of this natural architecture, and their fringes drape the sides, flank the towers, adorn the buttresses, and fill the crevices of the magnificent masonry. These forests are mementos of the time when the life-giving ocean winds swept free across the young continent, and wove a green garment for all its surface. The same winds still touch what is left of their old haunts, and their breath has still the same magic power. But before they sink into the dry depths of the later plains their moisture is wrung away. Meanwhile the ruins of man's buildings crouch pitiably bare at the feet of the mighty structures, with no leaves to cover their nakedness, as if Nature denied her consolation to man, the desecrater of the forest temples she reared for his protection—man, who by his sacrilege is covering the world's fairest fields with desolation, and hastening the day of the planet's death. May there not be prophecy in the Northern myth that when Iduna with her youth-giving apples is gone, leaving the gods gray and weak in the twilight of their power, then on the last day shall come Surtur from his realm of Muspelheim—the flame-world—and destroy the gods and the earth with his fiery sword? For the gods are but the powers of nature, and the last day is Surtur's day.

At Fort Wingate—whose clustered buildings of light gray adobe look cheerfully out from a mountain-side background of dark green pinos across a brown plain to a panorama of this architectural sublimity—while sitting in the officers' club-room one warm afternoon, we saw a striking figure walking across the parade ground: a slender young man in a picturesque costume; a high-crowned and broad-brimmed felt hat above long blonde hair and prominent features; face, figure, and general aspect looked as if he might have stepped out of the frame of a cavalier's portrait of the time of King Charles. The costume, too, seemed at first glance to belong to the age of chivalry, though the materials were evidently of the frontier. There were knee-breeches, stockings, belt, etc., all of a fashion that would not have an unfamiliar look if given out as a European costume of two or three centuries ago. But it was a purely aboriginal dress, such as had been worn on that ground for ages.

Answering our inquiry, the army officer with whom we were talking said: "That is Frank H. Cushing, a young gentleman commissioned by the Smithsonian Institution to investigate the history of the pueblo Indians as it may be traced in their present life and customs. He is living at Zuñi, that being the best field for his researches. It is no streak of eccentricity that prompts him to dress that way; no desire to make himself conspicuous. He is one of the most modest fellows I ever knew, and the attention attracted by such a costume is really painful

Frank H. Cushing.

to him. But he bears it without flinching, as bravely as he has borne many perils and privations in the cause of science. He has an end in view, and wisely adopts the means best suited to its attainment. That is the course taken by all men successful in whatever may be their chosen pursuits. Stanley would have been a fool to wear the fur clothing of the arctic regions, or even his native starched linen, on his expedition into the heart of Africa. Neither would a miller follow his trade in a suit of black broadcloth. So Cushing, to make a success of his investigations, can not stand contemplating his subjects from the outside, like a spectator at a play. He must go on to the stage, and take his own part in the performance. There are no people more distrustful of the motives of strangers than are the North American Indians. One can only learn anything trustworthy from them by gaining their confidence and sympathy; so Cushing has adopted the only sensible course. He has become one of the Zuñis for the time being, has conformed to all their observances, and learned their language thoroughly. He has been made their second chief, and is a recognized leader among them. His reward is that the curtain of a mysteriously hidden past and present has been lifted for him. To a primitive people rank and authority are most powerfully indicated by their outward symbols. To maintain his influence, Cushing must out-Zuñi the Zuñis, so to speak. A man sent to them from the great father at Washington, and with means and leisure, as he seems to have, must dress according to his station. And it pleases and flatters them to see him always arrayed in the full traditional costume of their nation—a dress such as they only wear on formal occasions. He is amply rewarded for all such conformities to their pleasure. As you are intending a trip to Zuñi, gentlemen, you ought by all means to meet him. To be there with him will alone make it worth your while to have come across the continent. His companionship will give you an insight into the life of a strange people whose strangeness is passing quickly away—a life which otherwise you could hope to know only by what the uninstructed, and therefore deceiving, vision might tell you."

We soon met Mr. Cushing, and spent a few pleasant days with him at the fort. The knowledge gained by our intercourse, which developed a warm mutual friendship, proved to be the finest preparation for the trip, like "reading up" before setting out on a tour to strange countries. Mr. Cushing was visiting his friend Dr. Washington Matthews, the post surgeon, and was engaged in packing some rare specimens to go to the Smithsonian Institution. Dr. Matthews was in hearty sympathy with Mr. Cushing's work, being himself an able ethnologist, who has made a reputation by his researches among the Hidatzas of the Northern plains, and is now making similar studies among the Navajos. Another energetic worker in the aboriginal field, whose duty happened to call him to Fort Wingate at the time, was Lieutenant Bourke, of General Crooke's staff, detailed to make special studies of the habits of the Indians. Lieutenant Bourke was modestly depreciatory of the value of his own work in comparison with that of Mr. Cushing, whom he termed the ablest American ethnologist. But Lieutenant Bourke's investigations, as recorded in his accurate and remarkably full notes, can not fail to form valuable contributions to ethnological science.

It was an early June morning, with hot sunshine, but clear, invigorating air, when we started in a four-mule ambulance on our trip of thirty miles to Zuñi. There were four of us—Mr. Cushing, a young lieutenant, the artist, and the writer. We were soon high up on the wooded uplands of the Zuñi range, enjoying on the ascent backward views over great plains expanding away to the blue distance of Arizona mountains. The forest scenery of the mountain heights was in delightful contrast to the dusty plain's dry waste. The road wound through shady groves of tall and sturdy pines, their trunks marked with clean red bark; also cedars with bark in queer gray scales, like the back of an alligator. The woods stood, not with closed ranks like an Eastern forest, but open and parklike, interspersed with beautiful grassy glades: just the places for grazing deer.

Time sped quickly in listening to Mr. Cushing's willing replies to our multitudinous inquiries. "If you are told that any primitive people is ignorant of its history, don't you believe it," said he. "They know all about it." And he told with what wonderful accuracy traditions are handed down among the Zuñis, the tales, repeated thousands of times, being transmitted from father to son without the change of a single word, for generation after generation. Reliance on written words seems to impair the retentive power of the memory of lettered races, and the marvellous memorizing capacity of illiterate peoples is illustrated in the handing down of the grand old Northern sagas by the Icelanders, until the acquisition of the alphabet enabled them to be recorded by that great author Snorri Sturluson; also the transmission for generations, among the same people, of the most intricate of genealogical details, involving the history of widely branched families for centuries, and covering all the lands of Scandinavia.

In the same way the Zuñis have an extensive unwritten literature, if the expression may be permitted. They have a vast accumulation of fables and folklore, and the past of the nation is given in what may be termed the Zuñi Bible.

This sacred work is publicly recited at rare but regularly recurring intervals. It is in four divisions, corresponding to four books, and each of these is divided into four chapters. Its recitation occupies two long evenings. It is in perfect rhyme and rhythm, and is highly poetic. When Mr. Cushing first came to Zuñi the charge of the Bible was officially intrusted to an aged, white-haired, and blind old man, a veritable native Homer. This was the sole duty of the bard, and he was supported by the public. He died, and the succession came to one of four whom he had trained up. These four are in turn continually instructing youth qualified for the high trust by birth and lineage.

To acquire and record this wonderful work, the Zuñi Bible, would be a Homeric task. Mr. Cushing has several times had the privilege of listening to its recital—it is very often recited informally; but to memorize it and write it down would demand the closest application. To get it repeated often enough for such a purpose would need the use of the nicest diplomacy. The Bible begins with the mythical origin of the people, and then enters upon what is evidently genuine history. This is brought down to comparatively recent times, but the work ends before the era of the Spanish conquest is reached. The story of the Zuñis is told from the time when their home was on the shore of the great ocean to the westward, probably in Southern California, and the various changes of abode are given during their migration to their present seat in the land of Cibola, as the country of the Zuñis, after much historical controversy, is now fully proven to be by Mr. Cushing. The sites of the seven cities of Cibola, described by Coronado and Friar Niza, have been accurately fixed by Mr. Cushing: they are in the immediate neighborhood of the present pueblo of Zuñi, which was established upon its present site not long after the Spanish conquest, having been removed from its location near by.

The accuracy of the information possessed by the Zuñis concerning the ruined towns where their ancestry lived is marvellous. These towns were successively settled and abandoned for various causes, chief among which were the pressure of hostile people, and the choking with sand of the springs upon which they depended. The history of these places, which are almost innumerable, is mostly back in obscure antiquity, as is certified by time's imprint upon the ruins. The region in which these ruins are found covers a large part of New Mexico and Arizona. Every investigation of ruins claimed by the Zuñis as theirs—their locations often having been unknown until Mr. Cushing was told that the Zuñis once lived in certain places, to be distinguished by certain marks and features—has verified their statements, their accuracy always proving unerring.

The language of the Zuñis is the reverse of barbarically crude, as might perhaps be expected of an aboriginal tongue. It has a finely ordered structure, and is very expressive, abounding in delicate shadings, and allowing fine distinctions of meaning. The order of sentences resembles that of Latin and German rather than English. The Zuñis are fastidious in their requirements for the correct use of the language, and are intolerant of ungrammatical speech; and, strange to say, they have an ancient or classical language, spoken centuries ago, handed down in the many sacred songs, and used to-day in their religious observances. This dead language bears a similar relation to their speech of to-day as Anglo-Saxon to English. It is not understood by the common people, but is familiar only to the priests and leading men. So here too is the Church the conservator of ancient erudition.

On every hand are met startling resemblances to the familiar civilizations of the East. The folk-lore, the recital of whose tales and fables begins after the frost comes, and fills the long winter evenings at the family firesides, offers many of these parallels. Some of their fables are, in substance, almost exactly identical with the fables of Æsop. For spells and incantations the Zuñis use short rhymed couplets, just as did our Saxon ancestors. Their religious ceremonials are strangely like those of the ancient Egyptians and Greeks. A striking analogy between the Zuñi and the Northern mythology is found in the characterization of the spirit of evil. The Zuñis have two names for the Evil One, meaning respectively "the maliciously bad" and "the stupidly bad." In the same way the Northern mythology has two evil spirits—Loki, the cunning demon, the spirit of intelligent wickedness, who often dresses evil in an alluring guise, and the strong but blind Hödur, in whom the evil coming from the possession of power by ignorance is typified, Hödur killing unwittingly his beautiful brother Baldur with the lance of mistletoe placed in his hand by the sly Loki. In view of these many resemblances, the query has been raised if the story of the lost Atlantis, the sunken continent, might not be something more than a myth. Might not this, the older continent, be the ancestral home of the oldest races of the Eastern world? Or do these resemblances simply show that for the mental development of man there are certain set forms, that these repeat themselves everywhere, and that the human intellect passes through regular stages of progression, of which these similarities are marks? These are questions which ethnology may be able to answer some day when it has become a more positive science.

Meanwhile we had begun to ascend the southerly slope of the Zuñi range, and the steepness of the way, together with its roughness, was calculated to arouse serious misgivings about arriving safely at the bottom. For a new sensation, driving on the plains and among the mountains of the Southwest may be commended. A team will fearlessly plunge, with brakes firmly set, down the banks of a deep arroyo—the dry bed of a torrent—and jauntily storm the almost perpendicular opposite bank. In an Eastern town the existence of such a road would fill the sleep of the selectmen with fearful nightmares of suits for damages to be brought by the owners of injured vehicles.

The beautiful valley of Las Nutrias (The Beavers) now lay smiling before us with fertile fields of growing crops, and ringed around by ruggedly picturesque mountains, sharp rocks and sombre pines contrasting with the peaceful beauty of the scene below. Las Nutrias is one of three or four small pueblos which, since the reduction of the tribe, have in recent years been abandoned as permanent abiding places, but are used as summer residences, where people live while they tend their fields. The entire population is now concentrated at Zuñi.

Crossing a brook whose waters irrigated the broad fields around, we halted at one of these "summer villas" to rest for lunch. Its structure was rather different from the regular dwellings we afterward became familiar with. Like them, its walls were solidly built of adobe and stone, but in front was a sort of veranda, and a wide space had been cut away in the wall of the principal room, a large apartment, which was thus made into a sort of airy, open hall. The noonday was hot outside, but within there was an agreeable coolness, the light, dry air of the altitudes not retaining the heat away from the sunshine. An old man and a white-haired wife welcomed us cordially, and chatted vivaciously with "Kuishy," as they called our friend, while a chubby brown boy of four or five years, with pretty face and black mischievous eyes, romped around us. To the lunch we had brought along, the old woman added by setting before us a basket of parched corn, which proved something like our parched sweet corn. They always slightly parch their corn before grinding it into meal, spreading it out in the dome-shaped ovens which stand outside their doors, and often on their roofs, forming, as in the Orient, prominent architectural features of their dwellings.

Lunch over, we set out again, but a sick mule made our progress tediously slow. Under the circumstances, finding that it would be impossible to reach Zuñi that night, we turned toward Pescado, another of the summer suburbs, named for a fine large spring near by, full of little fish. This spring gushes out beautifully from beneath a great lava rock, giving fertility to a large district. Though eating many strange things, as we soon had opportunity to see, the Zuñis together with other Southwestern Indians, have their own ideas of fastidiousness; and one thing which neither they nor the Navajos will touch is fish, showing the most intense disgust at the idea of eating it. Therefore the finny inhabitants which give their name to the Pescado spring remain undiminished in number.

The Governor of Zuñi, whom we had already met at the fort a few days before, was at Pescado attending to his farm. He was at work in a field near the road as we approached, and came to meet us. A joyful gleam illuminated his dusky face as he recognized "his young brother," and as he walked along beside our slowly moving team he humorously responded to Kuishy's playful queries. A member of the most powerful family of Zuñi, Patricio Pino is a man of middle age, with a thoughtful, reflective face, and a profile that is almost classically Greek. We reached Pescado none too soon, for the moment we stopped, our sick mule fell to the ground, and in a few minutes was dead.

The cloudless sunset was speedily followed by calm moonlight, and the night air had begun to have a touch of chilliness in it when we were summoned in to supper—climbing up a ladder, and entering through the roof of a house that probably antedated the Spanish conquest, for Pescado is much older than the present Zuñi. A large L-shaped room, with a low ceiling, and dingy walls hung with blankets and weapons, was lit by the flickering flame in a corner fire-place, where a large kettle was steaming and sending out an odor of stewing meat grateful to the nostrils of hungry men. Two large bowls of the smoking stew were dished out; one was set before us, and we drew around it, sitting on sheepskins and blankets spread over the earthen floor, while the dusky members of the household formed a circle around the other, close by. The dish was really excellent, a kind of thick mutton broth, with whole grains of wheat to give it body, and agreeably flavored with a kind of herb highly prized by the Zuñis. Rolls of the peculiar "paper bread" were given to us. In eating it, it is the custom to dip the end of the roll into the broth. The liquid part was eaten with a sort of spoon made of pottery—a spoon without a handle, but at the upper end of the bowl, where the handle should be, it was curved over backward so that it could be hung on the edge of the dish. There were, of course, no knives and forks, and the meat was taken out with the fingers. We learned that we had quite won the hearts of our hosts by doing in Rome as the Romans did; for they had been accustomed to see white visitors manifest much squeamishness about their food, and not unfrequently gingerly refuse to touch it at all.

As an "entrée," a dish of roasted locusts was handed around. The writer did not venture to try them, but his companions did. They are said to be as delicate and delicious as shrimps, with a similar flavor. Mr. Cushing confessed that, although he made it a rule to eat everything that the Zuñis did, he never could get over a certain repugnance to the idea of eating these locusts. But as lobsters, crabs, and shrimps are insects as well as locusts, there seems to be no logical reason why the latter should not be as edible as the others. To catch them, the holes where the locust larvæ lie are watched in the early morning. Just as the first rays of the sun strike the ground, they all appear simultaneously, as if at a signal call. The ground is suddenly covered with them, and they are captured by thousands, and taken home in baskets and bowls. They are put to soak in cold water, and left to stand overnight. This fattens them, and in the morning they are roasted in a dish over the fire, the mass being continually stirred until of a nice uniform brown.

After supper we lay back upon the sheep-skins quietly enjoying the novel scene about us. Sticks of pino wood had been placed on end in the corner of the fireplace, and their bright crackling flame sent a ruddy light through the large room, touching up the nearer side of all objects in sharp relief against the intensity of the shadows. Gay-colored clothing and blankets, hung on poles suspended from the ceiling, caught the dancing light; curious pottery was ranged along the door by the walls; and here and there in the walls were little niches, just as we had seen them in the walls of ruined cliff dwellings. In these little niches were conveniently arranged little articles of domestic use, which had a delightfully bric-à-brac suggestiveness. The scene was just the same now as it had been within those walls hundreds of years before. We were away back in the centuries, and living the life of the remote past.

We started late the next morning. In the distance, here and there among the mountains, thin blue smoke curled up in the calm air. It came from fires which the Zuñis had made to burn over the ground for planting their peach orchards in favorably situated cañons, where the trees would be sheltered from the blasting winds. In these places the Zuñis raise an abundance of peaches of a delicious quality.

We passed along the base of a mesa whose steep sandstone sides were fantas-

Portal and plume of the Goddess of Salt.

tically worn. In one projecting angle there was a large opening in the rock, through which the sky on the other side could plainly be seen. The Goddess of Salt, say the Zuñis in one of their myths, was so troubled by the people who lived around her home on the shores of the great ocean that she foresook them, and came to live in this region, where she wedded the God of Turquoise. They lived happily together for a long time; but at last the people here also became troublesome to her, and she left them, and disappeared in this mountain, making this hole by her entrance. But in passing through, one of her plumes was brushed off, and it remains to this day in the shape of the high monument of stone standing in the plain close by. The resting-places of the goddess are marked by the salt lakes, including the large one to the south of Zuñi-land, from which the Zuñis gather their salt. In recognition of the ownership of the Zuñis in this lake, other Indian tribes who get salt there have always paid them toll for the privilege, and the lake has thus been a considerable source of revenue for them. The favor of the goddess for the Zuñis was markedly shown in this bequest. The footsteps of the God of Turquoise are marked by the turquoise deposits in the mountains.

We reached Zuñi at noon. The pueblo lies near the foot of the majestic mesa

Tá-ai-tä-lo-ne, or Thunder Mountain

of Tá-ai-tä-lo-ne—the sacred thunder mountain.[28] Close to the town flows the Zuñi River. Whoever knows the stream will smile broadly at the instructions given a government exploring expedition sent out soon after the annexation of New Mexico. The commander was charged expressly to examine the Colorado, Chiquito, and the Zuñi rivers, with particular reference to their value for steamboat navigation. The stream is generally so shallow that in most places its waters would hardly reach above the ankles, and for considerable stretches in its course it loses itself in the sand altogether. But in the wet season the river often becomes a powerful torrent; it was for this reason that the pueblo, which once stood on the left bank, where it was subject to inundations, was, not long after the conquest, removed to its present site on the right bank, which is somewhat bluff-like at this place. The knoll upon which Zuñi stands seems higher than it really is, owing to the way in which the houses are terraced above each other, giving the place a commanding appearance as it is approached. The prevailing tone of the pueblo and the surrounding landscape is red. Such is the hue of grand old Tá-ai-tä-lo-ne's face; the pueblo is built chiefly of red sandstone largely excavated from the ruins of the elder-Zuñi across the river, the thin slabs, about the thickness of ancient Roman bricks, being laid in red adobe mortar from the tawny soil; and the wide stretching plain around is red, and worn bare of all vegetation by the thousands of sheep owned in Zuñi, and kept in the corrals, made of scrawny upright sticks, surrounding the place like a girdle of thorns.

Mr. Cushing's room at the house of the Governor was a picturesque mingling of culture and barbarism. A writing-table, a case of book-shelves with the books necessary to his studies, and the volumes of valuable notes that recorded his investigations, a stool, a student-lamp, and a hammock, completed the inventory of the civilized furnishings. But there was the wonderful addition of a telephone which Mr. Cushing and his brother, who was visiting him, constructed out of a couple of old tin cans and several hundred yards of twine, to prove to the Zuñis the truth of what he had told them about the triumphs of American invention. The telephone was connected with the house of one of the caciques on the opposite side of the pueblo, about a quarter of a mile away. The Zuñis found it the most marvellous thing they had ever seen, and an old fogy among them, who had scoffed at it as beyond reason, on satisfying himself of its reality, stood beside it all day when it was first tested, watching its operation with intense interest. The hard earthen floor of the room was covered with Navajo and Pueblo blankets, their bright hues making them admirable for rugs—a purpose for which they are used with artistic effect in the quarters of the officers at various military posts in New Mexico. The walls were also hung with some choice examples of the blankets, giving a novel tapestry effect. With the photographs of some home friends adorning the wall, the room had a charmingly bright and cozy look.

Against the outside wall of the house were built large cages for the eagles, which are kept for the sake of their highly valued plumes. Eagle-farming is carried on among the Zuñis to a considerable extent. The majestic birds had lately been plucked, giving them a comically disreputable look, by no means in concert with the piercing, fearless gaze of their bright eyes. They were by no means tame, and even the tormenting spirit of the Zuñi children could not tempt those imps of mischief to transgress the bounds of a respectful distance from the cages. A blow from those powerful beaks would leave a mark never to be forgotten. The dignity of these eagles was unruffled—something that could hardly be said of their plumage just then—and a slight turn of the head was all the notice their majesties condescended to take of by-standers.

The Zuñi children sported around the streets in cherubic nakedness. They were as rompingly mischievous as any children can be, and their delight in torment seemed abnormally developed, perhaps because their elders saw nothing out of the way in it. Most likely the savage love of torture in warfare may be ascribed to this. The poor dogs fared hard at the children's hands. Not unfrequently during our visit a succession of piercing yelps would be heard, while a poor cur disappeared rapidly around the corner, fleeing from a terrorizing piece of ancient pottery tied to his ruined tail, while a crowd of urchins yelling with delight followed at his heels. And the unhappy hogs straggling around in the outskirts, which nobody seemed to feel a proprietary interest in—no wonder that they were gaunt and razor-backed and never grew fat! no wonder that the Zuñis had no appreciation of the delicacy of pork! The wretched grunters were chased and hectored by the children from morn to night, until they became too exhausted to resist, and would submit listlessly to the wills of their tormentors. With such sharp, bristle-covered backs as characterized these swine, it was a marvel how the naked brats could take such pleasure in riding them.

It was a prettier sight to see the chubby brown bodies of the children as they lay by the dozen dabbling in the tepid waters of the river all through the hot hours, soaking in the pools, or scampering along the alkali-incrusted banks, noisily splashing each other. One thing to be said to their credit is that in their disagreements they never came to blows. The admirable Indian trait of considering it beneath the dignity of a human being to strike another seems to be inherent. The children are tenderly loved by their parents, and their training is carefully looked after. They have the universal child-love of toys and the little girls cherish maternally rude woolen dolls. A favorite toy for the babies is a little stuffed kid.

Outside the line of the corrals for the ponies, sheep, and goats were the queer little gardens of the women. They were divided into small rectangular lots, separated by stake fences, and often by substantial walls of adobe, with narrow alleyways running between. These little gardens looked for all the world like collections of gigantic waffles, being divided into rectangular beds, each bed cut up by intersecting ridges of earth. The little spaces thus formed appeared to be of almost mathematical exactness in size and were planted with onions and herbs. These little squares were thus ridged about to hold the water with which the ground was kept moist, each square receiving the contents of a large water jar. The gardens were carefully tended by the women, and looked wonderfully neat. All around on the plain were the corn fields, where crops were raised without irrigation, a remarkable thing for such a dry climate. The corn was planted very deep in holes punched with a sharp stick, and was very low in growth, the ears branching out from the stalk close to the ground. Maize had been raised in this way for ages. There are no irrigating ditches about Zuñi itself, but at Pescado, Las Nutrias, and Ojo Caliente the crops are elaborately irrigated. The labor in the fields is done by the men, who in all the pueblo tribes do not consider, as the savage Indians do, manual labor as something fit only for squaws.

The street scenes of Zuñi seem thoroughly Oriental. Narrow winding ways and irregular-shaped plazas, all of which have characteristic names, give the town a quaint picturesqueness. In places the terraced buildings tower to a height worthy of metropolitan structures. Low passageways carry the thoroughfare under the buildings here and there, giving artistic contrasts of light and shade, while the oddly costumed figures in the streets make a striking picture. The monotony of blank walls is here and there broken by the rude but massive stairways leading to second stories, rows of round projecting roof beams, and the gaunt ladders leaning against the buildings everywhere, each stretching two thin arms skyward. All the inhabitants have a sailor-like agility in the use of the ladders. The women go up and down with water jars on their heads without touching a hand to support or steady themselves; little children, hardly out of babyhood, scramble fearlessly up and down; even the dogs have a squirrel-like nimbleness, trotting in a matter-of-course way down the rounds of a steep ladder. If there were any more trees in Zuñi than the solitary cottonwood standing in the yard before the ruined Franciscan chapel, it would hardly be surprising to see the dogs climbing them like cats!

All through the day there is an unceasing carrying of water, the women passing and repassing through the streets on the way to and from the springs with the large ollas, or water jars, so nicely balanced on their heads as not to spill a drop, and walking with a fine, erect poise. But toward sunset is the time to visit the great spring on the hill-side just outside the city. It is a Scripture-like scene. Descending by a path between steep banks of clay, we come upon a large pool in an excavated cavern, a round chamber in the hill-side, and entered by a great arch-like opening. Here in the cool shadow crowds of girls come and go, dipping up the water, and pausing to gossip as they meet in the path or beside the well. Their soft voices fill the air like the chatter of swallows, and their white teeth gleam as they laugh. As they come down the sloping path the slanting sunlight touches up the bits of bright color that adorn their dark costumes, and their figures are bathed in a mellow glow, while those further down between the high banks are dusky in the gathering shadows.

Wandering through the place, we enter, according to the custom of the natives, any of the open doorways at pleasure, stroll quietly about the house, examine the pottery, blankets, and other household goods, the family meanwhile looking on with courteous curiosity. "I-mu" (be seated), they say; and if they are at their meals, one is welcome to join them, even though it chance to be their last crust. The woman of the house is perhaps at work baking paper bread. She takes a fresh sheet just off the fire, and making a roll of it, hands it to us. In her work she sits by the fire-place with a dish of the pasty corn-meal dough beside her made rather thin. She has no superfluous raiment, for the fire is hot. With a quick motion she takes a handful and skillfully spreads it over a large smooth stone slab, underneath which the fire is burning. It is baked almost immediately, being spread so thin. As soon as done, the sheets are laid above each other, until they form a considerable pile. They are in various colors, yellow, blue, green, or red, according to the color of the corn, which is carefully sorted, when shelled, with a view to this effect.

In their way the Zuñis are paragons of politeness, and the most polished nation of Europe could hardly excel them in genuine courtesy. One of them after shaking hands—they are great for hand shaking—may be seen to lift his hand to his lips and reverently breathe upon it, an action designed to breathe into himself whatever superior influence from the other person may have been received by the friendly contact. Here is a dialogue between two Zuñis about to smoke. Says one:

"Why do you not light your cigarette?"

"Are you older than I?" asks the other.

"Yes."

"Then light yours first, for whoever goes before his elder brother will surely stumble."

The Zuñi houses have large rooms and real doors, contrasting agreeably with the close little cells of many of the pueblos in the region near Santa Fe, which are entered only through the roof. It is not uncommon to see a large room with three or four fire-places, each of a different pattern, one designed for roasting meat, another for baking bread, another for boiling, etc. These fire-places have a quaint mediæval look. They are generally built in the corner, with a large square hood flaring out over them from the chimney. A double fire-place may be built against the centre of a long side wall, and an immense broad fire-place often takes up the entire end of a room. A style consisting of a little arch in the corner is like those of Mexican houses; the other varieties are native, and are found in the oldest ruins.

The houses are owned by the women. The Zuñis are strictly monogamous, while savage Indian tribes are polygamous. This contrast between two branches of the same race, one living a settled and the other a roving life, shows that monogamy is an essential condition of the former, and is an effective argument against one of the cardinal doctrines of Mormonism. The Zuñi women are by no means the slaves of the men. They have their rights, and maintain them. When a man marries, he goes to live with his wife, and if dissatisfied with him, she has the right to send him away. Therefore a husband is pretty careful to keep in his wife's good graces.

As one of the great annual dances was to come off, we waited a week for the sake of seeing it. Its regular time was at the full moon in May, but the two boys whose duty it was to repeat certain long prayers belonging to the ceremonials in the estufa had died, and novices had to be trained up in their places. Since the two prayers had to be committed word for word as they had been said for centuries, it was a long task, and the dance had to be postponed to the full moon of June.

Meanwhile the time passed quickly for us. During the day a mild hum of industry pervaded the place. The Zuñis take life easily, and never overwork; therefore they find no necessity for a periodic day of rest, but they are not lazy. Their wants are simple, and their work is ample to satisfy them. One of the most interesting things was to see them weave their fabrics on their hand-looms, producing beautiful designs by the nice calculation of the eye, but with no regular measurement. Our principal excitements during the week were the searching

Making pottery.

out of attractive blankets either Navajo or Pueblo, and the opening of kilns of new pottery. Each family makes all its own pottery, as a usual thing, and every day kilns were burning all over the place. The news that a finely decorated olla had been seen going into a kiln in a certain street was enough to set us agog, watching to see it come out freshly burned. One household had a special reputation for making fine ollas, another for small ware, another for figures of animals and one woman was famed for making very nice turtles. The vessels to be burned were arranged carefully on the ground, and a circular, dome-shaped structure of dried sheep's dung built up around and over them. This fuel is preserved carefully in hard-pressed, flat blocks, and is kept corded up for use. It gives an intense heat, and a kiln is baked in two or three hours.

Archæologists have been puzzled by the occasional discovery of fragments of hard pottery with glazed decorative lines, and theories have been formed that among the ancient Pueblos the art of glazing their pottery was known. But Mr. Cushing has discovered that this glazing is accidental, occurring only in the broken pieces of old pottery used to cover the articles in the kiln and protect them from the falling of the structure when it has mostly burned away. These fragments are made harder by the second firing, which also glazes certain mineral pigments used in their decoration.

Another interesting industry was the grinding of meal or flour. A row of girls, sometimes half a dozen or so, is often seen at work. They all kneel beside and over a series of bins, each of which has a bottom of smooth stone hollowed in a semi-circular shape. Each girl holds a bar of stone in her hands, and grinds the corn by rubbing it up and down with a motion much like that of a washerwoman at a scrubbing-board. The meal, ground course in one bin, is passed on to the next, where the stone bar is of a finer texture, and so on to the end, when it is often ground as fine as flour. The jet-black hair of the girls, cut off about half-way down their face, forms a short thick veil, which is tossed up and down by the violent motion, their eyes showing brightly through as they regard the strangers.

The artist's work was a source of wonder to the Zuñis, and they looked upon his spirited portrayals with intense interest. They were, until recently, extremely superstitious about portraits, and nothing would induce any of them to allow their pictures to be made. They believed that something of their actual personality went with their likeness, and that whoever possessed it would also possess a certain control over themselves—a control which might bring evil upon them. But Mr. Cushing, who has a talent for sketching which has been of great service to him in his notes, banished this superstition. It nearly cost him his life one time. But they saw that no evil came of it, and so they outgrew their objections. There seems to be no Chinese conservatism about them, but when they see the light, they readily accept it. In Mr. Cushing's earlier days in Zuñi his sketching caused a secret resolve to be made to kill him for practices that might bring disaster to them all. It was to be done at a great dance that was soon to come off. He sat upon a neighboring house-top with sketch-book in hand, when two hideous figures among the dancers, painted in diabolical black, came to the foot of the adjacent ladder and pounded upon it with their war-clubs, shouting out something which caused the multitude to look toward him. He thought it a jocular part of the performance, and smiled good-naturedly. But he understood enough of the language at the time to distinguish the cries among the crowd: "Kill him! kill him!" It was part of the performance to kill a symbolical Navajo, the Navajos being the ancient enemies of the Zuñis. Mr. Cushing had no idea that he was cast for the part of that Navajo, and did not comprehend the real gravity of the situation until he heard the women echo the cries, "Yes, kill him! kill him!" The people rose up and looked his way. The assemblage was silent with expectation. He glanced behind; there was a wall of dark figures frowning down upon him, half muffled in their blankets, and standing as immovable as statues. The twin fiends below made ready to come up the ladder. Mr. Cushing now saw that his life was really threatened. A thousand against one! Attempt at escape was hopeless. He thought his last moment had come, and in his heart was terribly frightened. But to give way to fear was useless, and something told him to face the danger coolly. So he leisurely laid down his sketch-book, placed a stone upon the leaves to keep them from blowing in the wind, produced a new hunting-knife which he had just brought back with him from Fort Wingate, where he had been on a trip—nobody knew he had it—and flourished it, at the same time breaking out into a loud, defiant laugh. The evident coolness of the act, his boldness in facing them, took his assailants aback; they paused, and uttered a word meaning, "a spiritual friend," that is, a friend possessing supernatural characteristic, making him more than a common earthly friend—qualities which would bring good to them as a people.

"A spiritual friend—we must not kill a spiritual friend!" cried the two; "but we must kill a Navajo!" they shouted.

So out of the court they rushed in search of a Navajo. A few minutes, and a fearful yelping was heard. In they rushed, dragging a "Navajo" in the shape of a great yellow cur half paralyzed with fright. They stunned him with their clubs; before he was dead they had him disemboweled, and in their frenzy were ravenously eating the smoking vitals. Mr. Cushing looked on in gratitude that he was not just then in the place of that dog, playing the part of a Navajo. But the event turned out to be the most fortunate thing for him; it fixed him in the affections of the whole tribe, and from that day was to be dated his great influence in Zuñi.

The superstition about portraits now lingered only among some of the old women—those conservators of the ancient order of things with all people. At Pescado the artist had made a sketch of a pretty little girl. At Zuñi Mr. Cushing showed it to the child's grandmother, a white-haired old crone, who looked at it intently for a moment, then left the room, sobbing wildly, saying, "My poor little Lupolita! how could you be so cruel as to let such an evil come upon her!"

One day the artist painted the portrait of Mr. Cushing's father by adoption, Lai-ui-ai-tsai-lun-k'iä, the high-priest, or medicine cacique, one of the "seven great chiefs of the Zuñi." He was the personification of gentleness, and looked the mystic that he was by virtue of his high office: the Zuñis are spiritualists, and their religion is in many striking phases identical with modern spiritism. In his

A Zuñi chief.

face, which in its strongly individual lines resembled Dante's, there was an indescribably kindly and lovable contemplative expression—a spiritual look like one who walked the earth with thoughts in another sphere. His affection for "Kuishy," his adopted son, was touchingly tender. One day when the lieutenant was admiring a handsome silver belt of native manufacture belonging to him, the old cacique said to Mr. Cushing, "Remember, my son, that whatever I have is also yours, to do with as you please."

And one night in the council, when Mr. Cushing was talking rather excitedly on a matter that caused him some vexation, the old man got up and walked away quietly. "Where are you going, my father?" Mr. Cushing asked.

"It grieves me to see my son show his anger," said the old man, gently.

While the artist was painting his portrait, he sat motionless for something like three hours. In this respect the Indians are ideal models. Old Pedro Pino, the Governor's father, who for many years was himself Governor, sat and watched the work of painting with the keenest interest, announcing his intention not to go away until the thing was finished. Old Pedro was gray and wrinkled, and must have been over eighty years of age. He was in his prime when the Americans took possession of New Mexico, and was Governor of Zuñi at the time. He was full of reminiscences of those days, and was never tired of telling the lieutenant about the officers he knew, especially about Major Kendrick, who, old Pedro was delighted to hear, was one of the lieutenant's instructors at West Point. Old Pedro had much of the garrulity of age, but his talk plainly showed the native eloquence which marked the days of his power, when he used it with the skill of a trained diplomat, keeping his nation absolute followers of his will. When the portrait was completed, he talked long and earnestly to the venerable cacique. He told him: "Though your body perish, nevertheless you shall continue to live on upon the earth. Your face will not be forgotten now; though your hair turn gray, it will never turn gray here. I know this to be so, for I have seen, in the quarters of the officers at the fort, the faces of their fathers, who have long since passed from the earth, but still were looking down upon their children from the walls."

The Zuñis delight in a council. These councils are frequently held, there being no specified intervals of time for their sessions. They are called whenever occasion arises, and all affairs of the nation are discussed and regulated by them. They are legislatures and courts in one, and furnish an extremely interesting picture of parliamentarism in its primitive form. When a council is deemed necessary, the Governor orders his herald to summon it. At sunset, when the air is quiet, the herald stands upon the highest house-top in Zuñi—a statuesque figure against the clear sky—and utters the call in a loud, measured, and resonant voice. The women all hear it, and the tidings quickly spread, so that in the evening there is sure to be a good attendance. The herald answers for the newspaper in Zuñi, for all proclamations and items of news deemed of general importance are announced in this way.

After dusk on the evening of the council dark figures with blankets wrapped about them—for the evening air is always cool—enter the Governor's house silently as shadows. A grave salutation and a grasp of the hand, and they seat

The herald.

themselves in the large room used for the councils. One evening about a hundred of the leading men were thus assembled, sitting on a sort of bench running along the side of the room, or squatting on their haunches in a circle. On the floor, in the midst of the circle, the Governor had strewn a lot of corn husks, and a bag of fine-cut being set out, cigarettes were rolled, and a constant smoking was kept up. The air would have been thick enough had not the large fireplaces given such excellent ventilation. The women and the young men gathered respectfully around the doors and windows and listened. As the evening wore on, the room grew warm, and the men gradually shed their garments, until about half the assemblage sat with naked bodies of a ruddy bronze hue. As it grew late, some arose and glided silently out of the room. But it was an important matter they were talking about, and the most of them staid until it was settled at a small hour of the morning. The subject was discussed earnestly and gravely, no emotion being shown either in the face or in the manner of speaking, although some would occasionally betray their excitement in a trembling voice. It was a will case under discussion, and the Governor sat motionless and speechless, being the judge from whose decision there could be no appeal. Early in the evening the two caciques who were present arose to go. In response to Mr. Cushing's question, Lai-ui-ai-tsai-lun-kiä said, "Though it is our place to elect our Governor, it is not for us to say anything that may influence his judgment." Would that all public men had as nice an idea of the proprieties of politics! It is not the voice of the people that chooses the Governor of Zuñi, but the caciques.

The pueblo Indians have been repeatedly characterized as fire-worshippers. But with the Zuñis, at least according to Mr. Cushing, the principal object of their worship is water, just as was stated by Coronado. And well may they worship it, living as they do in the midst of a sun-parched land, their life dependent upon the life-reviving element so scantily bestowed! The writer will never forget how one day, as he was standing in the door of the Governor's house, the clear sky became overcast with black clouds. The Indians standing around cast anxious glances at the heavens; with the first drops of rain they all said, with an expression of unspeakable reverence and gratitude, "E-la qua! e-la qua!" which are their words for thanks.

One day there was a great excitement over a race between two fast ponies. A large crowd was collected, and betting was going on at a lively rate. All sorts of things were staked on the contest—cloth, skins, dresses, blankets, jewelry, har-

Around the council fire.

nesses, etc. These things were deposited in great heaps on the ground, and then, after all the bet had been arranged, everybody went down on to the plain to see the start. The riders were two lithe, light youths, entirely nude, and with long black tresses flying in the wind. It was a spirited, graceful sight as they dashed away at full gallop on their tough little steeds. They were soon out of sight in the distance. It was some time before they came to view again, for the course was a long one of about six miles. At last they appeared, two black dots, and coming nearer they were seen to be still neck and neck. The race was close, and there was but little distance between the two horses as they dashed past reeking with sweat. The crowd was intensely excited, and greeted the finish with a tumult of shrill yells. An old fellow, fat and good-natured-looking, who had taken an exceptional interest in the race, perhaps because of large stakes, cantered down to meet the contestants as they came in. But while away it seems that his mare threw him, for she came tearing back riderless and with saddle hanging loose, kicking it off as she neared the crowd. Some time after the old man came running back afoot, and as he came to a stop he said, emphatically, "Goddamn!"—an expression which constitutes about all the English known in Zuñi.

Chief on horseback.

And as they do not know the meaning of that, its use can hardly be said to be sinful.

It was the day before the great dance. Everybody was getting ready for the holiday. All were to appear in their best clothing and with flowing hair, released from the little queues in which it is usually confined. Late in the afternoon we saw a young man sitting on a house-top with beaming face, while a brown beauty was carefully combing his hair as she stood behind. So the young man was a newly accepted lover! When a youthful Zuñi falls in love with a girl, he hints that it would be a real nice thing to have his hair combed. If she takes the hint and proceeds to comb it, it is a token that he has won her favor. The youth of Zuñi are just as sentimental, just as "spooney" in their love affairs, as fond of moonlight rambles and whispered nothings, as any lovers well can be.

As dusk deepened into night and the full moon rose over the roof-tops of Zuñi, there was a strangely beautiful sight. The narrow river meandered in a bright silver thread over the mysterious indefinite expanse of the plain. The stars glinted brightly in the intense blue of the marvellously clear sky, and looked down upon a new constellation. Fires gleamed on every house-top, lighting up great wall spaces with ruddy reflections, and sending tall shadows flitting round everywhere from the watching groups. The whole town was dotted with the fires, and it looked as if a mild conflagration were in progress, feeding scantily upon such unpromising material as stone and adobe. These fires were kindled for the baking of the *hé-per-lo-ḳi,* or sacred festival bread, baked on the evening of every festival by the young maidens of the pueblo. Everywhere there was a contrast of strong light and deep shadow, the effect modified and softened by the floods of white moonlight. The groups of silent figures standing and sitting around formed compositions ready for an artist, and they were touched with Rembrandt lights.

Hé-per-lo-ki looks, and is said to taste, like Boston brown-bread. It is made by a rather peculiar process. The corn meal of which it is composed is chewed up by the young girls. The object of this is to sweeten it, for the acid of the saliva, uniting with the starch of the corn, forms sugar. Some of the Zuñis, including the Governor's family, who can afford to buy sugar, make their hé-per-lo-ki in the way less economical, but more acceptable to civilized palates.

The morning of the festival dawned, and we were out early to see everything that was going on. All the town was in holiday dress. Everybody had his hair nicely combed, after washing it with amoli, the root of the yucca, or soap-plant,

Baking Hé-per-lo-ki on the house-tops.

which makes the finest shampoo in the world, leaving the hair soft and glossy. The festivities were ushered in by the appearance of the "Mudheads," nude men painted a uniform mud-color from head to foot, and disguised with drolly hideous masks of the same hue, while several great knobs, like enormous wens, adorned a smooth head with a snouted countenance. The effect was irresistibly mirth-provoking; the characters looked like pantomime clowns just coming under the spell of Circe. The Mudheads ran through the streets cutting queer antics, while they shot arrows into a bunch of feathers which they kept continually throwing on to the ground ahead of them. Then, after a while, the dancers made their first appearance, standing in a line in the street, and dancing and singing much as we had seen at Pescado. But now they were all arrayed in full costumes and every performer was masked. After dancing solemnly for some time, they broke ranks and went back to the estufa, where the time was passed in their mystic solemnities until they appeared in another part of the town and continued their dance. Thus it went on through the morning, until the dancers had made the round of all the principal places of the town. At noon there appeared on the streets some frightful figures, hideous in the extreme, and made diabolical in aspect by the buffalo horns which they wore on their heads. They ran along armed with great bunches of reeds, and everybody scattered at their approach, for they were privileged to strike any person they met, and could inflict a blow not to be despised. There were shrieks of laughter as the crowds dispersed, running up ladders and scrambling over the house-tops. Whoever could get indoors was safe, for the horned creatures could not pursue them beyond a threshold. Courtesy toward the "men-from-where-the-sun-rises" would not have permitted them to molest us, had they overtaken us, but to please the people we joined in the fun, and pretended great fright, clambering ladders and fleeing until we were breathless. The spectators were convulsed with mirth at our apparent dismay.

The Zuñis have one annual dance expressly to frighten the children and keep them in good behavior the rest of the year. Characters even more horrible in appearance than those with the buffalo horns are the chief actors. They represent fearful goblins who come to devour and carry off the children. They make the round of all the houses in town, and at their approach the parents conceal their little ones, pretending to fight the demons off and defend their offspring desperately. This makes a lasting impression on the children, and the mention of these creatures has thenceforward the same quieting effect as our nursery bugbears, only the bugbears are made a reality to them. Formerly the Zuñis had a certain dance which took place once in thirty years. Its ceremonies required the sacrifice of a child. For the victim the worst child in the place was always selected. The mention of this festival was very apt to produce instantaneous good behavior in a contrary child.

The ceremonies of the morning were ended with the disappearance of the horned monsters, and there was a recess of about two hours. At about three o'clock began the most imposing part of the exercises, which for the rest of the day were held in what is called the Dance Place. This was a large rectangular court; on all sides the houses rose in terraces, forming a picturesque amphitheatre for such a solemnity. It was the most gorgeous natural spectacle we had ever seen in real life. Everything was so thoroughly in earnest about it; there was nothing that savored of the stage, nor was there evident any of the tawdry display customary to the parade days of civilization. It was a genuine manifestation of the deep religious feeling of the people. The costumes, which were generally highly grotesque, were splendidly elaborate, brilliantly beautiful in color, and rich in material. The genuineness of their make [up] and the reality of the "properties" would put to shame the tinselled pretense of our gala days. There were wonderful varieties of headgear—plumes, crests, beards, fantastic masks checkered off in various colors, evergreen decorations of spruce twigs arranged around the neck in a sort of a sylvan ruffle, or in a girdle around the waist; ingenious devices in the decoration of kilts, sashes, fine skins, while various kinds of antique-looking weapons, such as war-clubs, spears, and bows, ornamented with bunches of reeds, gave the scene a sort of heroically classical aspect. Many of the beards were of a pale Scandinavian blonde, while the hair was of the same color in a number of instances. Perhaps these might have represented mythological characters who were albinos. But the albinos had no beards. Is it not possible that they may point back to a time when a light haired and bearded race existed in America? The albinos of Zuñi—there were several in the place—were droll-looking figures; they looked like the Dutch peasants in the paintings of Teniers.

Thronging the terraced roofs of the Colosseum-like Dance Place were the spectators, their best apparel with its brilliant hues stood in intense sunlight against a deep cloudless sky. All were gazing intently upon the dancers in the arena below, a line of stately rhythmic movement of rich colors, kaleidoscopic in its dazzling effect. From the dancers' throats arose a weird swelling song, accompanied by the jangling and rattling of rude instruments held in the hands and attached to the heels. This particular dance was called "the all-in-one," all the various dances of the Zuñi religion being represented in it. Each figure impersonated some character in the Zuñi mythology. There were, for instance, the God of Water, the God of Fire, the God of Air, the God of the Cactus, the God of Turquoise, the Woman from the Moon, and the Echo God. A dance would last about ten minutes, during which the only motionless figures would be the Mudheads, who would stand around in groups, or sit upon the ground with a comical open-mouth air, and the priest of the dance, who was the only unmasked participant. The priest was a handsome youth with flowing hair, dressed in a picturesque mediæval-looking costume of black buckskin, touched off with red sashes and an abundance of silver buttons in rows. He wore knee-breeches and leggings, and looked as if he might have come out of the days of the troubadours. He stood statue-like at the head of the line of dancers, his position one of easy grace, and he held a vessel of sacred meal in his hand. From this he would occasionally scatter a pinch of the meal on the ground. At a signal, which seemed something like that given in a theatre for a change of scene, the dancers would stop and retire for an interval of ceremonies in the estufa. As they were leaving the place, a bit of pantomime would always occur. The Woman from the Moon, who wore a skirt, and had a crescent-like mask, and long yellow hair streaming down her back—her whole aspect very Mother-Goose-like—would have a by-play with the God of the Cactus, whose place in the line was just in front of her. The legend was that she had come down from the moon to gather cactus; therefore the God of the Cactus was trying to avoid her as she endeavored to pluck the cactus adornments of his head-dress, and place them in the large basket she carried on her back. Meanwhile the Echo God, who was the last figure in the line of dancers, and kept invariably half a note and half a step behind the singing and dancing of the others throughout the whole, was at the end of the dance obliged to echo everything that was shouted out to him. He was thus often kept behind for several minutes after the others had gone in. The mischievous Mudheads took a leading part in this diversion. We shouted out to him in English, and although ignorant of the language, he proved himself a remarkably clever imitator. But when one of us whistled, that was beyond his mimicry, and it seemed to disconcert him a little. Each of the impersonators had come into Zuñi in the early morning from the direction of the place where the respective gods were supposed to live. The Echo God, for instance, came from his home in the valley near the sacred mountain.

The intervals between the dances were filled out by the antics of the Mudheads, whose functions corresponded exactly to those of the clown in a circus. Here was another of those inexplicable resemblances between Zuñi customs and those of our race. The Mudhead was an institution with them as far back as their traditions reached, and they had never seen anything in the nature of a circus. But, like our clowns, the Mudheads would burlesque the performance; they would make the most awkward blunders, always resulting in failure and discomfiture. They would make a deal of clownish fun, showing that an acute sense of humor enters into Indian nature, the spectators greeting every sally with shouts of laughter as merry as ever resounded from the benches around a canvas-covered ring; and in their nude bodies, and heads smooth and bald, with the exception of the knobby excrescences, they resembled the make-up of the traditional clown. As soon as the dancers appeared again, the Mudheads would subside, but would at once resume their indecorum with the beginning of the next pause. So it went on until the declining sun left the Dance Place in shadow. When its last ray had gone from the arena, the dance was ended. The handsome young priest approached the group of Mudheads, who stood with reverently bowed heads, and appeared to give them his benediction, sprinkling them with sacred meal. Performers and public then dispersed. That was our last day in Zuñi.

ZUÑI REVISITED

LATE IN NOVEMBER OF THE PAST AUTUMN [1882], I arrived at Fort Wingate with the intention of paying a second visit to Mr. Cushing, at Zuñi. The weather was uncharacteristically capricious, considering the stable nature of the New Mexican climate as I had known it in summer. One day the sky was a stony gray, with cold, dusty gusts and spits of snow; the next would show the familiar over-arching cloudless blue, with welcome warm sunshine tempering the bracing air; again, the sky was overcast, but softer, and the warm southwest wind blew, laden with the moisture of the Pacific. New Mexico is popularly supposed to be a warm country all the year round, but it should be remembered that the Zuñi land lies among the summits of the "continental divide," and is higher above the sea-level than the top of Mount Washington. Therefore the winter at such an altitude comes nearly as early as in New England, but it is a far milder season than it is here. Although in a dry country the distinction between winter and summer is not so marked as it is with us, nevertheless it was very perceptible, and Nature's fallow season was noticeable in the absence of hundreds of living,

From the *American Architect and Building News,* 17 March 1883 growing things which had characterized the region without particularly emphasizing their existence. Although the arborescent growth of the country is evergreen, and therefore its aspect was unchanged in that respect; nevertheless even the mountains and *mesas* had a sterner and a repellent look; their solemnity unrelieved by certain qualities which in the summer had invested their grandeur with a fascinating charm. Perhaps it was because the grasses and shrubs, now sere and withered, had given a certain tone to the landscape, and although their presence was not noted distinctively then, their absence had changed the whole scale of values in the picture. In the presence of the frowning mountains, the mythological fancy arose that the great gods are ever present, but at this season their troops of attendant spirits have fled, and the mood of the deities has changed.

Major Powell has pointed out, in his paper on the study of anthropology, printed in the first annual report of the Bureau of Ethnology, issued last year,[29] how environment has been an important factor in forming the mythology of a people. It is a life of unknown centuries amid such surroundings as these wild ranges—now tumultuously tossed by volcanic convulsions, at their feet great plains stretching away calm as eternity; now expanding into wide and lofty tablelands, worn remnants of an older continent, seamed with chasms and rent by awful cañons—that has shaped and colored the religion of the Zuñis; dreary, contemplative, and often strangely poetical. But whence came one lovely trait that pervades all their myths and folk-lore, as related by Mr. Cushing, like an interwoven golden thread, gleaming through every fabric—the idea of the ultimate good existing in everything, and that even evil-working causes are but transitory, and become the means to the accomplishment of final good? It seems strange to find a feature like this in the faith of a barbaric race, and it appears to be a proof of an innate gentleness of spirit. Army officers who are familiar with the Indians in peace and war tell me that the more they see of them the more they are impressed by the fact of their common humanity, as evinced by manifold traits brought out on acquaintance, though to the average frontiersman the red man is no better and no more entitled to human consideration than any wild brute. The frontiersman, however, has good reason to fear his hatred, but I regard both his view and that of the "sentimentalist" concerning the noble savage as equally erroneous. It is only by close and sincere ethnological study, such as Mr. Cushing is giving to the subject, that the Indian nature will be seen in its true light. The real value of this study of the races of mankind on lower steps of culture is the light which it throws on many secret springs and motives of human nature, laying bare the processes of development of man on his long journey to the high conditions of civilization. To find a parallel for the same treacheries and savage cruelties which we condemn in the Indian we have to go back but a few centuries and look at our own ancestors.

The sandstone architecture of this region, carved by time with the mighty tools of the elements, is wonderful. I should think it might offer some valuable hints to the student, especially in the way of composition and the arrangement of great masses.

Looking at an *arroyo,* or gully, worn in the hard, firm soil by a water-course born in the rainy season—the plains and valleys are ploughed full of such furrows—I saw the same effects repeated in miniature, the steep sides worn and cut out of the baked red earth by the rains of perhaps but a single summer, being almost identical in form with the huge cliffs of red and yellow sandstone slowly worn by the processes of ages. So it was all only a question of relative magnitude and time.

The humble animal to whose brief life days are as years, and a league's journey a task like the traversing of a continent, toiling along at the bottom of such a gully, may look up at the towering heights of a few dozen inches with the same reverent, awe-struck gaze with which we behold the wonders of the Grand Cañon, or of the Yo Semite; and as that lowly being is ignorant of the features of this structure, the world, which impress us with wonder, because they are beyond the range of his small vision, what greater marvels may there not be in the universe of which our limited senses can know nothing. And perhaps some bright, superior race looks down upon our insignificant doings and strivings, and upon the small features of this contracted drop in the ocean of space, with the same calm contemplation and pity which we bestow upon these lower orders.

I did not expect to see Mr. Cushing until I reached Zuñi, but he arrived at Fort Wingate unexpectedly one evening, having received directions from Major Powell to visit Oraibe, one of the Moqui pueblos, and make a collection of pottery, etc., for the National Museum.[30] The people of Oraibe, unlike those of the other pueblos, have a great fear and distrust of the Americans, owing to the representations of the Mormons, who are incessantly using all the influence they can exert to incite the Indians everywhere against the national government. A recent expedition which visited Oraibe found the place entirely deserted, the inhabitants having fled at its approach, and concealing or taking with them all their valuables. It was therefore a difficult place to make a collection in, and Mr. Cushing, by reason of his standing as a Zuñi, was peculiarly fitted to do the work, which would have been hardly possible under ordinary circumstances.

Having a friend with me who was desirous of seeing the place, I decided to visit Zuñi, although Mr. Cushing was not to be there. He said that we should be cordially received and well provided for, since he was now comfortably established in his own household, where his wife would be found, together with her sister,[31] his brother's wife, and Mr. W. L. Metcalf, the artist. Together with Mr. Graham,[32] the local trader, and Mr. Wilson,[33] the teacher appointed by the government, with his family, there was now at Zuñi a considerable little American community.

The day of Mr. Cushing's departure for Oraibe we were to set out for Zuñi, but the threatening weather of the past week culminated in a severe snow-storm, the first of the season, and therefore we were delayed. That evening Mr. Metcalf appeared at the hospitable door of Dr. Washington Matthews, the post surgeon, numb and half senseless with the cold, having ridden in from Zuñi to see about his trunk with his painting-materials, and got lost in the storm while crossing the mountains. The next morning we started in an ambulance, taking Mr. Metcalf and his trunk along; Mr. Cushing's brother, Dr. Enos Cushing,[34] accompanying us on horseback. It was still snowing slightly, but there were prospects of clearing off. It was a cold, dreary drive across the mountains, and wrap ourselves in all the blankets that we might, it was impossible to keep warm, for the keen wind searched every opening and cut like knives of ice. The protracted misery of the trip contrasted sharply with the delights of the previous year's journey over the same road in the sunshine and exhilarating air of early June.

It was dusk when we came in sight of Zuñi from the elevation of the Black Mesa, and dark when we arrived. As we drove up to the town the windows gleamed with the cheery, ruddy light of hearth-fires within, and out of many of the stumpy chimney-pots leaped lurid tongues of smoky flame. Around these fires were probably many groups of old and young, listening to the wonderful tales of folk-lore as they had been handed down for centuries from generation to generation. The sight of a Zuñi fireside in winter goes far to reconcile one to the discomforts of the journey thither. The blazing piñon stick, whose pitchy wood gives a beautiful flame; the changing light dancing over the antique interiors; the great hooded corner fireplace, and the picturesque groups, form a striking sight. The houses are comfortable, the thick walls retaining the heat from the fires which also afford the best of ventilation, and if the Zuñis should learn habits of cleanliness and adopt civilized methods in sleeping and eating they would need no commiseration.

We found supper awaiting us at Mr. Cushing's house, Dr. Cushing having taken a short cut over the trail from Las Nutrias, and arriving about an hour before us. It was the same house, that of the Governor, where we had visited Mr. Cushing before, but how changed it was. For twelve dollars and a few handfuls of broken clam-shells Mr. Cushing had bought four large rooms, which had taken about three months' labor to build—pretty cheap real estate that! Clamshells are better than gold and as good as silver in Zuñi. "If you ever want to do us a favor," said the Governor to me in Washington, one day, "send us some of these shells, but not too many, for we do not want to spoil their value by making them common." The Governor shrewdly did not want to bear the market.

The rooms were filled with civilized furniture, and where before we had slept on the floor exposed to sundry crawling things, and had eaten from primitive dishes set on a blanket spread on the same, there were now beds, tables and chairs, with an abundance of nice crockery and cooking utensils. A negro cook brought from Washington, and trained in an old Virginia family, presided at the fireplace, whence he conjured up the nicest dishes, and a cooking-stove was on the way for his benefit.[35] The refining touch of woman's hand was everywhere manifest. The room which was occupied by Mr. Cushing on our former visit had been transformed by his wife with charming artistic taste into a luxuriant little boudoir, in the decoration of which the local resources had been availed of in a way that gave it a peculiar interest. The floor was covered with the finest of soft sheep-skins; the walls were hung with Navajo and Zuñi blankets, whose rich and varied hues gave an effect much like Oriental tapestry. A broad divan was also spread with similar blankets, and on easels stood excellent oil-paintings, while rare and curious pieces of pottery were on the mantel-piece and arranged in nooks and corners, with decorations of rich scarfs and draperies tastefully disposed. Pictures, books, and magazines, Japanese screens and a handsome lamp completed the cozy, home-like effect.[36]

The Governor, Pa-lo-wah-ti-wa, soon came in and welcomed me with an embrace, and a gleam of pleasure lighting up his large, dark eyes and dusky face, showed his joy at meeting an old friend. I regretted that Mr. Cushing was not there to interpret the dear old fellow's remarks, but we had to content ourselves with our mutually spare Spanish, and the Governor used, to the best advantage, the few English phrases and words he had picked up in the East. He was very proud of this accomplishment. The Governor had been pretty homesick for the East on his return to Zuñi; he was glad to get back to Zuñi, but the scenes in the "lands of the Eastern Americans" had made a powerful impression. He said that he had brought back but one side of him, and the side where his heart was was still in the East.

The next morning I found Nai-iu-tchi, the senior priest of the Order of the Bow, at his house, and he welcomed with delighted surprise the young man whom, in the East, he had adopted as his son, with the name of Thli-a-kwa, the Turquoise, or "Sacred Blue Medicine Stone." I also saw Ki-ä-si and Na-na-he, but the other two pilgrims to the East, Pedro Pino and Lai-iu-ai-tsai-lun-k'ia, were out of town.

It had been a wonderfully prosperous harvest—one so great had not been known for years, and all the store-rooms were piled full with corn in the ear, looking with their many colors like great heaps of jewels—red, green, yellow and blue. The prosperous harvest had been regarded as a proof of the pleasure of the gods at the result of the pilgrimage to the Ocean of the Sunrise, and the bringing of its sacred waters to the keeping of the priests to whose prayers they would give the power to bring bounty to the Continent; for the Zuñis, like the Hebrews, regard their small nation as a chosen people. This happy result of the pilgrimage, as they regarded it, has contributed to advance Mr. Cushing's influence among them.

Poor Na-na-he, however, the giddy-headed Moqui, whose grace and agility had made him a favorite in the East, was in deep disgrace. When he returned with the other three in May, he immediately hastened to his old Moqui home to relate the wonders of his journey to his people. As seven large demijohns of the ocean water had been given to the party by the city authorities of Boston, Na-na-he believed himself entitled to a share out of such an abundance, and he promised the Moquis, whose religion is the same as the Zuñis, that when the water came they should have one demijohn of it.

When Mr. Cushing arrived in September with Pa-lo-wah-ti-wa and

Nai-iu-tchi, who had remained with him in Washington and the East, the party was received with great state, and extensive rejoicings were instituted; and when the demijohns arrived there were elaborate solemnities in the honor of the water. To attend these the Moquis sent a deputation of their leading men, who were also to receive and bring back the vessel of water promised by Na-na-he; but Na-na-he had promised without the power of fulfillment. The Zuñis said that the water was theirs; they should have the entire credit and glory of bringing it, and the honor thereof should rest with the Zuñi people. If the Moquis wanted any water from the Ocean of the Sunrise they could go and get it themselves, but from Zuñi not one drop should they receive.

The result of this was considerable coolness between the two nations, but the Moquis acknowledged the justice of the Zuñis' position in the matter, and friendly relations were not interrupted. The wrath of both peoples fell upon Na-na-he. He lost the importance which the honor of making the journey had given him among the Moquis, while in Zuñi he forfeited the promised and coveted promotion to high orders, and went about in deep disgrace.

It was the height of the dancing season in Zuñi.[37] There were dances at night in the houses and in the temples, and frequently by day in the open air. There was a public dance that day, and in the clear, crisp morning air we could hear the weird rhythmic chants of the dancers, strikingly like the voices of the wind, sounding over the house-tops from the Dance-Place. Climbing over the roofs we found the terraced sides of the amphitheatre-like rectangular Dance-Place covered with a blanketed multitude—an intense contrast of bright-hued raiments, brown faces, and glossy black hair against the sunny blue sky and dazzling snow. Down in the Dance-Place was a line of strangely-costumed dancers, all arrayed uniformly with the exception of the priest of the dance, who stood at the head of the line unmasked and motionless. All the others were masked, and upon their heads were tall mitre-like arrangements of thin, brilliantly painted and decorated pieces of board, cut into a trinity of scallops at the top. Their bodies were naked and painted a dark brown, and their necks and girdles were surrounded with fringes of spruce twigs, giving a ruffle-like effect. Gourd rattles in their hands and tortoise-shell rattles on their heels gave a strongly accented accompaniment to their singing, and to their solemn, measured steps. There was an orchestra of about half a dozen Indians dressed like women, all beating drums. This dance was probably the ceremonial of some single order. In the dance which I witnessed in the summer of the previous year, and described in an article printed in *Harper's Monthly* for June, 1882, each figure was differently costumed and masked, and represented some mythological character.[38]

The intervals between the dances, when the dancers retired to their estufa for devotional exercises, were, as usual, filled out by the clown-like characters known as "mud-heads;" men curiously masked with laughter-provoking and piggish-looking faces, entirely nude, and painted from head to foot a light clayish color. These grotesque fellows played the most amusing tricks, and cracked jokes which provoked the merriest laughter from their public. One of their performances was particularly interesting. There were eight mud-heads altogether, and at the conclusion of a dance they came into the court, each with a number of bright-colored ears of corn tied together at the ends and hanging horizontally. They also bore large baskets filled with squashes and dried fruits. Eight women, matrons and young girls, were selected out from the spectators. Their blankets were taken from their shoulders and placed in one pile; then a sort of lawn-tennis line was made across the centre of the court by scattering meal. On one side of this stood the eight "mud-heads," and on the other side the eight women. Each side stood in a line, single file, the one behind grasping the shoulders of the one in front; the two files faced each other, and all the men jumped simultaneously sideways to the right, the women at the same time jumping in the opposite direction, as if to avoid them. This play was kept up some little time, until the men caught the women. Then followed a sort of "tug-of-war," each side trying to pull the other across the line; the men made mock efforts at stubborn resistance, but the women pulled them across inch by inch until their line was about half-way upon the women's side, when it broke and the rear half fell upon their backs while the front ones were jerked suddenly across. The victory of the women was hailed with laughter and applause, and they gathered up as trophies the corn-ears and baskets of the men, together with their own blankets—all of which had evidently been deposited as a wager—and retired. During one of the intervals two ferocious-looking figures, with masks of infernal aspect and painted entirely in black, walked across the court and entered the temple, or estufa. They were followed by several boys, ten or twelve years old, clad in the brightest and cleanest of new blankets, and walking as if being led to slaughter. They were probably children who by right of their hereditary rank—members of a sort of aboriginal nobility—were to be initiated into an order where they belonged. Poor boys! according to all accounts their ordeal was to be no child's play. One of the "mud-heads" crept cautiously to the window of the estufa and peered in, but started back in affected terror as if the sight were too awful to behold.

The dancing ended at sunset. We spent another delightful evening with the Cushings, and the next morning we set out for Fort Wingate.

Sylvester Baxter

PART III

Reporting from Camp Hemenway, 1888–1889

Introduction

Two years elapsed between Cushing's return from Zuñi pueblo in late April 1884 and the beginning of serious planning for the Hemenway Expedition in the summer of 1886. While he published very little in that time for his nominal employer, the Bureau of Ethnology, and complained constantly of prostration, he did publish *Zuñi Breadstuff,* a brilliant ethnographic treatment of the use of corn in Zuñi life. It appeared through much of 1884 and 1885 in *The Millstone,* a midwestern agricultural trade journal.

During much of this period, Cushing was seriously ill with stomach problems. At this point Eben N. Horsford, a former professor of chemistry at Harvard's Lawrence Scientific School, came to his succor. Horsford (1818–1893) had several personal enthusiasms that overlapped with Cushing's: breadmaking, Indian languages, and North American history (especially Norse discoveries).[1] To remove Cushing from the hot Washington summer, Horsford invited him to stay at his summer home, Prospect Grove, on Shelter Island on Long Island Sound. Here Frank and Emily lived from August through October 1885, always talking of better health and making plans for Palowahtiwa and Naiiuchi to join them for continued work on Zuñi linguistics and folklore.

But Cushing was unable to produce any work and felt, as he apologized to Powell, like "a fly in a web"—the more he struggled, the more paralyzed he became.[2] In November, Horsford decided to place Cushing under the care of Boston physician T. P. Oliver and invited him to move to his family home in Cambridge. In accepting, Cushing abandoned any immediate plans he had for the Indians to come east.[3] At some point he moved to Mary Hemenway's estate, Old Farm, near Milford, Massachusetts, and in the spring of 1886 Hemenway suggested to him that, instead of returning to Shelter Island for the summer, he invite the Indians to her estate on the North Shore at Manchester-by-the-Sea. "She wished," Cushing later explained to William T. Harris, "to have the Zuñis as true guests like other visitors whom she also wished to have at Casa Ramona, and that the interest of entertaining them would alone suffice even were there no other result to accrue."[4] By June the Cushings were living there and planning again for several Zuñis to sojourn with them in order to resume the long-postponed studies in language and folklore.

With the arrival on August 13 of Palowahtiwa, Waihusiwa, and Heluta at Casa Ramona,[5] the Hemenway Expedition began to take shape. In addition to Mary Hemenway, Frank and Emily Cushing, Emily's sister Margaret Magill, Baxter, and the three Indians, the group included William Torrey Harris, the neo-Hegelian philosopher and theorist of education who in 1889 would be named U.S. commissioner of education; Martha LeBaron Goddard, a close confidante of Mary Hemenway, a prominent Boston social figure, and the widow of publisher Delano Goddard; Mary E. Dewey, a childhood friend of Mary Hemenway and a daughter of Reverend Orville Dewey, pastor at the Tileston family parish in New York City; and Professor Edward S. Morse of the Peabody Museum in Salem, a noted expert on brachiopods, natural history, and Japanese culture. Over the next two months, Cushing and the Zuñis worked on relating and interpreting folktales. Mary Dewey recalled that "[t]he life at Casa Ramona soon took quiet and regular form. Mr. Cushing, with an amanuensis, spent the morning over his papers, with the help of one or more of his Indian friends. An unwritten language was to be put into shape and belted in with vocabulary and grammar, its traditions secured, its historic and religious myths preserved, and its folk-lore carefully noted down."[6] In November the advisory board for the Hemenway Southwestern Archaeological Expedition was formed: Harris, Goddard, and Augustus Hemenway, with Baxter as secretary-treasurer.[7]

Baxter kept a two-year record of the expedition beginning in August 1886, a log of correspondence that indicates his central role in the affairs of the expedition. Baxter became Mary Hemenway's voice and representative, alternately exhorting and soothing Cushing in his work. For his part, Cushing came to depend on his friend to represent his interests and his often-grandiose plans to their patron, and to present his excuses when necessary. By the end of 1887, when Cushing had been in the field nearly a year, the Hemenway board felt such concern about the progress of the southwestern work that they dispatched Baxter to Arizona. He stayed nearly five months, engaging in some archaeological reconnaissance with Dr. Jacob Wortman near Florence for a week in April 1888.[8] The purpose of the visit was to check on Cushing's progress and health and to provide some prognosis for the Hemenway investment in southwestern archaeology.

The essay "The Old New World" was in effect Baxter's report, written in Camp Hemenway,[9] published in April 1888 in the *Boston Herald,* and reprinted later in the year by Salem Press. In Baxter's judgment, the Hemenway Expedition was fulfilling all of its promise. Nevertheless, while his glowing reports of life at Camp Hemenway brought positive public attention, they could not stem the tide of doubt and disappointment on the board. In the fall of 1888 he traveled to Germany with Morse to deliver Cushing's programmatic statement to the International Congress of Americanists in Berlin. Then Morse went on to survey European anthropology museums as models for the proposed Pueblo Museum. Baxter returned home in October and was removed from the expedition board at the end of the year.

Neither Baxter's perceptions nor his writings were entirely shaped by Cushing's charismatic enthusiasm. Both "The Old New World" and "Archaeological Camping in Arizona," which appeared the following year in the *American Architect and Building News,* are strongly flavored by the nostalgia that was Baxter's usual strategy for resolving aesthetic conflicts. In these pieces he establishes this sense through temporal shifts: by moving backward and forward in time, at one moment portraying desert scenery or life in camp, at another picturing an imagined prehistoric community steadily at work building irrigation ditches, at another describing Cushing at work, and at yet another projecting forward to a future vision of a valley of water and orchards. Throughout, he emphasizes both Cushing's unique abilities and the indispensable value of the Hemenway work to ethnology and the future of humanity.

The Hemenway Expedition, as portrayed by Baxter in these colorful on-the-spot reports, serves to bridge the human past and future: as the Salt River Valley once was, so shall it be once again. The painful confusions and distractions of the American present, so notably absent in his imagined prehistoric past, will give way again to future harmony and prosperity. In Baxter's eyes, the fundamental unity of humanity in space and time emerges as the final truth from the desert, the home of earliest human cultures. Anthropological knowledge only strengthens the "bonds of universal brotherhood" that lie "beyond the turmoil of the clouded currents of passion and strife for individual advantage." Thus, just as Mary Hemenway's project spoke to the very heart of human understanding and philanthropy, so too did daily life in Frank Cushing's desert camps serve as a contemporary model of cooperative, focused enterprise. At the center of Baxter's southwestern romance always could be found a strongly reformist, didactic streak.

Curtis M. Hinsley

THE OLD NEW WORLD

An Account of the Explorations of the Hemenway Southwestern Archaeological Expedition in 1887–88, Under the Direction of Frank Hamilton Cushing

Preface

this account of the hemenway Southwestern Archaeological Expedition in the Salado and Gila valleys in Arizona is the result of observations made by the writer during three months spent with the expedition in the early part of the year. It was originally printed in the Boston Herald of April 15, 1888, and is reproduced in this form in response to various requests. Within this compass it was, of course, impossible to give more than a synopsis of what has been accomplished. Various important features have here been simply mentioned which will demand treatment in detail for the satisfaction of earnest students. These requirements will be fully met in the forthcoming report by Mr. Cushing, who also intends to treat separately certain interesting aspects of his discoveries. Meanwhile the writer hopes that these indications of what has been done in little more than a year's research may contribute somewhat towards awakening a sense of the importance of the vast mines of treasure relating to the primitive conditions of mankind and the early cultures of the race—so essential to an understanding of what man is and guidance to a knowledge of what he may become—awaiting the attention of serious investigators in our Western World.

From the *Boston Herald,* 15 April 1888, reprinted by the Salem Press

Sylvester Baxter
Secretary of the Hemenway Southwestern
Archæological Expedition.
Ledgewood Terrace,
Malden, Massachusetts.
July 18, 1888.

THE TRAVELLER ENTERS THE VALLEY OF THE RIO SALADO surrounded by wide reaches of sage-brush and greasewood, interspersed with thickets of mesquite. A dreary, unpromising spectacle! he thinks, and here, tawny ground beneath the bushes has all the unfertile aspect of the traditional desert, to eastern eyes. A moment more, and behold a transformation as sudden and as magical to the astonished vision as was ever worked by change of scene on theatre stage! The desert has vanished, and smooth fields expand with the floorlike evenness of a Kansas prairie as far as the eye can see toward the distant bases of the surrounding mountains. Under the calm blue of the Arizona midwinter sky the young grain spreads away in broad acres of tender green; sleek kine are browsing contentedly in rich alfalfa pastures, and long, straight lines of alamos and Lombardy poplars intersect the fields in pleasant perspectives. It is a picture of peace and plenty.

This magic has been wrought by the touch of life-bringing water, which sparkles on all sides in the tree-bordered canals that tap the abundant river and spread their contents over the land in rapid streams. And still the change goes on. Wherever the water can kiss the land, there the soil stirs with new life and clothes itself with a beauty that appeals to all eyes because it is the garb of bounteousness. Daily the rich fields widen and the desert shrinks; at night the burning brush on the clearings dots the horizon with its flames like the lamp-lines of a city's environs. For every acre now yielding fat crops, a score will soon be under cultivation, and the river's capacity for irrigation is still beyond estimate.

Yet the valley was not always a desert. Centuries ago it was fair, with a fertility like unto that which is again overspreading it after a long fallowness. So the two chief towns of the region are not unfittingly named. Phoenix justifies its designation with the fact that all around it, out of the ashes of a long dead civilization, our mightier modern culture is arising and founding one of its fairest abiding places; while the beautiful fields amid which Tempe sits, carpeting the feet of ruddy and purplish mountain walls that rise in slopes of bare rock and craggy peaks, make a scene not unlike the typical landscape of ancient Hellas, whose fair and famous vale has a namesake here. Then, too, the fervor of the summer is very encouraging to a classic paucity of attire!

The investigations of the remains of the ancient civilization that peopled the valley plains, mountain gorges and mesa tops of this vast desert region of our national domain is [*sic*] the object of the Hemenway Southwestern Archaeological Expedition, of which considerable has been heard of late. The expedition has been in the field but a little over a year, and the results already reached indicate how deeply indebted the scientific world will be to the wise munificence of the Boston lady who instituted it. Mrs. Mary Hemenway, perceiving that the present unrivalled opportunities for the study of the aboriginal cultures of America would soon be lost forever through the destruction of their monuments and the absorption of their surviving representatives under the waves of our modern civilization advancing over regions that, until recently, have been deemed uninhabitable, and recognizing in the person of Mr. Frank Hamilton Cushing one rarely qualified for the pursuit of such investigations, quietly established this expedition late in the year 1886, and its operations in the field were begun in the second month of 1887. So rich did this region prove in its opportunities for systematic excavation that Mr. Cushing, alive to the scientific value of a collection that should be thoroughly representative of a typical locality, has confined himself, throughout the first year, chiefly within a radius of a few miles of this spot. Through the knowledge thus gained he will be able to work up more rapidly, and with a more complete understanding, the other regions comprised in his proposed undertaking.

II

The Hemenway Southwestern Archaeological Expedition is probably the most thoroughly equipped undertaking of the kind yet instituted, and as such it will probably mark a new era in ethnological science; for, as Mr. Cushing says, archæology is simply ethnology carried back into prehistoric times. This unprecedentedly thorough equipment of the Hemenway expedition is not by virtue of the outlay involved, for other archæological enterprises of a far more extensive character have been undertaken. It lies in its well considered and comprehensive scope in the coördinate pursuit of several branches of research, each helping the others in its progress, and contributing to a result that promises to be the most complete working up of any region, and the race of man that has chiefly occupied that region, yet known to modern science. Therefore, it is not too much to expect that in this work, when well advanced toward its consummation, we shall have a new point of departure for the guidance of all future researches of ethnology—the study of mankind: the youngest, the least formulated, and yet the greatest of all the sciences, including them all, with the student of them all as its subject.

The branches of research involved in the scope of the Hemenway expedition are mainly four:

Ethnological; or the study of man as a race, including all features constituting the peculiar characteristics of that race, whether physical or psychical, and therefore broadly comprising all circumstances affecting the race.

Anthropological; or the study of the characteristics of man, considered as an individual, and naturally including in its line of research those elements which have caused those characteristics.

Historical; comprising a careful study of all that has been recorded, so far as may be ascertained, concerning the region to be investigated, its primitive occupants and other races with which they have come in contact; the study including not only documentary records, but that most important factor in the historical investigation of a primitive race, the guiding thread furnished by its oral traditions, which have repeatedly proven, under their correct interpretation by those competent to understand them, infallible witnesses to the past.

Archæological; or the study of the prehistoric remains of a race as instrumentalities for the understanding of what that past has been. But these, it is assumed by the expedition, can only be properly understood when viewed in the light obtained by present knowledge; when regarded in that light a fragment of pottery may often tell a tale more plainly and eloquently than a written record.

Beside these four main lines of research there runs the study of the topography and physical geography of a region—the characteristics of soil and climate and its natural history—for these features of environment are potent in affecting, and even sometimes originating, the racial and national traits of a people. All of these lines of research will be found here and there running into each other, one requiring the practice of the methods of the other for the determining of questions that may arise; and, embracing them all, stands ethnology, the science of mankind, making its demands when need be upon all the vast store of human knowledge accumulated in the structure reared by modern science.

Other archæological enterprises have been, in the main, exploring or collecting undertakings; the Hemenway expedition is archæological in the truest sense, its object being not only the careful collection of material for the study of the past of the race whose remains compose that material, but the study and mental reconstruction of the past as necessary accompaniments of the collection and exploration of that material during the very progress of the work.

III

The scientific corps of the Hemenway expedition is organized with reference to the most efficient prosecution of these several lines of inquiry. It is nearly seven years since the present writer had the privilege of meeting Mr. Cushing at Zuñi and making public, through the columns of the *Herald,* the first account of his remarkable investigations in that isolated pueblo of New Mexico. Mr. Cushing's discovery of the esoteric societies existing among that people, together with the remarkable fund of information secured by his intimate association with them, proved a revelation to the scientific world, throwing a flood of light on the nature of primitive man, and giving a new impetus to ethnological research. His course was the first example of how ethnological studies should really be pursued; it showed the necessity of conducting such investigations from the inside, and the absolute futility of external observation in all work of the kind. The object of Mr. Cushing's researches among the Zuñis, adventurous and attended by exceptional hardships as they were, has in some quarters been somewhat misapprehended as to its bearings. At the time of my visit, however, I fully understood that his purpose was not merely to study the Zuñis as a peculiar and mysterious people; his chief design was to study primitive man through the Zuñis, the thorough knowledge of a typical stock affording a firm basis for obtaining a knowledge of other stocks or races through the application of the principles thereby obtained. It happened that his choice of an example was exceptionally fortunate, for the Zuñis turned out to be representative of the most complete survival of the ancient sedentary culture of the southwest, and as such so regarded by a majority of the other existing Pueblo races. Their designation as the "Father of the Pueblos," which I employed when first writing of them, is therefore appropriate as a substantially literal version of their appellation by cognate peoples.

The fault of much of the best of the ethnological research previous to Mr. Cushing's has been that it has been conducted upon purely materialistic lines, and the assumptions thus made have necessarily led to false, or, at best, inadequate conclusions. Mr. Cushing, however, through a thorough acquisition of the language of the Zuñis, and identification with their modes of life and even thought, was enabled to look at their institutions from the standpoint of primitive man himself, which, in its conception of all appearances as realities, is precisely the reverse of our modern standpoint. Without this thorough knowledge thus gained by his Zuñi studies, his line of important archæological discoveries made during this first year of the Hemenway expedition would have been impossible. These discoveries have been the result of the application of the knowledge of the institutions of a living, but primitive, sedentary people, to the interpretation of the remains of an ancient race of a similar character.

The anthropological work of the expedition is in charge of Herman F. C. ten Kate, M.D. and Ph.D., a native of Holland, and the son of the distinguished artist of that name resident in the Hague.[10] Dr. ten Kate is a graduate of the University of Leyden, and has a thorough medical training, which, of course, is of the greatest advantage in his line of research. Though a young man still in his twenties, he has attained eminence in his branch of science through his reports upon investigations conducted in the course of extensive journeyings in various quarters of the world, from Algeria to Lapland, from the East to the West Indies, and among numerous Indian tribes of the United States, Mexico and British America. In some of these travels he has been the companion of Prince Lucien Bonaparte, who is an earnest and munificent ethnological student. Dr. ten Kate has acquired a store of highly important material through a line of anthropometrical investigations pursued largely among primitive races, making a series of accurate measurements and other records, in the course of which various specially designed instruments of delicate adjustment are used. These data, which include also close observation as to the color of eyes, hair and skin, quality of hair, form of face and features, etc., when collected in large quantity, form valuable material for the classification of different varieties of the human species, and the distribution of those varieties and their modifications through the intermingling process which has been going on for ages in nations and races.

These researches, together with others, Dr. ten Kate will pursue amid the various Indian tribes now living in the territory covered by the scope of the expedition. The anthropological work enters the archæological field of skeletons exhumed in the investigations, and the correlation of the results of this with those of the work just described.

In this work Dr. ten Kate has the coöperation of Dr. J. L. Wortman, the comparative anatomist of the Army Medical Museum at Washington, who, in view of the great importance of these osteological remains of an ancient American race, has been specially detailed for the purpose by the curator of the museum, Surgeon J. S. Billings, U.S.A. Dr. Wortman, who, like Mr. Cushing and Dr. ten Kate, is also a young man, is one of the foremost of comparative anatomists and osteologists in the country; for several years he was the assistant of Prof. Edward Cope, the eminent palæontologist, and he has achieved a high reputation in his line of science by reason of both his original research and the nicety of his laboratory work.

The historical work is in charge of Mr. Adolph F. Bandelier, a gentleman who is preëminently fitted for the task. Mr. Bandelier is one of the foremost of American ethnologists, and the thoroughness of his work in the historical field has given him a high reputation in Europe, as well as in this country. He unites with his deep erudition a brilliant capacity for the marshalling of facts in that unity of aspect which makes the true historian. Probably no other man living is so thoroughly conversant with the materials of Spanish-American history; and his work now in hand on the documentary aboriginal history of Zuñi, and, following it, of the Southwest generally, can hardly fail, when completed, to place him in the ranks of great American historians. His work for the expedition, in conjunction with his preparation of a history of the Church in New Mexico, presented to the Pope by the archbishop of Santa Fé, on the occasion of the recent jubilee of His Holiness, gave him access to a vast amount of valuable material in the archives at Mexico, hitherto inaccessible, and the notes thus obtained, bound and arranged in several volumes with the careful exactness of the true historian's method, form a most interesting feature of his choice historical library at Santa Fé, where his home has been for several years. Mr. Bandelier was one of the first to recognize, after due examination, the great scientific importance of Mr. Cushing's work at Zuñi, and it is an interesting fact that the work of each—the one upon purely ethnological, and the other upon purely historical, lines—has, when they have entered upon the same field, tallied with and corroborated that of the other. Both history and archæology thus stand in similar relations to ethnological research; the latter goes back and clears up the mysteries of the former, and they in turn, help to make the present intelligible.

Another important member of the expedition is Mr. Charles A. Garlick, until recently of the United States Geological Survey. Mr. Garlick, who is a brother-in-law of Major J. W. Powell, the director of the United States Bureau of Ethnology, and of Prof. A. H. Thompson, who is in charge of the United States Geological Survey, besides having care of the practical affairs of the expedition, is its topographical surveyor as well, and has made excellent maps of the ground covered by the work. In his engineering work he has had the assistance of Mr. Fred. Hodge, Mr. Cushing's private secretary, who has turned a good training as a draughtsman to account in the plotting of carefully made plans of the excavations. Mrs. Cushing and her sister, Miss Margaret W. Magill, are also members of the party, and in the classification and care of the specimens they have rendered important aid, while Miss Magill's artistic talent with pencil and brush has been of invaluable and constant service. The immediate supervision of the force of laborers, consisting entirely of well trained Mexicans, is intrusted to Mr. Ramon Castro, a fine type of young Mexican manhood, who, under the guidance of Mr. Cushing, has developed what might be called an instinct for the presence of archæological remains so keen that the faintest traces are usually sufficient to reveal to him the nature of what will be found beneath the surface.

IV

Mr. Cushing's researches here constitute the second great step in what he has chosen for his life work. They have already enabled him to disentangle important leading threads from the skein which involves the mystery of the nature and origin of the sedentary peoples in the great American family of mankind. Here in the valley of the Salado he came across the vestiges of a group of ancient cities, akin in character to similar groups whose ruins are to be found by the score throughout all the fertile valleys of this southwestern country. This group, amid which Camp Hemenway lies, has lain forsaken for untold centuries, its walls gradually uniting with the soil of which they were made until nothing was to be distinguished but a low mound in the midst of each city, ill-defined heaps of earth at close intervals, various depressions in the surface here and there, irregular lines of old irrigating-canals, and the ground covered with pottery sherds, remains of stone implements, etc., scattered far and wide among the mesquite forests and brush thickets.

As shovelful after shovelful of earth has been removed, revealing more fully the remains of the life which animated the spot with its doings and strivings, a life as engrossing and important to its actors then as ours is to us in the larger activities of to-day, and, perhaps, after all of just as much account in the economy of the world, Mr. Cushing has by degrees been enabled to reconstruct that life of the dim past, until many of its features already form coherent pictures before our mental vision.

Some of the printed accounts of his investigations have, doubtless, appeared tinged with sensationalism, but for that Mr. Cushing cannot be held responsible.[11] Even in this corner of the world such operations cannot be conducted without attracting attention, especially when Phoenix, the chief city of Arizona, is but a few miles distant. There is a natural tendency to exaggeration among the witnesses of any operations that are out of the usual order of events, but Mr. Cushing has exercised due scientific caution in reaching his conclusions, and the sober facts are interesting enough without embellishment.

Without his Zuñi experiences, the clear light which Mr. Cushing has cast upon much of these primitive peoples would be impossible. The facts of the daily life and religious institutions of the Zuñis, their keramic and other industrial arts, and things plainly recorded in the structure of the Zuñi language and thus handed down through the centuries from remote antiquity as plainly to one who knows the linguistic ground as though they were graven in stone—all these have been indispensable means to the attainment of his striking results. What he has found here has also, in turn, made plain to him the meaning of various facts observed by him in Zuñi, and which he hitherto could not understand.

V

Could we behold this valley as it appeared when it was peopled by that ancient race, we should see a cluster of cities standing upon the level, or slightly and evenly sloping plain, separated by distances varying from a mile or two to five or six miles. The intervening spaces would be occupied by carefully cultivated fields, bearing crops of corn, beans and pumpkins. In the midst of the valley courses the rapid river, with its shores marked by tall trees, undergrowth and cane-thickets, just as to-day. From its banks broad irrigating-canals meander through the valley, adapting themselves to irregularities of the surface and not running in such straight lines as their modern successors. The branches of these thread the fields in like sinuosity, and dispense fertility far and wide.

When the fields are green with the young crops, the cities stand out in sharp contrast, like islands of tawny yellow amid the verdure, glowing in the sunshine under the azure, and with the mountains rearing their purple walls in the background. In the winter, however, they are like parts of the ground amid which they stand, and of which their walls are formed. In the midst of each city there rises a massive structure prominent above the rest, with walls thick and fortress-like, and six or seven stories in height. Around this there stand the dwellings of the people in enormous blocks, with flat roofs and rising in terraces three or four stories in height. One of these blocks may cover acres of ground. In each city we find another public building, a great oval structure of one story; and again, outside of all the high massive walls enclosing each block, huts not unlike the great oval structure and covered with sloping thatch instead of flat earthen roofing. Between, around, and beside the blocks there run the canals, their course marked by trees. Whoever has seen the pueblo of Taos at the foot of the Rocky mountains in New Mexico, with its two blocks of terraced buildings and the stream running between them, may, if he but imagine the ovens and sheds standing about the hut described, gain something of an idea of the aspect of these dwellings; but one of these ancient structures would contain within itself many like those of Taos. Beside each block of dwellings there is a reservoir filled with water, and occasionally there are two, the canal either entering or running through. Near the reservoir is a heap of earth, and each building has close by a large circular pit. Far off, on the borders of the fields, stand hamlets of thatched huts, with sides of wattled cane, precisely like those clustered nearer the central buildings. Such is the general aspect of the scene, but in two or three of the cities, instead of one great central structure, there stand several smaller edifices of similar aspect in various parts of the town.

The population is of a race like that of the Pueblo Indians of to-day, but theirs is a stone-age civilization and more highly organized than that of its surviving remnants. The people are industrious, peaceable and contented, but they have their full share of the pain and suffering which must have been the lot of mankind in all ages. The men till the fields and engage in the chase; the women attend to the household-duties, cook the food and grind the maize into fine meal in the stone handmills or metates, and they make and bake the pottery, decorating it with the designs which have been handed down from a still remote past, and which are yet faithfully repeated by the Zuñis and to less extent by some of the other pueblos to-day.

There is a deal of mechanical activity always going on among the men, for the fashioning of the various implements of stone and bone, for instance, the grinding or rubbing down of the stone axes to their symmetrical shapes and true lines necessitates an amount of patient, painstaking labor that would be the despair of one of our nineteenth-century workmen. But the work done with these clumsy tools is much more expeditious than would seem to be possible. With these tools we see them hewing trees and chopping and working wood into the various materials used in their house-construction, shaping it into bows and arrows and making various utensils, or breaking it into fuel; we see them chipping stones into nicely formed arrowheads, spearheads and knives; we watch them making their highly prized articles of adornment from sea-shells and turquoises and other stones precious in their eyes. They have, in all probability, by the evidence furnished by petrographs and tradition, as well as analogy, driven in long lines, single file, strange "little beasts of burthen" which perhaps, have carried water and these same precious stores of shell and stone material over long journeys; and then, as now, the dog is man's faithful companion. Men are coming and going, bearing heavy burdens on their backs—deer and antelopes from the chase, grain from the fields, or staggering beneath the weight of heavy stones from the river bed, or rough blocks of hard, porous lava, to be shaped into the indispensable metates, for generally these things are too heavy for their "little beasts." Occasionally a man comes in from a long journey to the distant gulf of California, or the shores of the Pacific in California, bringing the equivalent of several small fortunes in the shape of loads of the most coveted varieties of shell, and which Mr. Cushing finds to be worked into bracelets, ear-rings, beads, small shells for use as strings of tinkling bells, and large ones for use in sacred ceremonials.

In their undertakings which concern the people as a whole, they are coöperative, and the individual, under such circumstances, subordinates himself completely to the community, which works as a unit, and thus constructs the extensive irrigating systems, the public edifices, etc., which even to us seem gigantic in their extent and conception, making us marvel that they could have been carried out with such crude implements. Without this unity of effort they would, indeed, have been impossible. One feature of their coöperative work is the public ovens belonging to each block of buildings, in the shape of the great pits above alluded to. Each block was occupied by a distinct clan, and in these ovens or baking-pits, enormous quantities of food are cooked, to be shared, perhaps, by the entire clan. The method of cooking is much like that of the New England clambake, which originated, it will be remembered, with the Indians of our coast; great fires are burned in the pits for several hours and then smothered in a shaft at the bottom; green branches are then thrown in to make a lining of considerable depth; on these are placed large amounts of green corn and other vegetables, together with meat. More branches are then piled on, and the whole finally covered with earth and packed hard. On this a great fire is built, around which at night a semi-sacred dance goes on. After twenty-four hours or so the pit is opened and everything is found to be deliciously cooked. So intense is the heat of the fires in these baking-pits, and so much are they used, that the clay with which they are lined has been melted throughout to a vitreous slag.

The great central edifices are the temples, the dwellings of the hierarchy of hereditary priests, containing the store-rooms for the share of the grain and other crops which is theirs on the tithing principle, contributed by the entire community, as well as rooms for sacred and public purposes. In time of war the building incidentally becomes the citadel of the place, and with its massive walls it is well nigh impregnable. As the dwelling of the priestly rulers it might perhaps be called the palace or temple; at all events, it may correctly be termed the germ of the palace and castle that came into being when monarchical institutions had fully developed out of a similar stage of culture in other parts of the world.

With the people whose past we are beholding, religion is the main thing of life, and every act, every movement, however insignificant or however slight, has its religious aspect and significance. So thoroughly are they pervaded by their devotional attitude that it requires no exercise of authority on the part of their priesthood to secure submission; their obedience is that of children to their parents, filial and reverential, and the voluntary outcome of their mythico-social life. They have their esoteric societies for the guarding of what they deem secrets of nature, methods of treating disease and fighting sorcery. These societies have their lodge rooms probably in each block of buildings, and in the great oval building we have seen is their meeting-place for more formal and public exercises; this building is what is commonly called the estufa in speaking of the modern pueblo, but the term, which means "stove," is a misnomer; perhaps sun-temple, the name which Mr. Cushing applies, would be more correct, since it is the headquarters of the Priest of the Sun, the spiritual head of the people, and standing apart in his functions from the hierarchy, the "six Masters of the House."

The burial customs of this people are of two kinds: the common people were cremated, and the priests and members of the hereditary priestly caste—the line of descent being always through the mother—and of the esoteric societies, were buried. For, according to their belief, in order to secure the complete liberation of the soul from the body immediately after death, it is necessary for the body to be burned, its destruction setting the soul free at once, while the priests have, by virtue of their spiritual powers, this knowledge, and so their bodies do not need to be burned. This knowledge also belongs to members of their caste by right of heredity, and sometimes by initiation sanctioned by them. Such persons are, therefore, always buried in the temple or beneath the floors of their houses. The low, gray earth and ash-mounds which we have noticed near the reservoirs are the "pyral mounds," or places where the bodies of the dead are cremated. After the funeral pyre, loaded with precious sacrifices, offerings of members of his clan, has burned out, the few remaining bones of the dead are gathered and placed in a jar of pottery and buried on the margin of the mound. Unless the burial-jar has been specially made or reserved for the purpose, it is neatly

A double burial; male and female.

Excavated cemetery at base of pyral mound, showing pottery containing cremated remains.

"killed" by drilling a hole in its bottom or otherwise partially breaking it, thereby allowing its soul to escape with that of the person whose remains it holds. The personal belongings of the dead are also burned with him, that their spiritual counterparts may be set free to accompany him into the other world. In the case of the house-burials, however, the vessels containing food and drink buried with the deceased are not "killed" except in the case of young children who may be considered too inexperienced to know how to exert the power necessary to taking the vessel and its contents with them upon their journey.

VI

All these facts have been acquired by Mr. Cushing through the knowledge gained in his Zuñi experience, enabling him to read the past in the light of what he there learned concerning the nature of primitive man. His principal excavations thus far have been carried on in two of the ruined cities of the valley about six miles apart, which he has respectively named Los Muertos and Las Acequias, or the City of the Dead and the City of the Canals, from local features, the former name coming from the large quantity of skeletons and cremated remains found there. Camp Hemenway is situated in the midst of Los Muertos, which covers an area of something over two square miles drawn out along the borders of a canal or artificial river, to a length of nearly six miles. According to the very conservative estimate made by Major Powell of what the population of an ancient ruin in the Cañon de Chelle, in the north of Arizona, must have been, judging by the number of dwellings, Los Muertos had at least 13,000 inhabitants, and it is not improbable that the number was greatly in excess of that figure. As has been stated, Los Muertos is one of the smallest of a group of seven cities, and, conceding an average of 14,000 inhabitants to each city, the population of the entire group would have been at least 90,000, and probably very much larger.[12] There are various very strong reasons aside from these for holding that the population of these fertile, universally irrigated valleys, was a dense one. One of these is the carrying out of large constructive works, a labor which, with the crude implements of a stone age, would have required the coöperation of large forces of men. Most conspicuous of these are the extensive systems of irrigation, with the great canals running many miles into the interior. One of these canals in the Gila valley is fully thirty-eight miles in length at the least calculation, and in other parts of Arizona there are ancient canals over seventy miles long. The construction of these canals to-day, with all our improved appliances even, would be a great undertaking, and their execution with simply stone implements for excavation and baskets or litters for carrying the earth would have been beyond the means of a small population. Moreover, a small population would have kept near the river and made but a short canal. One of these ancient canals has been partially utilized by the Mormons of Zenos, or Mesa City, one of the towns in this valley, in the construction of their own irrigating system, and they say that, at a single point where the old canal had been cut through a bed of hard, natural cement, it saved them an expense of between $10,000 and $20,000.[13]

The irrigating systems furnish another strong argument in favor of a dense population, by reason of the great economy of water that was practiced, and consequently the large area of land that was brought under cultivation. The ancient people were content with a fall of but one foot to the mile, whereas the fall thought necessary by the white inhabitants of to-day is twice as great—an extravagance which must be remedied in time with the growth of population and the increased demand for land. The primitive inhabitants, therefore, carried their irrigation to much higher levels than is feasible under the modern methods. But even thus it appears that the supply from the river did not wholly meet the needs of the ancient inhabitants, for they still further husbanded water by storing up the rainfall from the neighboring mountains as it flowed down from the ravines in the gullies, or *arroyos,* worn in the ground. They thus were enabled to irrigate additional tracts of land. Sufficient amounts of water were diverted from these *arroyos* at practical points and led into large tanks or storage basins, generally oval in form and made with high banks of earth, lined at the bottom and sides with puddled clay, which was often rendered still further proof against leakage by filling the basin with brush and making a fire that baked the clay into terra-cotta.

Another feature of the great public works of this class was but recently discovered by Mr. Cushing. It is still more significant of vast population operating coöperatively. The unusual rainfall of the past winter has caused a luxuriant growth of small flowering plants upon the plains surrounding Los Muertos and other ancient cities of the southern Salado system. Mr. Cushing observed, however, that while this growth is always most luxuriant where ancient buildings have stood, it is absent along the inner borders of the banks of what were the once extensive irrigating canals, whose lines could previously be traced no farther, so obliterated had they become in the course of time. Following out one of the canals of Los Muertos by this means, he found that it led off to the southwest some three miles farther than it had been explored, terminating in an enormous *represo,* or storage reservoir, irregular in outline, something like a mile in length and averaging nearly half a mile in width.[14] Apparently, advantage had been taken of a natural depression for the creation of this reservoir. Considering that its banks were built of earth excavated by stone implements and transported in baskets, it is evident that an army of laborers must have been required for its construction. The reservoir was evidently designed to store the surplus water from the canals, and it is not improbable that one of its purposes was to enable the canals, without waste of water, to be run bank-full, for the sake of the navigation, which naturally would have existed under the need of transporting building and other heavy material from the river and crops from the fields to the towns, and with the facilities offered by water-ways of such magnitude. It seems likely that the craft used in these canals were rafts of bundles of reeds, since enormous quantities of reeds from the river were used for roofing and other constructive purposes, and floating them down the canals would suggest their availability for transportation purposes. Thus, under such conditions of irrigation, in a timberless region, probably originated the balsa or raft of reeds, universal among the Peruvian aborigines and in the Gulf of California.

These ancient canals may often, or almost always, be traced by the large and small, black river pebbles or cobble stones that are found in profusion on their banks, when not covered, together with the worn-out digging implements of stone. The reason for the existence of these river stones in such places is to be found in one of the many peculiar beliefs held by primitive man in the taking of appearances for realities. Just as they are sometimes found to hold that the motion of the trees causes the wind, instead of the wind moving the trees, and that the butterflies bring the summer, rather than the summer the butterflies, so as they see the apparent motion of pebbles in flowing water, they hold that the water is urged along by the pebbles. Therefore, they placed the pebbles along the banks of the canals, particularly in places where there was danger of breaking, under the belief that the stones, or "water-tamers" as Mr. Cushing calls them, would exert their influence in repelling the water as it leaped up against the banks, and urge it along in its proper course down the stream. At the entrance to their reservoirs and all around the great reservoir above described, little heaps of these river-stones are to be found, put there to show the water the way out of the canal into the places where it is wanted to go. The Zuñis of to-day hold this belief, and the existence of the "water-tamers" among the vestiges of these people shows that the belief was handed down from very ancient times.

The study of the methods of irrigation and agriculture pursued by the primitive races of the Southwest is highly interesting and instructive. The subject has been followed closely by Mr. Cushing for several years, and the results of his investigations thereof will, when made public, have not only scientific, but also a genuine practical value in indicating improved methods for bringing large tracts under cultivation, and showing that, with all our boasted nineteenth century civilization, the modern man can profitably go to school to the occupant of the soil in an age when they used hoes of stone and planting sticks, instead of steel ploughs, seed-drills, cultivators and harvesters.

Of late years it has been a favorite theory among ethnologists to hold that there never was a large aboriginal population in America, and that the enormous number of ruins found here in the Southwest is to be accounted for by successive occupations of a small number of inhabitants. The ancient history of the Old

World, however, shows that the population of fertile portions of desert regions was compact and dense; the valleys of the Euphrates and of the Nile—the former as desolate and waste to-day as our own Southwest—sustaining enormous populations in ancient times. Similar natural conditions exist here, and what was there to prevent dense populations in these valleys? Then, too, a successive occupation by migrations of small populations, building city after city, pueblo after pueblo, of those whose ruins exist to-day, would have necessitated a period of time so great, even giving but a few generations of habitancy to each place, as to confer upon many of these ruins an antiquity so vast as to be beyond the bounds of probability and the lasting qualities of the materials employed in constructing them.

It is certain, however, that some of these ruins do possess a very considerable antiquity, while on the other hand Mr. Bandelier's recent researches would seem to show that cities of the general character of Los Muertos—with the feature, that is, of the central temple or citadel—were in existence, and inhabited when the first Spaniards invaded the land.[15] At least there were people dwelling about such places, though perhaps only as the Pima Indians dwell about these ruins to-day. On the other hand, then, the theory of successive occupations holds good, with the qualification of large populations. It is seen that the institutions of this people required a contemporaneous inhabitance of an entire group of their towns, but that inhabitance was subject to termination through a regard for a peculiar article of faith, which must have existed with them from a very remote period in their past, and which must have been a controlling motive in the migrations which dispersed them over such wide areas of the continent.

This was a belief in the necessity of maintaining their abiding place at the centre of the world. Should the stability of the natural conditions of the locality inhabited by such a people be undermined through the occurrence of disturbing phenomena, and should religious ceremonials and sacrifices be unavailing in persuading the gods to cause a cessation of such phenomena, then the place would be abandoned with all the belongings of the people, and however desirable the region might be for residence, however rich the soil, a taboo would be laid upon the towns and the fields, and no one of that race might longer dwell there or till the soil. A removal to a short distance, no farther away than a neighboring valley, for instance, would be enough to comply with the self-imposed edict, and there the people might live even for centuries, perhaps, about a stable earth-centre, rejoicing in the favor of the gods.

Skeleton of man crushed by wall probably overthrown by earthquake.

Earthquakes were one of the main causes of the instability of the "centre of the world," and it was evidently that which occasioned the abandonment of the group which has been the scene of the investigations of the Hemenway expedition for the past year. Mr. Cushing first came to this conclusion through finding the household utensils left in their regular places, unbroken and undisturbed, just as they would have been in the case of such a deliberate abandonment under taboo. That earthquakes were the cause was shown by the nature of the sacrifices which he also found, the same sacrifice that the Zuñis make to-day to the gods of the lower regions, the divinities who produce and control the phenomena of earthquakes, whenever a great landslide or other allied disturbances occur in their country. The walls of many of the houses were also found to be overthrown and the roofs burned, as if from the fires on the hearths, and now and then the skeletons of persons were found who had been caught and crushed beneath the falls. That of one man thus excavated appeared to have been held to the ground alive and mangled, as if struggling to free himself.[16]

When at San Francisco on a visit last autumn,[17] Mr. Cushing, at a dinner given in his honor by members of the Academy of Sciences, gave some account of his work here. President Holden of the University of California, and Professor Davidson, in charge of the coast survey on the Pacific, were particularly interested in what he had to say concerning the earthquake idea, but were evidently disposed, and very properly, to receive his theory with scientific caution, the subject being a specialty with them both, they having recently returned from elaborate investigations of the great earthquake of Sonora at its centre of disturbance at Bavispe, that had occurred the preceding spring. Therefore, they asked Mr. Cushing if he had observed in which way the walls had fallen. "As if hinged at the bottom, and, opening outward, they had let the roof fall inside," he responded; whereupon they assured him that his theory was absolutely correct, for an earthquake was, generally speaking, the only cause which could make walls and roofs fall in that manner. This fact was a discovery which had been made by them during their observations at Bavispe, and it was not until after this dinner to Mr. Cushing that their report announcing it was published.

In this connection a singular occurrence deserves noting. On May 3, 1887, two gentlemen, resident in Arizona, were visiting Camp Hemenway, and were dining with Mr. Cushing. They listened with interest to what he told them about the ancient earthquakes, but they said that they could not accept his conclusions, since this was a region free from such disturbances. Ever since the first occupancy of the territory by the Spaniards, even such a thing as an earthquake had not been known. They had scarcely finished the discussion when the flag on a staff over a neighboring tent, visible from the table, was observed to be fluttering violently, although not a breath of air was stirring. Then a strange motion of the earth was felt beneath them, accompanied by a rumbling noise. "An earthquake, gentlemen," exclaimed Mr. Cushing, drawing his watch and timing the disturbance. The shock lasted something like two minutes; it was the great Sonora earthquake whose effect was felt far up into Arizona and New Mexico. "I believe you now!" exclaimed the guests, and one of them looked at Mr. Cushing with an expression that might have been interpreted to proceed from a suspicion that their host was a wizard, who had conjured up the earthquake expressly to prove himself right.[18]

VII

Speculation naturally arises as to the probable age of these remains. That is, of course, a difficult matter to determine, and, in the present stage of the investigations, little more can be looked for than an approximate minimum estimate. The culture itself represented by these remains is undoubtedly very old upon this continent. When the Spaniards first came into this country the most notable edifice in the Southwest among the ancient structures, Casa Grande, on the Gila, was even then a ruin, and it is, after nearly three centuries and a half, still standing.[19] Mr. Cushing's researches have proven the Casa Grande to be a typical central temple and citadel of the ancient civilization, and all the others have long since crumbled into mounds which give only slight indication of their structural character. The condition of the articles taken from the ruins, particularly of the pottery and the skeletons of the inhabitants, is such as to betoken an age of between 1000 and 2000 years at least.[20]

An indication of the possible age of these remains may be found in a consideration of the remarkable archæological discoveries reported from the Spanish province of Almeria, made last summer, so shortly after these of Los Muertos as to be almost simultaneous. The account of those reads like a repetition of the story of these, for there, too, it was a stone-age culture whose remains have been brought to light; that people also practiced both cremation and house-burial, and there, as here, the house-burials often included both husband and wife, or at least man and woman, side by side. As the conditions of soil and climate in southern Spain and our Southwest are remarkably alike, both regions being dry, hot and desert-like, and conducive to the long preservation of buried remains, it is quite possible for relics of the past to last as long here as there. And for European archæology there is set an interesting task in estimating the possible period of a stone-age civilization on the borders of the Mediterranean, in a land subject to the influences of the iron-age Latin cultures and the bronze-age pre-Latin people. It is a striking fact, that at nearly the same time there should be discovered the remains of two cultures so closely resembling each other in their institutions, both in new Spain and in old.

There are evidences in the habitable valleys of the Southwest, of superimposed occupations of the same sites, as in the great centres of population in the old world, and for the same reason—the character of soil and other natural conditions being such as to invite population by successive peoples. And as race-history almost universally shows that more or less of the blood of preceding peoples passes into the veins of successive occupants of the same soil, this seems sufficient to account for traditions among the latter pointing to descent from a race whose culture often occupied a higher grade than their own.

Mr. Cushing's studies have led him to characterize this primitive sedentary culture, for convenience of designation, as Shiwian, or Toltecan,—not as Toltec, not as recognizing a distinctive Toltec race—but as distinguishing a culture, though not necessarily a race, as the parent of the Aztec, Maya, Peruvian and other civilizations of Mexico, Central and South America. Of this he is firmly convinced, for by comparing his own studies here with the explorations of others conducted in those regions, he traces by the sure and gradual lines of natural development the evolution of those civilizations from this root and stock, which formed an ample framework for the elaborations there supplied. The word Shiwian comes from the Shiwi, the name by which the Zuñis call themselves. As the Zuñis furnish conclusive evidence, both in their language and institutions, as well as in the way in which they are regarded by neighboring Pueblo races—which have adopted not only their religious customs, but the very words designating those customs—that they, of all existing Pueblo nations, preserve in the greatest purity the heritage of the ancient sedentary culture of the new world, it is most fitting that they should give the generic name to the ethnic groundwork upon which the autochthonous American civilizations are based.

VIII

It will be seen that the results of the Hemenway expedition are of importance, not so much through what has been found, as by what has been *found out* in the progress of the work. The collections, however, are remarkably rich and extensive; their great and paramount value rests upon the knowledge of their collector, and thereby the circumstances under which they were collected. Without this, they would be simply like the great majority of other collections—merely curiosities, or museum bric-a-brac. The collections of the Hemenway expedition, however, will rank among the few that may be said to have a soul; that is, deriving their value more from their intelligently recorded history than from their objective interest, great though that may be. One of the other notable exceptions to the general run of archæological collections is that which Professor Putnam of the Peabody Museum at Cambridge is making with such admirable system and exactness among the ancient aboriginal earthworks in Ohio,[21] and the results of Mr. Cushing's labors here cannot fail to throw much light upon the meaning of what has there been found.

All the facts concerning each and every article in the collection are ascertained and noted with as much detail as possible, that it may be enabled to tell its story; for, although that story may be veiled in mystery at the time of its discovery, there is no telling at what moment some other discovery may remove the veil if the history of that article is carefully preserved for reference. This has occurred again and again in the course of these explorations, and the records that have been preserved will prove invaluable aids for the guidance of investigations. And the fact that may prove the key to a vexed problem is not unlikely to be a seemingly unimportant detail. Therefore, all objects are carefully labelled and catalogued, and in the catalogue all the circumstances concerning their finding are noted. This record is also checked and amplified by the daily report of the director, written carefully by Mr. Cushing, giving the history of each day's work. So far as practicable, photographs are made of the excavations and the objects found; plans are also made of the buildings whose ruins are excavated, and these are shown collectively in maps of the localities.

The importance of having archæological work proceed under the direction of a man thoroughly conversant with the institutions and characteristics of the race, whose remains are under investigation, is shown by the knowledge brought to the task by Mr. Cushing. One not familiar with Indian life and methods of thought would, in a field like this, be fumbling blindly in a labyrinth. The knowledge of the motives that would actuate primitive man under given circumstances tell him why certain objects are placed in certain positions and relations as plainly as if he had seen them put there himself. For instance, he finds a skeleton buried with adornments that he recognizes as belonging to the paraphernalia of a certain priesthood that he knows among the Zuñis, and held sacred to that purpose, while on the facial bones of the skull is found the dry, colored dust of a pigment with which the members of that priesthood paint their faces during certain ceremonials of the order. Mr. Cushing therefore learns, by this observation, that the same priesthood existed centuries ago among this people, and that the remains of one of its priests are before him. Again, by certain articles found about the skeleton of a female, he recognizes that here was an Indian Iphigenia—the articles are sacrifices to the gods of the lower regions, and the maiden was probably the best-loved child of a priest, slain to gain the favor of the deities and avert the earthquake dangers. So, also, from his knowledge of the Zuñi conceptions of the regions in space; of the tendency of that race, for the sake of protection as well as agriculture, to locate its towns and camps in certain relations to one another and generally in the midst of the plains, then to distribute around about these homes their cave-sacrifices and shrines according to certain local conditions and to their ideas of the regions of the world, he is

Skeleton of maiden sacrificed to prevent earthquakes.

able to enter a valley-plain in the Southwest before unknown to him, and find there the cities of the ancient occupants—even though these be buried, with scarcely a trace on the surface. Having thus found these towns, he is then able, by looking at the mountains with Zuñi eyes—"dividing the horizon mythologically"—thus to choose, as would a priest of the old Shiwian cultures, the places of sacrifice; and when, according to this choice, he rides off to these appropriate places, he finds, readily and almost invariably, the round and square god-houses, the ritualistic petrographs, and even the cave-shrines placed there centuries ago, with their rich accumulations of textile, feather and wood paraphernalia in the shape of vessels, symbolic weapons, etc., preserved as thoroughly as if they had been kept in the cases of a museum.

The collections include pottery, stone implements, turquoise and other stones held in esteem in the ancient days, shells and shell ornaments, and human and animal remains. So great is the age of the ruins that but slight remains of textile fabrics have been found—two or three precious scraps—and pieces of wood and other vegetable remains are also very scarce for the same reason. Those that have been found are in a charred condition, for the greater part, and it is this charring which has preserved them, enabling the burned roofs, for instance, to tell the tale of the earthquakes.

The pottery is found, for the greater part, in houses, buried beneath the floors as food and drink vessels for the dead with whose skeletons they were found, or in use as domestic utensils; or discovered buried at the bases of the pyral mounds, containing the cremated remains. It makes a rich collection; one of the finest in the world, when its typical character and the circumstances of its discovery are taken into account. In general characteristics it is the same as that of the ceramic art of the Southwest, both ancient and modern, and many of the designs are identical with those made by the Zuñis of to-day, some types not varying in a single detail, illustrating the power of tradition in the conservation of design among a primitive people. One of the most important things is the discovery here of nearly all the types needed to complete the chain of development in the evolution of pottery-forms and designs out of basketry, traced with scientific exactness by Mr. Cushing in his paper on pueblo pottery, contributed to the fourth annual report of the Bureau of Ethnology, recently published.[22]

The collection of stone axes and other tools is already unquestionably one of the finest in the world, both in variety of form and in nicety of finish, as well as in number of specimens. The articles of personal adornment show that the race

Examples of decorated pottery excavated at Los Muertos.

possessed considerable artistic skill in that direction, as well as in pottery. Seashells were the favorite material for the manufacture of these, and much of the shellwork shows traces of having been used as a base for inlaying. Fortunately a very precious example, one of the gems of the collection, tells just how this inlaying was done. The article is a figure of a frog made by creating the back of a shell with an excellent kind of black cement, manufactured from the gum deposited upon the leaves and twigs of the hediondillo, or grease-wood, by a species of lac-insect. In this gum were embedded little mosaic fragments of various shades of turquoise and of red shells, and then rubbed down smooth. It makes a realistic figure, as well as a very beautiful article of primitive jewelry. Probably no public collection in the world has any example of this peculiar inlaid work, a few articles of which are held in priceless esteem by esoteric orders among the Zuñis and other pueblo tribes.[23] A unique example of the art of this ancient people was found the other day while excavating the ruins of an interesting temple, in the shape of the only specimen of their basket-work thus far encountered. It was protected by the charring of the contents, a kind of marmalade of pitahaya fruit, as it lay in the storeroom of the temple, but unfortunately it was badly broken by the shovel of a workman before it was observed. The fragments have a great scientific value, however, since they show that the decorative coloring was protected by a kind of lacquering, probably also made from the hediondillo gum, the first yet discovered among the prehistoric remains of this country.

The anthropological value of the large collection of human skeletons—nearly 200 having thus far been found—may be seen from the fact that the ancient pueblo skeletons have been extremely rare and correspondingly coveted heretofore, but three or four skulls having been found previous to the work of the Hemenway expedition. The collection of skeletons has particular worth, from the excavation and preservation of the remains having been personally superintended by two such eminent scientists as Drs. Wortman and ten Kate, so that every possible bone has been secured. This circumstance has, indeed, enabled those gentlemen to make a discovery of great importance, the nature of which, however, it would be unbecoming in me to indicate before its announcement in proper scientific form by its discoverers.[24] The doctors also declare that the number of anomalies they have encountered make it the most interesting collection of skeletons they have ever examined.

IX

As carrying out the work begun by Mr. Cushing in Zuñi and confirming the conclusions reached there, the following list, prepared from data furnished by his notes, will show the nature of some of the chief results attained by the Hemenway expedition in but little more than a year:

1. The finding of extensive groups of petrographs, or rock-inscriptions, existing throughout central Arizona from Prescott to the Salado and Gila valleys identical even to detail with the Zuñi groups, and thus establishing that their purpose was, like that of the latter, ritualistic, and to be interpreted, when of Pueblo origin, mythologically, and not as records of events.

2. That the class of ruins typified by the Casa Grande remains is universal in the valleys of the Gila and Salado and neighboring watercourses, and equally so in lines extending southward far into Mexico. The chief characteristics of this type are demonstrated to be (1) the use by their constructors not only of stone and of hand-made adobe, or sun-dried brick, but also in the building of their main earthen walls by forming them within a framework of slight timber and wattled cane, thus characterizing their architecture as derived, like their pottery, from original basketry types—in this case, of hut structures; (2) the occurrence of enormous central citadel or temple buildings in the midst of (3) groups of dwellings distributed within walled enclosures, and (4) in their vicinity clusters of houses or huts of an inferior type, unenclosed, inhabited by an ultra-mural outcast, or laboring class; and (5) in shape these entire groups of structures or cities invariably conform to the lines of extension of the main irrigating canals, thus being of great length relative to their width; (6) that these ancient canal cities are universally located along the outside limits (that is, farthest from the river) of the irrigation tracts lying between the canals and the river; (7) that these cities invariably occur in groups, contemporaneously occupied, of six or seven, thus exactly corresponding to the mythico-sociologic division of the "seven cities of Cibola" or ancient Zuñi, and the still preserved division into seven corresponding parts of the one modern Zuñi pueblo; (8) of the universal prevalence among their inhabitants of the significant dual system of burial of the higher social and sacerdotal classes by interment beneath the floors of the houses wherein they dwelt and their relatives continued to dwell, and in gentile cemeteries surrounding the bases of sacrificial mounds—designated by

Excavated house-ruins.

Mr. Cushing, in consequence of their use, as "pyral mounds"—of the ordinary classes, whether intra- or ultra-mural.

3. The occurrences, as in Zuñi, throughout all these pueblos, associated with their appropriate structures of (1, in temples), tribal; (2, in urban houses or quarters), of clan, or gentile; (3, in dwelling rooms and house sepulchres) of family; (3 [*sic*], in pyral sacrifices) of individual, amulets or fetiches, consisting of concretionary stones of high natural colors and peculiar shapes, and held sacred because derived from the "source of life" in the sea, lakes and rivers. In correspondence with this institution there occurs a decorative symbolism on pottery identical with that of Zuñi.

4. Conforming with the grouping of their cities, the ancient inhabitants practiced an elaborate and thorough system of coöperative irrigation, superior, in some respects, to that of the present white inhabitants; in addition to which they practiced an elaborate and even more ingenious system of rain irrigation.

5. That from the form of their canals and distribution of their canal-systems, as well as the evidences, direct and indirect, of the transportation of bundles of

reeds and canes, they seem to have had a crude, yet effective, system of canal navigation.

6. That, from the evidences furnished by (1) the traditions of the Zuñis, (2) stray allusions in old Spanish narratives, (3) petrographic herder-rituals, these people had domesticated animals, notably the turkey, and probably also the rabbit and a variety of the auchenia or llama,[25] as shown by (4) the petrographic inscriptions observed by Mr. Cushing in western New Mexico and central and southern Arizona, and the repeated finding of sacrifices for herd-increase or reproduction, of actual figurines strikingly resembling the last mentioned animals.

7. The practice of an entirely indigenous metallurgic art, evidencing a crude knowledge of the reduction of ore by smelting, working of the resulting metals by beating or repoussé treatment with stone implements, and fusing or brazing with terra-cotta and cane blowpipes, showing the beginning of the extremely interesting transition, within and from the stone age toward the metal age, in this, the working of the softer metals chiefly for ornamental purposes solely with stone-age appliances; the utilization of metal for implements being considered as marking the beginning of the metal age.[26]

8. The establishment, by Dr. ten Kate, of the types of crania belonging to the remains of these people, as being of the peculiar brachycephalic pueblo, older Mexican and Peruvian type, and also the discovery, by Drs. Wortman and ten Kate, of new and strongly distinctive anatomical features that promise to be of extreme value in racial determination.

These, which are only the chief among numerous interesting discoveries and observations, all evidence, as above narrated, a continuous desert culture, the direction of whose growth and elaboration lay from north, southward, finding its most immediate course and its clearest and most perfect development and exemplification at its extreme limit, in Peru, especially among the Chimu and other Yunga remains—its most primitive and representative living example in the little tribe of Zuñi, to-day, though to a greater or less extent still traceable as an absorbed element among nearly all the tribes of the Southwest.

Beside the strictly scientific fruits, and the fact that probably there is no really scientific achievement without a thoroughly practical aspect in the shape of benefits to human progress—although they may not directly appear—the Hemenway expedition has accomplished directly "practical" results which may be turned to great economic account in the very region where its researches are prosecuted. In investigating the remains of the primal desert culture of our continent—and Mr. Cushing holds that, from the necessities of environment, the origin of all great civilizations is to be sought in the desert—it is bringing to life the facts concerning a people who had learned all that the desert had to teach them, or at least all that it was needful for them to know. And the desert-craft of the aborigines is not to be despised. A single example may suffice. When Mr. Cushing's researches concerning their methods of irrigation are made public, it will be seen that, with their economy of water and their knowledge how to utilize and husband the rainfall for irrigation through simple and effective means of storage, in addition to the water brought in canals from the streams, the facts acquired by them through ages of experience can be adapted to our modern resources, to the great advantage of the multitudes who are now repopulating these valleys. And this knowledge will be of enormous benefit to the Southwest, vastly increasing its population, and enabling the cultivation of extensive tracts that are still regarded as hopelessly desert.

X

All that promotes an understanding of man by men strengthens the ties of sympathy that are destined to overcome, in the course of the ages, the mutual prejudices of individuals and the mutual hatreds of races. These ties will form the bonds of universal brotherhood, the attainment of which has been the aim of the masters of life, who have towered like mountain peaks above the levels of their kind, and, in the calm, clear air that lies beyond the turmoil of the clouded currents of passion and strife for individual advantage, have seen that human happiness can have no lasting home where it is not plainly recognized that only that which is for the good of all men is for the good of any man. Dislike is dispelled by knowledge; and ethnology, the science of mankind, is, therefore, essentially the most philanthropical, as well as the greatest, of the sciences.

To understand any subject we must first go to its beginnings and work from the foundation upward. In tracing the history of the human race and the development of the human mind back through the long volumes of Nature's book, that, with their baffling pages of strange though plainly inscribed records precede our few chapters told in familiar speech called history, we must first go to primitive man and study the race in its childhood if we would understand the true meaning of that blossoming of humanity known as modern civilization. In making this work its task the Hemenway expedition is rendering an invaluable service, and the results already reached give promise of grander results to follow, as the strands now grasped in the light of discoveries made are brought together to form the line that shall lead far back among the vanished peoples of the very old "new world."

Written at Camp Hemenway, near Tempe, Arizona
April 4, 1888.

ARCHAEOLOGICAL CAMPING IN ARIZONA, PARTS 1–4

I

THE WRITER HAS ELSEWHERE given an account of the work of the Hemenway Southwestern Archaeological Expedition to Arizona, under the direction of Mr. Frank Hamilton Cushing: its purposes, its composition, and the results reached in the first fifteen months of its operations.[27] Some details about the country, pictures of life in camp, and the methods of exploration pursued—rambling though they be—will probably help the many who are interested in the important prehistoric story of our continent to gain a clearer conception of the character of the researches.

First, then, a glance at the country: The scene of operations has chiefly been in the neighborhood of the flourishing young towns of Phoenix and Tempe, in the valley of the Rio Salado, now usually called the Salt River by the American inhabitants. I prefer, however, to keep to the more euphonious Spanish name. To the northward and eastward the mountains rise grandly in compact ranges, the main peaks having about the same relative height, as seen from the plain, as Mount Washington when viewed from the Saco Valley at Conway, in New Hampshire. Out of this mountain wall the Salado breaks from a wild cañon,

From the *American Architect and Building News,* 5, 12, 19, and 26 January 1889 whose neighborhood was the scene of some fierce and momentous struggles between the gallant troops of General Crook and the wild Apaches fifteen years ago or more, at the time when that splendid soldier gave the country its first relief from their incursions; a peace which would probably have remained unbroken to this day had it not been for the wicked mismanagement of the Indian Department, under the control of corrupt rings.

Not far from its exit into the plain the Salado is joined by the Rio Verde near a huge ruddy rock, that looks like a Cyclopean fortress, called Mount McDowell. The military post, Fort McDowell, is near its base. A few miles below Phoenix the Salado joins the Gila, the former being really the main stream above their confluence, although the latter gives its name to the river in its further course down into the grand Colorado. From the southeastward around to the northwest the mountains rise in detached groups, with the land sloping away evenly and gradually from their feet in a way that may, perhaps, be best illustrated by imagining a great carpet with heaps of sharp stones placed here and there beneath it, and their ragged tops appearing above the sagging surface they have torn through.

It is a semi-tropical region, the latitude being that of Southern California, and the altitude in the neighborhood of a thousand feet. The winters are delightful in temperature; a fiercer summer heat is hardly to be found in North America: dry and oven-like, at times rising to something like 130 degrees, but, on account of its dryness, it is not so oppressive as a temperature of 90 degrees in the humid air of the Eastern States. The vegetation is the monotonous growth of the desert: sage-brush, greasewood, forests of stunted mesquite, and clumps of ironwood and palo verde near the mountains, cottonwoods along the river, and many varieties of fantastic-looking cactus almost everywhere on the plains. But where the land has been brought under irrigation a new and luxuriant growth appears: fertile fields of grain and pasturage, vineyards, orchards of peaches and apricots, and already, in spots, date-palms, fan-palms, orange-trees, oleanders, and cypress are imparting a new aspect to the landscape.

It is in the early afternoon of January 11 when I step from the train of the Maricopa & Phoenix Railroad—a branch from the Southern Pacific—onto the platform of the new brick station at Tempe, at present the only regular stopping-place on the line between Maricopa Junction, about twenty miles away, and Phoenix, the terminus, nine miles farther on. I am greeted by Mr. Fred. Hodge, the stalwart young private secretary of Mr. Cushing. We proceed to Camp Hemenway in a buckboard drawn by two stout mules. The weather seems to be a strange commingling of early summer and late autumn. The sky is serenely blue, the air is quiet, and the sun shines with a warm, southern friendliness. But the ground is brown and the trees are bare, though some sparse yellow leaves still cling to the alamos, or cottonwoods, here and there.

The town has enjoyed a "boom" from the building of the railway, and its evidences are seen in many new buildings; the railway has made the great timber-supply of California and Oregon available, and, frame construction being a novelty here, its attainability has given it a proportionate desirability in the eyes of the inhabitants. Wooden buildings are, however, totally unsuited to this hot and dry climate, and the folly of substituting them for the thick-walled and comfortable adobe structures, so despised as "mud-houses" by the average settler, must soon be made manifest by experience. It is possible to make an adobe building architecturally attractive, though, as commonly constructed by the American or the somewhat Americanized Mexican, they are about as ugly as they can possibly be made, with their bare walls contrasting with the bony whiteness of painted door and window-frames, and the inconvenient sliding sashes set even with the wall-surface, thus giving no shadows or depth to the openings. Houses with such windows have a vulgar impertinence of expression. The conservative traits of ordinary humanity are shown in hardly anything more than in their methods of construction, and the presumably wide-awake and progressive American will cling to the customs of his predecessors with all the tenacity of the most primitive races, though he has no other ground than that his fathers did so before him, and therefore, it must be good, reasoning no more about it until experience in a changed environment slowly teaches him more convenient ways. The unintelligent savage builds like his fathers because his fathers were taught to build like the gods, and, therefore, those ways are sacred, and must not be changed. The northern origin of the American population that is now filling up this region is shown by its adoption of details of construction totally unsuited to the climate, who reason, of course, that that is the way things are done in a "white man's country," and, therefore, must necessarily be superior to the ways in which Mexicans do things. So they go on stifling and sweltering all through the long, hot summer days in their boxy little houses, survivals of the habits brought from regions where timber is plenty and the climate fickle.

Considering these things, I have thought I should like to settle down in a place like this long enough to set an example of how it is possible to live comfortably with pleasant surroundings by adapting the ordinary materials to modern means and taste. For instance: a one-story, wide-spreading house of thick adobe walls, with large, high, airy rooms, and casement-windows opening to the floor, giving the full benefit of the air-space; above the flat roof, supported on posts or thick adobe piers, with a space of eight to ten feet between, a second roof of corrugated tile, such as is used so extensively in Spain and Spanish America, sloping gently, and with wide eaves. This would answer the purpose of a double-roof, the shaded air-space keeping the rooms below cool, and would also give a second story, open to the air. In the summer this open story would be used for sleeping purposes, divided by screens in the Japanese fashion to give privacy, if need be, and with mosquitoes, flies, and other insects kept out by wire-netting surrounding the whole. People in this region find it impossible to sleep in their houses in the summer now: they take to the open air with their mattresses, either on the roofs or on the ground outside. By this means, however, they would have all the advantages of open air combined with shelter, for drenching rains come up in the night-time not infrequently. Care would be taken, in such a house, to leave no interstices for the concealment of tarantulas, scorpions, centipedes, and other things of the kind. An agreeable exterior would be given by coating the walls with cement, colored with some pleasant-hued paint or wash so common in Mexico and other Spanish countries. A beautiful feature could be introduced in the shape of a large central hall, running up to the second roof, with a handsome staircase to a gallery communicating with the open space on either side. Instead of the hand-made adobe, a much cheaper and better material might be obtained by making the blocks in an ordinary brick-machine, like common bricks, thus saving the very considerable expense of burning them, while the pressure used in making them would give them a compactness, assuring a lasting quality far greater than that of the common adobe. I have seen an unburnt, machine-made brick that has been kept for years without crumbling, as hard as when first turned out. I wonder something of the sort has not been adopted in countries such as this, where the dry, frostless climate renders burning the brick for ordinary purposes really superfluous. Like many other most useful and simple things, the idea has probably never occurred to makers.

Several rocky hills rise abruptly around the town, the main portion of which lies at the base of one of them. Here, as elsewhere throughout the West, the

French term "*butte*" is applied to such isolated hills, although here one might expect to find the Spanish "*cerro*" fully domesticated. It is in all probability a lingual acquisition from the French trappers and *voyageurs,* handed along from the time when the French were in possession on the Mississippi Valley, and incorporated into the vernacular of the plains by the Missourians, who are the pioneers in all the trans-Missouri migratory movements. The Missourians have the reputation of being a nomadic, semi-vagrant people, and might be called the gypsies of the Western World. Possibly this trait may be due to an absorption of considerable of the French half-breed blood by much of the Missouri population, inoculating it with the same roving impulse that characterizes the French-Canadians. The word *butte* appears to be one of the few things in the vernacular of the plains—which has become that of the entire far West—taken from the French, Spanish being the most fruitful foreign source, due chiefly to the influence of the Texan vaquero, of which "cow-boy" is a literal translation. The reception of the word through immediate racial contact is proved by its pronunciation throughout the West, *bute*—as near the French *u* as Anglo-Saxon could be expected to approach. Had it been a literary acquisition, the pronunciation of *but* would have been given the word, for we invariably strive to phoneticize—a tendency which, with our unspeakable orthography and ill-formulated phonetic rules, has thoroughly distorted our English tongue. Thus the plainsman talks of the States of *Coloraydo* and *Nevayda;* but, hearing the name of the celebrated Ute chief spoken as it is in the Spanish dialect of the Mexican peasantry, he calls him Colorow, which is really nearer to the proper pronunciation of the State.

The rapidity and luxuriance of vegetable growth in a region like this encourages the use of ornamental plants, shrubs and trees; the streets are well shaded, and dwellings are usually surrounded by pleasant gardens. The formally located roads are all straight and rectangular in their intersections, running due north and south, east and west, as throughout the West, following the "section-lines," the surveys of the National Land Department cutting the country up into sections of a mile square. So the roads are a mile apart, and, in going to any places not lying in the direction of the cardinal points, one has to travel along two sides of a triangle, necessitating much superfluous travel and consequent expenditure of time. This does not speak well for the American "practicality" of which we are accustomed to boast, especially when we are so used to regard time and money as equivalents. This difficulty might have been avoided, and the distance saved, by providing for a second system of roads traversing the sections from corner to corner, making the quarter-sections triangular in shape. All portions of the country would thus be within convenient reach of each other.

Where the land has not been taken up and brought under cultivation, of course, the roads are free to run across country at random, and in an open country like this it is easily done, for the making of a road involves no more than to drive along the same path until tracks are made; but as soon as the land is occupied the roads must confine themselves to section-lines, so that in a journey between two places that lie, say, twenty miles apart from northeast to southeast one would have to travel nearly thirty miles. This, to be sure, is not so serious as it would be were it not for the railways, the great modern highways, which, when a country becomes so well settled as to necessitate the rectangular system of roads, are certain to cover it with their network, and, as they are subject only to the limitations of the most convenient grades, they take the straightest possible course between two points. It would probably be hardly practicable at this late day to adopt such a system of roads in our country, but, as there is a tendency to lay out new towns in a way to provide amply for future growth, it ought to be possible to plan them so as to give streets between the corners of the squares as well. It seems strange that our rushing Western communities, where people are so intent upon making the most of their time, should not from the start have avoided one of the greatest wastes of time and exertion to which the planning of their towns subjects them.

Our road takes us first to the eastward. Facing us are the Superstition Mountains, their name another mistranslation, from the Spanish: Sierra de la Encantacion is the original designation, suggestive of sacrificial caves and weird rites held there by the Indians, as they undoubtedly were. It is, however, a matter for congratulation that the English name is not of the average commonplaceness, but also, like the Spanish, has a mystic significance. The Superstitions have a broad, cliff-like frontage, rising abruptly from the plain, with high banks of steeply sloping detritus at their feet. Their tops are mesa-like, though broken, and on their faces are plainly traced the strata-lines that indicate their geological history. Their forms are suggestive of some grand primitive architecture: castle-like towers and pinnacles stand out from the ruddy mass in the bright sunlight of the afternoon; in the clear atmosphere the mountains seem close at hand, but they are a day's journey distant by wagon! A prominent landmark to the northward of the Superstitions, rising just over the Salada cañon, is the great mountain mass of the Cuatro Picos, the Four Peaks—four clustered summits, beautiful in the Alpine purity of their winter snow-mantle that seems flung over them like some graceful drapery. A similar garb is worn by the Sunflower Peaks, still farther northward, and by others of the mountain wall that extends in compact ranges across the northern horizon, ending in the lofty Bradshaws off beyond Phoenix in the northwest. Beyond and above the Superstitions, to the eastward, rise the Pinal Mountains, and, then, to the southeastward, the detached masses of the high Santa Catalinas, near Tucson, with the Tortolitas and the Picachos intervening, and the Zacaton near at hand; southwesterly, just across the Gila, is the abrupt wall of the Estrellas frowning in the shadow, and close at hand are the humbler Maricopas. These mountains are nearly all full of mineral treasures awaiting some lucky prospector to reveal them; several rich mines are being worked, and in the Pinal mountains is the famous Silver King mine, one of the great silver-producers of the world.

Now and then we pass, by the road, traces of ancient ruins, in the shape of low mounds of earth that the ordinary observer takes for natural irregularities of the surface. Tempe is partly built on the site of one of the ancient cities, and the Mexican quarter, locally known as "Sonora," in token of the neighboring Mexican State whence nearly all the inhabitants immigrated, covers long rows of these mounds.[28] Beyond, we pass a house of one of the well-to-do American residents, built on the summit of a large mound formed by the crumbled walls of a ruined temple, which have been nicely graded and terraced, and planted with shrubs and fruit-trees. At first thought it seems a pity that the sites should be so occupied, but there are in the open more than can at present be explored, and, in reality, the ruins thus covered are reserved for the future explorer whom science may send, effectively guarded against the burrowings of relic-hunters—those pests of the archaeologist, who simply destroy, confuse and disturb for the sake of what are to them but mere "curiosities."

The irrigating canals, or *acequias,* are marked features of the landscape. They give the soil its fertility and are again converting these valleys into luxuriant gardens. The night-frosts of January are just strong enough to check the growth of most things, but the fields of barley and wheat are mantled with the tender verdure of the infant blades, and the darker alfalfa covers expansive pastures with its velvety garb. The land spreads away in floor-like evenness to the feet of the mountains on all sides, towards which it rises in a gradual incline, the direction of which would be almost imperceptible did not the purling water in the ditches tell the tale. Where the canals or ditches have been established a few years, long lines of trees mark their course and give beauty to the landscape. These trees are mostly cottonwoods, which, under the stimulus of plenty of water, attain a height of fifty feet or so in a comparatively short time. They are usually planted along the water-ways, their shade and their shelter from the dry winds preventing evaporation. Where not planted, they spring up themselves in the course of a few years from seeds scattered by the wind, or borne by the water to the banks. The settlers are beginning to plant other varieties than the cottonwood, which will make better timber, among them the catalpa, which grows as rapidly and makes a handsome tree, particularly beautiful in flowering time.

The main canals cut across country regardless of section-lines, following the course that enables them to irrigate the most land, but the supply-ditches, for the most part, keep along the margins of the fields, and the line of trees that mark their course relieve the monotony of the level expanses, making hollow squares of the farms.

Our mules, though stolid enough in aspect, show that experience has not been an unheeded teacher. Tough are their hides, but their feet are small and delicate, and they have a horror of mud as of the evil-one. At a harmless-looking wet place on the road, they shy in alarm. Well they may, for this peculiar soil, stable as it is under ordinary conditions, is converted into something like quicksand when water flows upon it for the first time. In such a place a mule-team will suddenly sink almost to the ears, and the animals will be likely to smother unless speedily rescued, floundering about without a foothold, and with every movement sinking deeper and deeper. After such a mud bath, a mule is a sight to behold, with skin and harness thoroughly plastered. A new ditch, into which the water has flowed for the first time, seems to present but a slight obstacle to travel, but it is something to be dreaded by the traveller, and hardly any amount of persuasion can induce a mule to venture across it. A well-travelled road, however, gets compacted so that water has no effect on it, or after water has flowed over a piece of ground for two or three successive times, something in the soil seems to be so affected as to give it stability. A mule has keen discernment and seems able to tell such a place from freshly-flowed land, for it will fearlessly enter upon a part of the regular road where water stands, perhaps from the overflow of a broken ditch, or will, unhesitatingly, cross an acequia or a stream at a regular ford. The liabilities of these mishaps, in a country where new land is being extensively brought under cultivation, gives an element of adventure to drives around the valley.

A half-mile to the eastward, two miles southward, another mile eastward, and then we turn southward again, following an irregular road across country after passing the great Tempe Canal. As we proceed, the country has become more open, for the trees have not yet had time to grow up on the newly-cleared land. The irregular road is, for the most part, through the original wilderness growth of the desert—which is not destined to remain so for many weeks more. A drive of nearly ten miles from town brings us through a low mesquite wood, and we emerge with the white tents of Camp Hemenway before us half a mile to the westward. The place has a pleasant look in the midst of a cleared plain, the military-appearing cluster gleaming in the light of the setting sun against the dark background of the Maricopa and Estrella Mountains.

Our drive ends in the space enclosed by the various tents like a parade-ground; the ladies, Mrs. Cushing and her sister, Miss Magill, advance to welcome their guest and receive the daily mail, and a handsome Mexican youth steps forward to take care of the team. Mr. Cushing is still out at the excavations, but in a few minutes he comes galloping into camp on his beautiful horse, "Douglass," and his eyes shine with happiness at meeting his old friend.

It is dark when the violent clattering of a cow-bell summons us to the kitchen tent to supper. All our little community, with the exception of the laborers, who wait for the "second call," are gathered around the board, and the presence of the ladies imparts an ameliorating influence rare in camp-life. There are two anthropological members of the staff, Dr. Herman F. C. ten Kate and Dr. Jacob L. Wortman. Dr. ten Kate I have known and esteemed for nearly two years,[29] and in Dr. Wortman I am delighted to find a man whose quiet, unassuming ways do not obscure the recognition of the remarkable scientific attainments of which I have heard from mutual friends in Washington. Dr. Wortman is the comparative anatomist for the Army Medical Museum, at Washington, and has been temporarily detailed to look after the preservation of the valuable ancient skeletons excavated here. Doctor Washington Matthews, also surgeon in the Army, and at present Curator of the Museum, himself a distinguished ethnologist, was ordered to this place by the Secretary of War, last summer, owing to the critical condition of Mr. Cushing's health. Dr. Matthews, who is an old friend of Mr. Cushing's, having been surgeon at Fort Wingate when Mr. Cushing was making his important investigations at Zuñi near by, was so impressed with the scientific value of the ancient skeletons unearthed here, that his representations induced Dr. J. S. Billings, the Director of the Museum, to enter into an arrangement whereby the Museum should secure duplicate series of the skeletons in consideration of attending to their preservation and classification. The result was the detail of Dr. Wortman for this purpose, a young man already known as the foremost comparative anatomist in the country, and one of the ablest of osteologists and paleontologists.

II

With sundown the air has suddenly become sharp and keen, much like that of late October at home, differentiating the midwinter night of this region considerably from the midwinter day. The stars glitter brilliantly in the clear, cloudless sky, and an impressive silence broods over the country, hardly disturbed by the slight sounds of the camp—the Mexicans quietly chattering in their tent, the cook setting things to rights in the kitchen for the night, and the "chomp, chomp" of the animals at their fodder in the neighboring corral. The lights in the tents shine through the canvass and give them a cheery aspect: from the inside there is heard the steady hum peculiar to blazing wood in confinement, for a genial warmth is maintained in little stoves simply made of sheet-iron fashioned into a cone shape and kept full of mesquite wood, which is almost as hard and heavy as iron and gives out a heat like coal. These stoves, with the pipe running straight up from the top of the cone, are simply inverted funnels, with a little draught-hole at the bottom. The cold of the nights would occasion no discomfort to house-dwellers in this climate, but it easily penetrates the tents, and brisk fires are needed for comfort, even late into the spring.

Mr. Cushing's tent, occupying the centre of the camp, has a cosy, home-like appearance, with the touches of decoration and aspect of order that betray the feminine presence. It is a large wall-tent, divided by a curtain into two rooms. A canvass covers the ground and makes a neat floor, cases of shelves contain a considerable reference-library for use in working-up the results of the excavations from day to day, and there is a convenient portable desk; shelves, desks, etc., all made so as to be packed into small compass and easily transported when camp is moved. Bright colored Zuñi blankets cover the two cot-beds, and there are tastefully displayed on the walls and shelves some handsome examples of the decorated basketry of the Pima Indians, mostly with bold, rich designs woven in black and white, and sometimes additional decoration painted in red and green. There are also a few specimens of the ancient pottery excavated near by. A sewing-machine lends an air of domesticity to the place, and several candles illuminate it.

Mrs. Cushing, who is the custodian of the smaller treasures of the collection and guards them with jealous care, brings them out and delights my eyes with some exquisite arrowheads, carefully chipped and graceful in form, made of quartz and agate, or other colored stone, evidently chosen with regard to its beauty; ornaments of turquoise and beads of shell; bracelets and finger-rings carved from sea-shells, and last and most beautiful, a wonderful frog found wrapped in asbestos in a sacred jar excavated from the ruins of the great temple of Los Muertos.[30] It is an exquisite piece of work, showing not only a genuine aesthetic sense possessed by the ancient people, but an artistic conception and decorative quality that would do honor to our own race and civilization if produced to-day. In making it a shell similar to that of a quahaug, or "little-neck clam," was taken and on its convex side the effigy of a frog was produced in lines of mosaic-like fragments of turquoise embedded in a black cement made from the gum of the greasewood, or hediondilla. The line down the centre of the back was made in red bits of shell, resembling coral in color.[31] The whole was worn down smooth by rubbing. The effect is extremely realistic—an exception to the conventionalism that characterizes most of the art of this, in common with other North American primitive cultures. Prof. Edward S. Morse, who visited Camp Hemenway in April, took this frog East with him for safe-keeping, and stopping over in New York he showed it to the people at Tiffany's, who expressed great delight and marvelled that such a thing could have been produced by an ancient people in this country.

The rest of Camp Hemenway consisted of a tent occupied by Mr. Hodge with his desk and records, a tent adjacent occupied by Mr. C. A. Garlick, the surveyor and practical superintendent, a small tent in which Miss Magill was domiciled, commonly known as the "dog-tent" from its diminutive size and fancied resemblance to a kennel, a tent occupied by Dr. ten Kate, a Sibley tent for guests,[32] a large tent for housing the collections, with a shelter of canvass, called by its Spanish name of *ramada,* originally meaning "brush-shelter," adjacent as an annex; a tent for the Mexican laborers, a tent for the photograph material and other stores, a shelter for the baggage, a little "dark-tent" for photographing operations, and a shelter for the harnesses. The mules, with the two horses, are tethered around a large crib under one of the few mesquite trees that have been left standing about the camp; they need no shelter in this climate and beyond an occasional kick or bite at an encroaching neighbor they live together in amity.

The next morning I make the acquaintance of Ramon Castro, the noble-faced young Mexican who acts as foreman of the laborers; faithful, industrious, and an innate gentleman. Later in the day Don Carlos, as Mr. Garlick is called, drives in from Phoenix, fourteen miles away, where he has been over night on his semi-weekly errand of purchasing supplies for the camp.

It is a typical morning of this region, clear, sparkling air, and the sun soon warms up the world—or all that portion that lies about us—into summerish cheeriness, melting the ice that has skimmed over the buckets in the camp and fringed the ditches with frosty lace. But off in the upland regions of Arizona, three or four thousand feet above our level, they are having some real winter, as the snow tells us that is glittering on the mountains.

A great mound lies about a quarter of a mile distant, rising in a low, broad mass of brown earth above the plain, and something like twenty-five feet above the general level. It is the ruin of the great central temple of the place, and Mr. Cushing takes me out to see it. It has been excavated sufficiently to show its construction. It was originally probably six or seven stories high, and divided into various rooms on each floor. Only the remains of two stories are now to be traced. The outer wall is very thick, something like three or four feet. The material is indurated earth, and in the course of excavation Mr. Cushing made a highly important discovery concerning the constructive methods of these people. Along the top of these outer walls is seen a double row of holes running down perpendicularly, and each row within the outer and inner face of the wall, respectively. These holes were found filled with the powder of decayed wood, and some large fragments of the wood itself were discovered. Further investigation showed that these walls were constructed by first driving a double row of stakes into the ground, and then wattling-in between the stakes so as to form two parallel lines of wattled work. Building this wattling up to a height of a foot or two, the space was filled with moistened earth, packed down firmly, perhaps by treading with the feet, or tamping with heavy stones. The wattling was then built up higher, and the process continued until the wall was carried to its full height. Thus a solid structure was formed with walls enclosed within a wattled surface. This surface formed a sort of lathing, and it was covered with a thick plastering of mud with a smoothly finished surface such as is still to be found on the walls at Casa Grande after a lapse of centuries.[33] It was unknown that this was the method of building these massive walls until Mr. Cushing made this discovery. As soon as he saw these double rows of holes he declared what their origin must be, and said that wattling must have been used in the way it proved to have been, as revealed by subsequent investigation, where the impress of the wattling was found plainly made inside the walls. Here, then, was a most significant fact. The origin of pottery in forms of basketry has long been made familiar. This discovery showed that not only did the primitive utensils of burnt clay, but also the primitive structures with walls of clay, find their origin in basketry types. For, just as the coating of baskets with clay suggested the making of pottery, so this form of structure bears the records of the story how the primitive wattled hut, first rendered more substantial and weather-proof by a coating of mud, suggested a more massive form of construction with a basketry basis. Possibly all mud or earthen walled construction may thus have been developed from basketry.

In this connection, a subsequent discovery deserves mention. Readers of the *American Architect* may remember an article that appeared in these columns a few years ago, briefly recounting how Mr. Cushing discovered that in the ancient Pueblos the doors to the houses were made of stone slabs, through an analysis of the etymology of the modern Zuñi word for door, which signifies "a wooden stone close," showing that before boards were made available for the construction of their doors, they must have closed their doorways with slabs of stone. Thus throughout their language the successive stages through which their methods of house-construction, their implements, etc., passed in their development from lower or ancient to higher or recent types are preserved in the structure of their words. In investigating the ruins of Casa Grande, one of these "stone closes" made of mud was found in the shape of a great and heavy block of adobe, nicely finished with square corners, and accurately fitting into the place where it filled a doorway from one of the rooms to another. Subsequently, in excavating the ruins of a smaller temple in Las Acequias, one of the ancient cities near Los Muertos, a similar door of adobe was discovered lying upon the ground close to the doorway to which it belonged, its position such that it might readily be raised to fill the opening. These huge blocks were probably made in moulds of basketry, and their surfaces afterwards smoothly finished by hand. Even if moulds of wood were possible, they would have been so difficult to make with their crude instruments that the idea would hardly have occurred when basketwork was so universal, and so easily made available for plastic purposes. The greater portion of the soil in these regions contains elements of clay and of natural cement, so that when indurated it hardens to an almost rock-like consistency.

From the top of the temple-mound there is a good view over the country. We are just about on the low divide between the Salado and Gila Valleys, and from this point the water in the irrigating canals, brought up gradually to this level from the Salado above, runs down toward the Gila, instead of back towards the Salado. When the operations of the expedition began at this point something like seven months ago, it was supposed by the settlers that the supply of the irrigating-canals would hardly reach much farther southward, but the researches showed that the irrigation works of the ancient inhabitants penetrated far beyond, and, in consequence, the available land in this region has all been taken up, and there has been a great development all around, with thousands of acres brought under tillage.

Therefore, the landscape has undergone a rapid transformation. When the camp was established here, the section upon which the main portion of Los Muertos stands was covered with a thick growth of very old mesquite trees. Only the great mound betrayed the existence of an ancient city on the spot. The other ruins were hardly discernible. The whole place has now been cleared and "brought under water," as they say here; that is, brought under irrigation. Only a few trees are left standing just about the camp, and the owner of the section, who took it up under the Desert-land Act, has sown the greater part of it with barley. Thus the land is resuming the fertility which characterized it ages ago. The settlers have made a mistake in making such a clean sweep of the mesquite. With a few dozen trees left on each section, standing singly or in groups here and there, the appearance of the landscape would have been much improved, and shade afforded for cattle in their alfalfa pastures during the summer heat. With its thirst amply gratified, as it is on irrigated land, the mesquite becomes quite a different tree from the scraggly, dwarfed growth of the desert-plains, with mis-shapen, unsound, contorted limbs. Given plenty of water, it becomes inspired with new vigor, and it lifts its head proudly high into the air, animated with health that becomes manifest in symmetrical shape.

Objects of considerable size soon lose themselves in the vastness of such a landscape as that spread before us; the white tents of the camp become mere specks on the plain, and the little shanties of the settlers on neighboring lands become so diminutive as to afford a scale for estimating a distance that otherwise would prove very deceptive in this clear air.

The land chosen by Mr. Cushing for his excavations has been kindly left undisturbed by the owner, beyond clearing it of its trees. Low mounds slightly rising from the level indicate the ruins, and large areas laid bare testify to the industry of the laborers whom we see, here and there, casting out the earth with their shovels. We stand a long time watching them at their work. The Mexican laborers have gained something of the enthusiasm of Mr. Cushing, and are eager for results. When something is found they gain new encouragement, and their shovels and picks are plied with greater celerity. They are gentler, more impressionable and receptive than men of a corresponding grade in our own race, and seem to have a greater natural intelligence. Their training has made them careful, and, when evidences of the presence of pottery, of skeletons, or other objects are encountered, they proceed cautiously, and do their best to remove intact what is found. Ramon, in particular, has been an admirable disciple under Mr. Cushing's schooling, and he has become a practical archaeologist, with an almost intuitive capacity for discerning the presence of ruins and relics. He can trace the course of walls unerringly by indications imperceptible to any one else except Mr. Cushing, and marks out with his shovel the lines for the men to follow in their excavations. He will likewise tell just where the skeletons are to be found in the house-ruins, and one day, at Las Acequias, I see him fill Doctors ten Kate and Wortman with astonishment and admiration; they are anxious to find some good skeletons, and are beginning to be discouraged at the prospect of encountering them in a certain excavation, where two badly-decayed ones have been found near the surface. "Let us dig deeper," said Ramon, "and we shall find three fine *difuntos:* one here, one here, and one here," indicating the places and the positions of their heads, and sure enough, they were soon found. "*Es usted un hombre de mucho talento!*" I remarked, in response to Dr. Wortman's enthusiastic request to "Just tell him he is a mighty smart man!" and a modest smile of gratification illuminated Ramon's expressive features.

The excavations of the house-ruins were usually carried to a depth of three or four feet below the present surface of the country, laying bare the remains of the walls, and showing their interiors. The only evidences of these houses, which had long been concealed in the mesquite forest that had grown up over them, perceptible at first sight, was a slight and gradual elevation above the surface formed from the gradually crumbling material. In the excavation work it was difficult to distinguish the walls from the material that buried them, being of the same color and quality of earth, and varying only in hardness. Therefore, the sense of touch was the determining factor in bringing them to light. One of the workmen, in his ambition to please by laying bare a goodly line of wall, would habitually be led astray by his imagination and frequently show a considerable stretch of "*pader*" as they called the Castilian *pared* or wall, in their Sonora vernacular; but the test of a not over-vigorous kick from the foot of Mr. Cushing or Ramon, whose practiced eye could detect that no wall belonged there, would bring the sham structure down into an ignominiously crumbling mass. The real walls would not yield to such an assault, but, after months of exposure to sun, wind and rain still showed the plans of the great blocks of buildings to which they belonged, often covering an area of an acre or more, and honeycombed into small rooms and narrow passages.

The domestic utensils would be found undisturbed in just the places where they belonged in a well-regulated Pueblo household, unbroken save by the falling walls or the weight of earth upon them. This fact indicated a deliberate abandonment of the place, under such a *taboo* as would be laid upon it by the priesthood in the case of a region made unstable and uninhabitable, according to their notions, by an earthquake or succession of earthquakes, such as Mr. Cushing found evidence of. Here, and nearly universally among all the ruins explored in this and the Gila Valley, the charred remains of the roofs were found. This might have happened by the roofs of earthquake-demolished houses falling in upon the hearth-fires, and communicated to the adjacent houses. The uniformity with which the roofs are everywhere burned, however, seems to militate against their destruction in this manner. It might have happened, however, that the whole region was overwhelmed by a savage horde like the wild and nomadic Apaches, who exterminated the inhabitants and burned their towns, or caused them to flee to other parts of the continent, possibly thus putting in motion the migratory movement southward that established the Mexican cultures. An investigation of ancient ruins at various stages southward in Mexico, beginning in Chihuahua and Sonora, as careful as that which has been pursued here, is of importance in settling these questions, for the conditions in which they were left, in comparison with those here, would tell much. It would seem that an invading horde would be likely to sack the houses and smash their contents. On the other hand, if the towns were left deserted they might remain unmolested even after the lapse of years, for the superstition of other tribes settling in the region would very likely prevent their venturing within the precincts of a place, much more across the thresholds of its dwellings, that had been abandoned because of divine disfavor, and over which still presided the powerful demons who would work harm to all who might be so rash as to defy them. But, whence, then, the universal conflagration that seems to have visited every one of these ancient towns? Possibly the departing inhabitants might have applied the torch themselves, making a final sacrifice of their abandoned homes in hopes of thereby regaining the favor of the gods for their new dwelling-places.

Beneath the floor of nearly every house are found buried at different depths and often in three successive layers the skeletons of members of the family that occupied it. The topmost skeleton was invariably that of a young person; on account of their immaturity, and also from the fact of being near the surface, these skeletons of the upper tier were in the worst state of preservation. It seems likely that, when the young persons of a household began to die the house was abandoned because of the misfortune that had come upon it, thus accounting for the fact that the last burials made in a house were those of young people. Another interesting fact was that it was the custom to bury an infant beneath the kitchen hearth. This practice of house-sepulture could not have been promotive of sanitary conditions, though, in this dry climate, the results would not be so disastrous as they might have been elsewhere. Mr. Cushing, while in Zuñi, was puzzled to account for the fact that graves were called the "houses of the dead," but the discovery of this custom of house-sepulture threw light on the subject. Ancient Pueblo skeletons have hitherto been very rare, for explorers, not suspecting the custom of house-sepulture, could not find where they were buried.

But a small proportion of the remains was disposed of by sepulture, for that was a privilege only accorded to members of the priestly caste or of the esoteric societies, whose control over the soul was believed to be such that they had no need of external aid to separate the soul from the body at death. The ordinary people were cremated, and the pottery vessels containing their remains were found buried near the bases of pyral mounds, or great heaps wherein were found the fragments of the personal belongings of the dead, burned with them to accompany them into the other world. These vessels in which the dead were buried were usually plain, while the food-bowls and water-jars buried with the skeletons exhumed in the houses were, for the most part, handsomely decorated.[34]

In Mr. Cushing's paper on the evolution of Pueblo pottery, contributed to the Fourth Annual Report of the Bureau of Ethnology,[35] the growth of form from primitive types was traced as clearly as is the course of development in a chain of species in natural history. Some of the types necessary to complete the chain were not to be found at that time, but he pointed out what they should be. All the missing types were found here in the course of these excavations, thus substantiating the correctness of his reasoning.

Owing to the nature of the soil, which is exceptionally rich and retentive of moisture, encouraging the penetration of the roots of vegetation to a considerable depth, and probably also to a great extent due to the antiquity of the remains, the pottery found here at Los Muertos is very tender, and falls easily into fragments, requiring particularly careful handling. Close examination of pieces freshly excavated will show how delicate little rootlets have wrapped their fine net-work all around them, and with their subtle acid extracted from the pottery some element that gave it cohesion. For the same reason the skeletons excavated here at Los Muertos crumble after exposure, so that it is almost impossible to preserve them, despite the utmost skill of Dr. Wortman. The potsherds found on the surface are as hard as when freshly buried. Both the pottery and the skeletons found at Las Acequias were much better preserved, owing to the more gravelly nature of the soil there.

III

An archaeological camp proves to be a very busy place, although it seems a very region of *dolce far niente,* under the serene sky, on the wide and silent sunlit plains basking in the sunlight. The landscape is a picture of peace. All nature is enjoying a delicious repose. No hum of insects is heard in the bright and quiet air. The ground is brown and bare; even the withered herbs have nearly all crumbled into dust and been scattered by the wind, leaving the brown plain bare and baked. The warm sun of the days cannot yet call forth the plants from the sleep induced by the cold of the night-time; only the brave blades of the grain have the strength to thrust themselves, little by little, day after day, farther and farther into the air, until March sees them undulating like sea-waves over the broad fields, their bloom showing foam-like and creamy green, while mid-April finds them golden and ready for the harvest. The brooding calm seems emphasized by the few glimpses of animation, the few sounds, that at intervals strike the eye or greet the ear; the scurrying rabbits, the timid little cotton-tails and the great jack-rabbit with his enormous ears and astonishingly long leaps; those pretty creatures, the "*juancitos,*" which word means "Johnnies," rat-like and squirrel-like, with long tails terminating in a tuft of hair like those of shaven poodles, and wee ground-squirrels dodging into their holes with which the ground is everywhere burrowed into a honeycomb that keeps horsemen warily on the lookout when dashing across country; that humorous fellow, the coyote, skulking among the brush or sauntering indifferently along a few dozen feet away when he seems to know you are not armed, making night anything but musical with his yelpings; and the birds that hover around, some with exquisite musical notes, and the numerous flocks of quail with their queer crests perked forward and looking like some prize carried in their bills, evidently aware that their meat is as dry and tasteless as sawdust, for they run across the roads as indifferently as barnyard fowl and rarely take wing.

But while Nature and her children are taking their ease, Camp Hemenway is well occupied. The laborers have early gone afield to carry out the instructions that Mr. Cushing has dictated to his secretary the night before; the two doctors are out with them looking after the skeletons of the Ancients; Mr. Hodge is at his desk in his neatly-kept tent writing out his notes or busy with the accounts; Don Carlos is looking after practical affairs, turning out some needed carpentry at the bench under one of the mesquite trees, or is on the way to Phoenix for supplies, or is at work on his surveys, while Mr. Cushing is out keeping the run of the work on the excavations, photographing the finds *in situ,* elated over some interesting discovery and drawing inferences therefrom in the light of his manifold ethnological experiences, ranging the plains in the saddle or on the buckboard with eyes alert for the slightest traces of ancient landmarks, or in his tent finding comparisons among his books or among his old notes that throw new light on fresh observations, or writing or dictating the daily reports that preserve accurate records of the work as it progresses. All this in the intervals left him for work by the delicate condition of his health, and often accomplished only by dominating over keen pain by the mastery of a strong will.

The ladies also are by no means idle, even a camp providing abundant domestic cares for Mrs. Cushing, while Miss Magill spends the day at her easel over the beautiful water-color drawings which she is making of all the important articles in the collections, with conscientious accuracy, and to scale. Of the pottery, for instance, she makes two or more drawings of each specimen, one from the side and the other from above or below, or perhaps both, while in the case of the decorated ware she makes a drawing of each different motive in the ornamentation, affording many beautiful designs and hints for decoration which could well be availed of by architects and painters. This idea of giving in a painted band the motives of pottery design, adopted in the reports of the Bureau of Ethnology, originated, I believe, with Mr. Cushing and it is extremely useful in affording an understanding of the decoration, which, when seen on the vessel appears often so complicated as to be difficult to elucidate, while, by presenting the motive alone it is made clear.

Another busy man is the cook, who has a difficult task in suiting the appetites of so many, some of whom have been made dyspeptic by the exigencies of desert fare. Cooks in camp appear to maintain the reputation of the craft for inconstancy and for perversity of temper, and the incumbency of the office often changes. Various nationalities have been tried: Chinamen, Mexicans, Americans, Irishmen, Germans, Frenchmen. The Chinamen bring the economy that they are accustomed to exercise in their own affairs into that of their masters; it seems a second nature to them, and they cannot help it. This is an admirable trait when not carried too far, as it is when they economize so as to half starve those dependent upon them. In his first months here Mr. Cushing had with him two of his Zuñi friends. The cook at that time was a Chinaman, and he held that men who were idle did not require so much food as those who worked, and he applied the idea very rightly to these two Zuñis. One of them rarely condescended to labor, while the other often went to the excavations and did good service with pick or shovel, receiving pay accordingly. To the worker Mr. Chinaman allowed two cups of coffee—a beverage of which the Indians are very fond—but the other was sternly denied a second cup, and when one evening he contrived to help himself to a second while the cook's attention was momentarily diverted, it was instantly snatched from his hand. The cook was likewise chary of pie to the non-worker.

When I first came to the camp a Mexican was temporarily in charge of culinary affairs, during a hiatus occasioned by the resignation of a much-esteemed American *chef* in consequence of a spree, and the fare was something unspeakable in the way in which good material was converted into various materials of indigestibility. A gaunt and pale young man next appeared on the scene, speaking one of the vernaculars prevailing south of Mason & Dixon's line, fond of talking of "the fine old family" to which he belonged, and expressing a sense of the degradation of the estate to which he had fallen. If he had had more respect for his calling and talked less about his antecedents perhaps his claim to gentlemanly rank would not have had to be so volubly expressed in order to obtain recognition—for I have had the fortune to encounter genuine gentlemen in nearly every walk of life. Poore's specialty was cakes and puddings, imposing in aspect and formidable in quantity—of their quality perhaps it is sufficient to say that our failure to eat any of them did not seem to discourage him in the least, and the same prodigious piles—that is, the same in appearance, though unfortunately for the resources in eggs and sugar, fresh-made each day—were triumphantly borne before us to cap the climax of each meal though left undiminished at its end. Perhaps the Mexicans disposed of them at their table, which accounts for the aversion they manifested towards the cook before he finally vanished in the cloud of the customary "tear" that usually serves to mark changes of culinary administration in this part of the world. Edward the Alsatian next appeared on the scene, and he proved a treasure; he took a pride in his work and knew how to give nice little attractive touches to his dishes and impart an appetizing flavor to his preparations. He was cheery and diligent, and far into the evening he would sing the German folk-songs of his fatherland over his work; pleasant to hear, for their melody's sake, even though he did invariably maintain the pitch a semi-tone below the key! Shortly after he came to us we had a little *fiesta* in honor of the birthday of Don Carlos, and Edward elaborated a magnificent cake for the occasion; with icing ornamented in the height of the confectioner's art. But alas, when cut it was like lead within! When Edward came in shortly after he saw a piece lying on a plate, and the transitions from astonishment, through disgust, to humiliation and grief that passed over his face would have furnished profitable study for a comedian. "Cheezus G-h-r-i-s-t!" he muttered slowly, inspecting it critically and then tasting it. We sympathetically assured him that the cake was good, the icing was fine enough to assure that, any way; but he refused to be consoled; he knew what cake was and when he said it was bad, it was no use to tell him it was good—he had forgotten the yeast-powder. "I mague you a gake domorrow!" he declared, and the next noon he set his success before us in justified triumph. But the spoiling of that cake gave us enough entertainment to atone for the mishap. Edward's weak point was his coffee, which was strange, considering the part of the world from which he came: as a guest expressed it, he was "coffee-blind." It happened that neither Mr. Cushing nor the ladies were coffee-drinkers, and so the rest of us suffered in silence rather than reveal the flaw in the one who gave such thorough satisfaction to them, until we received the delightful visit from the afore-mentioned guest, to whom a good cup of coffee was the main dependence at breakfast, and he frankly declared that it was the most abominable stuff it was ever his fortune to taste; a declaration which was concurred in by the rest of the table with astonishingly hearty unanimity. Whereupon Mr. Cushing, who included a good knowledge of cooking among his many accomplishments, proceeded to give Edward a course of instruction in coffee-making, with some degree of success, for the time being.

Rafael Castro, the handsome, stalwart youth who takes care of the animals and attends to the many wants of the camp, is a favorite with us all, like his brother Ramon. He is faithful, diligent, and a natural gentleman. Watering and feeding the animals, hauling water and wood, driving into town after the mail, and doing the daily chores of the camp, time does not hang heavily on his hands. In the morning the animals are set loose, and they repair in a herd to the neighboring acequia for water, Rafael riding bare-back on Jack, one of the largest of the mules. The other mules lie down to indulge in a roll the first thing, kicking the dust up in clouds. Jack, a solemn-faced creature, deliberately follows their example, Rafael stepping from his back as he nears the ground, and patiently holding the halter until the exercise is finished. "Get up, Jack!" he finally exclaims out of his limited English vocabulary. But Jack has not yet got enough, and proceeds to take another roll, while Rafael smiles indulgently. Rafael's English is limited to his remarks to the animals, and I observe that the Mexicans hereabouts seem to think it the proper thing to use our mother-tongue in addressing horses and mules. Possibly they learn it from the American teamsters, or perhaps it is because the horses and mules are American-bred, and understand the phrases better! Does not the proverb say that Spanish is the language of heaven, Italian of love, French of social intercourse, while English was designed to be spoken to animals!

Mules are devoted admirers of horses, and Mr. Cushing's herd is ardently attached to Douglas; oftentimes the latter will set them a bad example when returning from water, and, feeling the need of exercise, go galloping in splendid style off to our neighbor's barley-field, whose greenness appeals appetizingly to his eyes. The others feel themselves privileged to follow, and there is a grand scampering and flourishing of heels, until, after great efforts on the part of Rafael, they are finally driven back to camp, each marching to his or her respective place at the crib with the sober decorum of beings who never knew what a frolic was. The mules are a fine-looking lot, and it is interesting to note their individual peculiarities, manifest when together in camp, or when driven or ridden, in sympathies or antipathies toward each other—the mutual friendship of one pair, the stolid indifference of another; the strong affection existing between Dr. ten Kate's horse Billy, *alias* Café, and the skittish and sturdy little mule Zuñi, who are near neighbors at the crib, and stand and caress each other by the hour; the nervousness and feminine eccentricities of handsome Mary; Bob's occasional outbursts of irritability; the incurable laziness of great Pete and Barney; the alert responsiveness of Chub and Thistle; the sullenness of Joe, and the omnivorous appetite of Jack, who has a fondness for bacon and for mutton stewed with Chili-peppers.

The skeletons exhumed at Los Muertos are so badly decayed that it proves next to impossible to preserve them, and so Mr. Cushing decides to establish a side-camp at Las Acequias, where the more gravelly soil affords better conditions for sound bones. True, no skeletons had yet been found there, for there had been no excavations on that site, and the two doctors, who are to have charge of the operations, express some doubt as to the result. "You shall find skeletons in abundance, and splendid ones at that," said Mr. Cushing, and the result proves the justification of his prediction.

The new camp is pitched in a pretty little hollow, amid a clump of old mesquite trees. The hollow is that of one of the ancient reservoirs, and the moisture retained there makes it a favorable place for the luxuriant growth of the mesquite trees, which always flourish particularly well in such a spot. Three tents are brought from the other camp, and gleam brightly amidst the trees: a small wall-tent for the Doctors, a larger one for the Mexican laborers, the main force being transferred to the new field here, and the Sibley has been brought for the storage of the collections. One of the Mexicans has assumed the duties of cook, and the kitchen is established between the first two tents in the open air, the apparatus consisting of a "tarantula," or great iron frame supported on legs, and placed over the fire for the support of the various kettles, frying-pans, etc., and a crib is built for the animals needed for service here. The name conferred on this ancient city, Las Acequias, comes from the great irrigating-canals that spread out, fan-like, among the ruins, and reach away to various parts of the plain to supply the other cities of the group. Their course may still be plainly traced here, and one of them runs close by the camp, connecting with the reservoir in which it is situated. It must have been an enormous labor to excavate them in those times, with nothing but crude stone implements and baskets for transportation of the earth. The present Tempe Canal follows the course of one of these old ditches very nearly for some distance from the river, and where another passed through a hard bed of natural cement. The Mormons of the neighboring settlement in constructing their canal adopted the old route, thus saving an expenditure of between $10,000 and $20,000.

In a short time the plain is dotted with the yellow heaps of earth thrown up by the excavations, and rich archaeological treasures are found in the shape of skeletons, pottery, stone-implements, and other articles. The two Doctors are found grubbing in the pits, industriously at work over the skeletons, over whose anatomical characteristics their enthusiasm is aroused to a high pitch. They are intent on securing and saving every bone, and are regardless of personal discomfort, not only their clothes being covered with the dust, but their faces begrimed and their hair and beards thoroughly powdered, making them look like some strange burrowing animals. The result of their painstaking is one of the finest and most complete collections of ancient skeletons ever brought together, and the consequent discovery of certain anatomical characteristics that promise to be of high importance in the determination of racial distinctions.

Las Acequias, like the other ancient cities, consists of groups of large houses, corresponding to our city blocks of dwellings, each of which was inhabited by a single clan. These are numbered in the course of the excavation, and the numbers are recorded on the plats of the ruins subsequently made. The skeletons and other specimens found are labelled with the numbers of the ruins and rooms where they are found, and the circumstances attending them are also recorded, so that each object is accompanied by a concise statement of its history, which, in conjunction with the preliminary and daily reports made by Mr. Cushing, will prove invaluable in the study of the collection, giving it a scientific worth such as few other collections possess. The circumstances under which objects are found, particularly when observed by one competent to make deductions from those circumstances, are frequently of even more value than the objects themselves in their relation to the main purpose of such explorations—the understanding of the people of whom they are relics.

The drive between the two camps becomes a familiar experience. It is made by some one in a buckboard almost daily, Mr. Cushing keeping close watch of the progress of the excavations. In the early weeks of my stay the intervening region is still a wilderness, with a clearing only here and there, so we cut straight across country through the various patches of mesquite, sage-brush, and greasewood that make up the wilderness. It is more difficult to find the way over these broad valley-plains than one might think, in spite of the landmarks presented by the neighboring mountains, for the spot one seeks is difficult to find amidst the general flatness of the land and the uniform character of the surrounding objects, which, amidst the various rambling cart-ways, make even the road itself hard to follow until one has made the acquaintance of its details through familiarity.

The landscape undergoes a rapid transformation in the course of a few weeks. Here and there, the plain is dotted with the camps of laborers engaged in clearing it, consisting of Mexicans at work for some contractor who has undertaken the job for the owner. Our nights are enlivened by the brilliant brush-fires gleaming around us in all directions, near and far. The mesquite trees are cut down and burned in piles above their roots, whose ramifications are followed by the smouldering combustion, leaving the ground ready for the plow when that instrument shall eventually be brought into requisition, which will probably not be for two, or even three years, for the mellow, rich soil needs no plow at first. A seed-drill rapidly sows the grain when the ground has been cleared, and the only labor then required is to irrigate and harvest; the next year, even the labor of sowing is unnecessary, for a luxuriant volunteer crop springs up from the self-sown, ripened grain, and often, the second year, there is still another volunteer crop as abundant as the first!

The growth of sage-brush or greasewood is cleared off with slight trouble or cost; a stout bar or beam is dragged across the land by a pair of horses, one attached to each end. The bushes are displaced by the powerful leverage at their bases as the beam is dragged over them. The team then follows the same course in the reverse direction and completes the destruction, either yanking up the bushes by the roots, or breaking off the brittle wood close to the ground. The brush is finally gathered into great piles and burned, making a strong, clear flame that shows across country for a great distance.

It is not long before the whole country is cleared, changing the aspect of the locality entirely. The land stretches away almost as smooth as a floor for miles, the very uniformity in contrast with the rugged mountain-chains around[,] giving it a certain attractiveness akin to beauty. The tents of the settlers follow those of the clearing parties. It is an easy matter to become domiciled in this region, with its mild climate, unlike the settling of the rigorous Northwest: no shelter is required for stock, and little for the people, who live at ease in the dry air, until their first simple cottage of adobe or boards is ready. Not unfrequently one sees a handsome new buggy standing with evident ostentation before the tent of a new-comer, looming up prominently from a distance.

The greater part of the land is taken up under the Desert-land Act, which, in order to encourage the reclamation of the desert, enables a citizen, or a man intending to become a citizen, to take a whole section of 640 acres, a square-mile, in the arid regions of the country, on condition that it be cleared, irrigated, and cultivated within three years from the time of entry, on the payment, at the end of that time, of either $1.25 or $2.50 an acre, according as the land is within the limits of a railway land-grant or not, the latter, or "double-minim" price, being charged in that event; so that, for $800 or $1,600, one can obtain a square-mile of land, and, as only one-fifth of the amount has to be paid at the start on making the entry, the land will, of course, pay for this, and also the expenses of clearing, beside a handsome profit, if it be brought under cultivation at once.

Much of the land is also obtained by settlers under the Homestead, Preëmption or Timber-culture Acts, each of which permits the taking-up of a quarter-section, or 160 acres. It is possible for one man to take advantage of all these acts, and so obtain from the Government 1,120 acres of some of the richest and most valuable agricultural land in the world. Many of these settlers, who came into this valley a few years ago with nothing but their blankets, have already handsome fortunes.

Before I leave the valley, in mid-April, the greater part of this land, which I first saw as a primitive wilderness, is green with young grain. It will not be long before it all presents the same aspect as the beautiful homestead-region of Mesa City, the Mormon town close by Las Acequias. Driving towards the latter camp from Los Muertos, we see Mesa City simply as a long line of trees in the distance, with a few houses of recent settlers scattered here and there in the open on the hither side. It seems but a single line of trees bordering some irrigating canal, but, when we have once penetrated it, we find that it is the border of a beautifully embowered town, with neat houses and long, shady avenues enclosing many a square-mile of vineyard and orchard. The little gurgling streams that run rapidly everywhere by the roadside beneath the rows of tall cottonwoods, which, with all their great trunks and spreading boughs, are but a few years old, are the secret of this prosperity. The gravelly soil of this spot was despised by the less intelligent Gentiles of the valley as comparatively worthless, but the more experienced Mormons saw that, for fruit-culture, it could hardly be surpassed. Mesa City, like scores of other Mormon towns that have sprung up in this part of the world, affords a practical example of what can be done by intelligent and systematic coöperation in a community, great economies being effected by the union of all the proprietors of the land in introducing a water-supply for irrigation, and economically administering it, so as to make it in the distribution utilized to the utmost; also by a well-devised arrangement of the land under common agreement, that enables great economies in the construction of boundary-fences, and also in its cultivation or use as pasturage; by carrying on other works in common, and thus effecting a great saving of labor; and again by establishing coöperative stores, where all members of the community can purchase the best of supplies in great variety at substantially cost-price, making, of course, a great saving in the expense of living. The Mormons accomplish all this by their superior methods of organization acquired in their years of isolation from the rest of the world; the necessities of their situation, as well as their devotion to a common cause, teaching them the advantages of working in coöperation, both for the individual and the community. For this reason the Mormons are, as a rule, far more prosperous than their Gentile neighbors.

IV

As the work proceeds, the obscure hints and indications concerning the life of this ancient people become more clear and plain. A beautiful instance of how history, archaeology, and the traditions retained by living peoples all contribute in their interrelation to reveal a picture of the past with graphic fidelity is afforded by a certain thread which Mr. Cushing followed out in its course hither and yon, until it led to the conclusion. Briefly it must be stated here. The narrations of the early Spaniards mention a certain pueblo, the "kingdom" of Cibola, or Zuñi, as containing a population of so many within and so many without the walls. Standing by itself, this statement has been accorded no particular significance by historical students. But here in these excavations Mr. Cushing came across frequent remains of a different class of dwelling than the urban houses, standing in clusters in the fields, or just outside the boundaries of the towns. Then he recalled a folk-tale of the Zuñis, about a maiden who herded turkeys, and belonged to the low-class dwellers outside the town. The Zuñis to-day have certain persons who, for various shortcomings, are compelled to live across the river, outside the town, though not now numerous enough to form a distinct community. All these facts combined to bring out certain evidence with distinctness: that these peculiarly situated and constructed dwellings were the habitations of an ultra-mural, low-caste, agricultural and herder population, and that domesticated animals were kept by the town-dwelling Indians in pre-Columbian days. Among these domesticated animals were turkeys, and probably rabbits, and perhaps still another very important kind, as we shall see. Mr. Cushing has found, in his linguistic investigations of the Zuñi language, how the past of a people may be recorded in the structure of their idiom as plainly as fossil-remains tell the story of the geological past, or contain the record of the development of a chain of species in the gradual modifications of the evolutionary chain. The Zuñi tongue has a word for this outcast, ultra-mural population, which conveys the meaning of "self-thrust out," or, "cast out by their own acts"; that is, voluntary outcasts. Such a people, by some circumstance, some act of desecration perhaps not even intentional, place a ban upon themselves which forbids either them or their descendants to live in contact with those within the walls. A permanent outcast class is thus formed. This is quite in accord with primitive religious beliefs. It is notable that in Peru there was also an outcast agricultural population, and Peru contains many resemblances to this primitive North American culture. It is also notable that the Sudras, the low-caste population of India, are tillers of the ground.

In excavating the remains of one of these ultra-mural houses, a group of animal figurines was found buried together. They were crudely, but realistically made animals with long ears and without horns. The Zuñis have to-day the practice of making figures of sheep, horses, and other domestic animals, which they sacrifice for an increase of herd. As these ruins were unquestionably pre-Columbian, and as, of course, there were no sheep here in those times, the problem was: What were these effigies meant for? Their resemblance to the llama was so marked as to be noted at first sight by Doctors ten Kate and Wortman and other observers. This, taken in connection with other evidence, led Mr. Cushing to the belief that among the domesticated animals of these ancient people there was a species of the llama family. The other evidence was found in the numerous petrographic inscriptions abounding in the Southwest, in the traditions of the Zuñis, and in the narratives of the early explorers, which speak of a domesticated animal answering to this description among the Pueblos of that day. To be conclusive, however, it needs the finding of the bones of the species among the ancient remains—something that has not yet been done—and, while the testimony of the old Spanish explorers is strong, it is notable that they do not mention seeing the animals themselves, so that at that time they must already have become rare. Mr. Cushing has, however, accumulated an important mass of testimony weighty enough to justify laying it before the scientific world to await the time when the required links shall be found, encouraging others to look in the same direction.

It is well known that North America was the home of the auchinea, or llama family, the ancestor of the Old World camel, and the fossil-remains of numerous species, large and small, have been found by paleontologists, while no fossils have, I believe, yet been found in South America, the present home of the family,—limited to four species there. Two of these species are domesticated there, and have been since prehistoric times—the llama, the only beast of burden that existed among the aboriginal population of the New World; and the alpaca, which was bred for its wool. As these species are, therefore, comparatively new in South America, and as it has been something of a puzzle for naturalists to account for their being there; and as, moreover, North America was the home of the family, it is not unreasonable to suppose that some one or more of the species of auchinea were already domesticated among the ancient populations of this part of the world; that they were taken to South America by the gradual spread of the primitive cultures thither in very remote ages; that the other species differentiated there from the original stock in consequence of escape from domesticity; that meanwhile, in North America, the climatic changes wrought by the advance of the glacial period drove the various species of the family into new environments, where the conditions proved unfavorable, and brought about their extinction. Some may have remained in domesticity, and possibly lingered here and there till about the time of the Spanish conquest, when descriptions of them were heard by the invaders of Cibola. As serious epidemics are often known to break out among domestic animals, it is not unlikely that something of the sort may have swept the last of them from existence, which would account for the fact that none of them were seen by the Spaniards.

One day Mr. Cushing, Don Carlos, Ramon and I, with a Mexican laborer, proceed to explore the great cave in the face of Central Butte, near the town of Tempe. By its position Mr. Cushing determines it to have been the "northern place of sacrifice" for the neighboring ancient town of Los Hornos. The butte lifts its head boldly from the plain, forming a lofty cliff. In its precipitous face the dark opening of the cave shows like the deeply recessed entrance of a Gothic cathedral, the pointed arch something like forty feet or more from the base. The customary slope of detritus, worn away from the rock by the slow friction of the ages as they pass, lies at the foot of the butte. Ascending this, and standing at the mouth of the cavern, we survey the surrounding country. The prospect is enchanting. It is the height of spring-time, the 9th of March. Verdant fields rich with young grain spread for miles around, embroidered by long lines of trees in full leaf, and silvery threads of irrigating-water gleaming in the sun. Here and there a house may be seen almost concealed beneath a mound of leafage, and not far away stands the clustered town, accented by puffs of steam from the train just arrived.

Don Carlos leaves us and drives into the town, regretful that routine errands prevent him from sharing our explorations, and the rest of us turn to the lesser mysteries of the cave where in their devoutness the worshippers of perhaps many centuries ago have stored the symbols of their faith that shall help illuminate the understanding of the seekers after knowledge of what man is as they delve in the soil where his being is rooted—the nature of primitive man.

The cave is a great crevice between the two monstrous masses of rock which lean against each other, and form the mass of the butte. It narrows gradually and runs in from something like fifty feet or more, far enough to make the light very dim at the farther end. The floor slopes upward from the entrance at a heavy grade. The air is dry, and at a considerable distance outside the entrance may be perceived the odor peculiar to caverns in this country, coming from the droppings of the bats and the terrestrial rodents that inhabit it. The rat-like juancitos have brought in the joints of the cholla cactus in great abundance. As this cactus bristles with its sharp spines like a porcupine, it is a marvel how they ever manage to transport it without lacerating their mouths or making pincushions of themselves after the style of St. Sebastian with his arrows, as portrayed by the old masters. Throughout Arizona the floors of such caves are found covered with a deep bed of chollas. But wherever white men have entered—and the prospectors for mineral have been about everywhere—they have almost invariably set these chollas on fire, for the sake of enjoying the spectacle of seeing the animals scamper out of the place in terrified swarms. The chollas are exceedingly inflammable, and blaze like tinder. The fire communicates to the accumulated guano, and smoulders down beneath the surface to a considerable depth. Thus, when the cave is a sacrificial one, as is apt to be the case, great quantities of precious relics are heedlessly destroyed to afford a moment's diversion for unthinking men.

This cave had, of course, shared the usual fate. But several months before, when Mr. Cushing had visited it, he had found a number of interesting sacrificial relics, and the indications were that a systematic search would reveal rich finds. So Ramon and the laborer took pick and shovel and began to dig over the floor from the entrance inward, and Mr. Cushing and I grubbed in promising-looking corners. The floor was covered with the broken fragments of rock that had been falling from the roof and sides through the ages, covering it to a depth of three or four feet. All this was embedded in guano and a surface of loose ashes. Our search was soon rewarded, for relics abounded everywhere. How long the cave must have been used for sacrificial purposes cannot be conjectured. The relics must have existed by the thousands before the fire, for savages never disturb a sacrificial place, even of an enemy, fearing to provoke the hostility of the gods and spirits that guard the spot. As it was, we found them in large quantities; both in charred fragments, in whole examples more or less charred, and many that had escaped the fire entirely, protected by their depth, or some intervening rock. The relics were chiefly sacrificial cigarettes, made of cane; also prayer-wands and plumes, and sacred tablets. Great masses of string and fragments of cloth were found, gnawed from the sacrifices by the juancitos to make their nests. Many of the cigarettes were wrapped with miniature breech-clouts, nicely woven of cotton, some of them with bits of turquoise and other ornaments attached. Some of the cigarettes were in bundles of four, others of six, according to the nature of the sacrifice, or, perhaps, of the rank of the man making it. Some were still filled with tobacco, which, when a bit was burned, had the familiar smell. In spite of the great age, the dryness of the air and, perhaps, the quality of the guano imbedding them, the uncharred relics were mostly as fresh in appearance as when new, even the woven cotton looking clean and white.

In these ancient cigarettes of cane, we find the prototypes of both the pipe and the cigarette. They are always made to include the joint of the cane, which is punctured with a small hole. The hollow on one side of the joint corresponds to the bowl of the pipe, being filled with tobacco, while that on the other side answers for the stem.

What a job we had! Our excavations filled the place with the dust of ashes and finely pulverized guano, which was perfectly dry, and the smell of ashes and guano mingled made a horrible odor. We were nearly suffocated; I felt myself growing sick and sicker, but in the enthusiasm of the search I hardly heeded it until the lengthened shadows, creeping over the plains as we looked from the entrance, warned us that the day was nearly ended, and we had nearly ten miles to go for supper. Don Carlos came with the team, and we emerged in about the most disreputable-looking condition imaginable, with hair and clothing filled with the malodorous dust, and faces grimy with it. But our treasure-trove was worth it; besides many other valuable specimens, it included, counting what were found the next day when Mr. Cushing completed the exploration of the cave, over 1600 of the sacrificial cigarettes.

Before we start for the camp, Mr. Cushing makes a reconnaissance of the butte and comes across a smaller cave. A rattlesnake is coiled up at the entrance, and above he sees a pretty tip of fur hanging from the edge of the shelf of a sort of niche. "Ah, a Pima sacrifice!" he exclaims mentally, and he is about to slay Mr. Snake and lay hands on the ethnological specimen, when the latter stirs and disappears, and in its place appears the other end, the head, of one of the most beautiful and most avoided of quadrupeds, for it was the tail of a sleeping skunk! As there is a chance that the cave may contain some real specimens, he concludes not to spoil it by the consequence of irritating the pole-cat, and he leaves both the occupants in peace.

We ride back in the mild evening air, in the white light of a wonderful silver sunset that seems like warm, glowing moonlight. The side-camp is now at Los Hornos, where the men are engaged in excavations; Dr. Wortman greets us with the news of an important find, in the shape of a fragment of a small copper bell, the first piece of metal-work discovered by the Expedition. A few days later a complete little bell of the same metal is found in the same place; peculiarities of its workmanship tell clearly an important story which Mr. Cushing interprets in the light of his knowledge of Zuñi silversmithing, in which he served an apprenticeship. It tells that it was of pre-Columbian origin, that the art of fusing, smelting and soldering metal was known, and that, while theirs was essentially a stone-age culture they were at the dawning of a metal-age, and that the art of metal-working practised by the Zuñis is, as they have claimed, of native origin handed down from ancient times, and not acquired from the Spaniards.

Among the important investigations made by Mr. Cushing is that of their system of irrigation, which was both elaborate and extensive. The lines of their canals are to be traced for miles and miles over the plains, and a map of the canals supplying the Salado group of ruins is made by Mr. Garlick. Sections of the canals are excavated to reveal the method of their construction, which proves to have been peculiar. The canals contained a smaller channel running along as a sort of groove in the centre, so that a cross-section resembled in outline that of a vessel amidships, the smaller channel corresponding to the keel. The purpose of this was apparently to secure the maintenance of a flow in the smaller channel when there was not water enough available from the river to give a flow in the large channel, the narrowness of the former giving a depth and a velocity, with the minimum of evaporation, such as would have been impossible with the shallow flow in the flat bottom of a broad canal without this supplementary device. It appears likely, also, that the canals were used for navigation by rafts of reeds, corresponding to the balsas in use in the Colorado River and the Gulf of California to-day, as well as in Peru and Bolivia. So long has been the time since these canals were in use that in many places they are filled by the action of the elements to a level with the surface of the country, and it was not until the growth of the vegetation of spring-time that their course could be traced, being then marked by lines of bare ground between masses of flowering plants caused by the gravelly banks, and the richer soil between and on either side. These lines were shown beautifully in some photographs.

In the excavations of the canals it was found that the supply-ditches led off just above the level of the supplementary, or keel, canal. To prevent the wearing away of the bank and consequent shoaling at the point of junction, the acute angle at the branch was hardened by burning it under a hot brush fire, being baked to a coarse terra-cotta, and a projection from the opposite bank to deflect the water into the branch channel was similarly treated.

PART IV

Conclusion

The Promise of the Southwest

▼

A Humanized Landscape

Curtis M. Hinsley

In the years following the collapse of the Hemenway Expedition, capital investment in the desert Southwest increased dramatically and a booster mentality occupied the region from Santa Fe to Los Angeles. As Edward Everett Hale had prophesied in 1878 and Sylvester Baxter had observed at firsthand in the 1880s, the railroad revolutionized the region within a short time, bringing thousands of tourists, speculators, and settlers. They, in turn, brought their personal investments with them, and the literature of the Southwest that grew up in the *fin de siècle* years projected their expectations and desires.

The process of forming a regional identity, however, is too complex to be expressed in immigration statistics or a real estate investment prospectus. In the American Southwest it involved, within a period of less than fifty years, the transformation of experience into narrative, and the tropes of narrative into new fictive genres. By the 1920s, in the wake of World War I, the Southwest had come to possess a set of distinctive images. For example, as the Indian arts movement took on momentum in the Southwest and as Santa Fe's Indian Market began to take off, the essentialism inherent in the notion that the Indian is "naturally religious" or "naturally artistic" began to emerge with some insistence. So too did the counterpoint of the "artistic" Indian and a machine-age society. By

1931, when the New York–based Exposition on Tribal Arts published its two-volume *Introduction to American Indian Art,* anthropologist Herbert J. Spinden had no difficulty with the logic of the Indian artist as a therapeutic Other for a machine-driven civilization. "We may safely trust these first Americans," he wrote from the Brooklyn Museum, "with a mandate of beauty. In a world which grows mechanical they seem able to keep contact with the great illusions."[1] But even when the results of the process of identity formation are fairly clear, the stages in its development may be less so. In attempting to understand more precisely how the experiences of one generation became the touristic prescriptions of another, no vista is more revealing than that of the mysterious cliffdwellers.

Mesas and Cliffdwellers

In 1909, twenty years after Baxter's last writings on Cushing and the Southwest, Willa Cather published a short story entitled "The Enchanted Bluff" in *Harper's Magazine*. Her narrator recalls his Nebraska boyhood of twenty years before: it is late summer as the boys, on the edge of manhood, sit by their sandspit campfire—"our last watch-fire of the year"—and confess their dreams for the future. Tip Smith, the buffoon of the group, who works hard in his father's store and collects things of "remote origin," reveals his plan to climb the Enchanted Bluff in New Mexico someday:

> There's a big red rock there that goes right up out of the sand for about nine hundred feet. The country's flat all around it, and this here rock goes up all by itself, like a monument. They call it the Enchanted Bluff down there, because no white man has ever been on top of it. The sides are smooth rock, and straight up, like a wall. The Indians say that hundreds of years ago, before the Spaniards came, there was a village away up there in the air. . . . They were a peaceful tribe that made cloth and pottery, and they went up there to get out of the wars. You see, they could pick off any war party that tried to get up their little steps. . . . Uncle Bill thinks they were Cliff-dwellers who had got into trouble and left home. They weren't fighters, anyhow.

One day, many centuries ago, Tip's uncle has told him, the men of the village atop Enchanted Bluff were stranded at the foot of the mesa by a terrible storm. While they were trapped at the bottom, a war party "from the north" massacred them as their wives and children looked on from above. The community above, unable to descend, slowly starved to death, and "nobody has ever been up there since."

After hearing Tip's story, the boys discuss techniques for getting to the mesa top (perhaps "a rocket that would take a rope over"), but then they are distracted by the scream of a whooping crane and eventually fall into sleepy silence. As they drift off, Percy speaks in the darkness:

> "Say, Tip, when you go down there will you take me with you?"
>
> "Maybe."
>
> "Suppose one of us beats you down there, Tip?"
>
> "Whoever gets to the Bluff first has got to promise to tell the rest of us exactly what he finds," remarked one of the Hassler boys, and to this we all readily assented.[2]

Neither Tip nor his friends ever saw Enchanted Bluff, and none of the dreams of their Nebraska boyhood turned out quite as they had hoped. Cather's theme—boyish enthusiasms and the dreams of adolescence fading (but not forgotten) in the face of a harsh adult world—to which she returned with more complexity in "Tom Outland's Story" (*The Professor's House,* 1925), fits snugly into a literary tradition of industrial-era nostalgia which in post–Civil War America included the works of such writers as Mark Twain and Hamlin Garland. But the southwestern location and inspiration for "The Enchanted Bluff" derived from a more specific tradition of experiences and storytelling that accrued in the last quarter of the nineteenth century. Tracing the development of the "cliffdweller-mesa discovery" trope demonstrates with some precision a succession from original experience through embroidered narrative to fictive re-enactment—a pattern that emerges in southwestern representations in general. Through this process, the experiences of one generation became the stories of the second and the expectations of the third.

In 1875 William Henry Holmes, serving as artist and geologist on Ferdinand V. Hayden's U.S. Geological and Geographical Survey of the Territories, took charge of the exploration of the San Juan Valley of southern Colorado and northern New Mexico. Here he first encountered southwestern cliffdwellings. As he clambered up to the cliffhouses, Holmes was stunned by what he saw, even more by what he imagined. His excitement was reflected in his journal:

> From the top of the wall we looked out and down; there was the deep Canoma Valley. The cliffs above the trees slope below, and the winding thread of the

> Mancos [River] in the green strip at the bottom. How secure; how impregna[ble]; one man with loose rocks at his command could keep off the world. I had the feeling of being in an eagle's nest and was tempted to take wing and fly, but only screamed and then started at the perplexing echoes. We admired the skill with which these fortresses were built and the hardihood, and were amazed that such means of defense could have been conceived and carried out with the nearest water far below, and only these great jars to contain a supply. With their fields and flocks and the supply of water within the hands of an enemy . . . [the cliff-dwellers] must have perished or have crept down the cliffs to fight or yield to the foe. They are gone now indeed and have been for centuries and now like vandals we invade their homes and sack their cities. We . . . carry off their earthen jars and reprimand them for not having left us more gold and jewels.[3]

The wonder and speculation of an archaeological treasure hunt were apparent as well in Holmes's published "Report on the Ancient Ruins of Southwestern Colorado, Examined during the Summers of 1875 and 1876" (1878). As he approached the cliffdwellings he found himself "led to wonder if they are not the ruins of some ancient castle, behind whose mouldering walls are hidden the dread secrets of a long-forgotten people; but a nearer approach quickly dispels such fancies, for the windows prove to be only the doorways to shallow and irregular apartments, hardly sufficiently commodious for a race of pygmies."[4] In 1876 Holmes collaborated with the artist and photographer William Henry Jackson in displaying photographs and models of the cliffdwellings as part of the government exhibit at the Philadelphia Centennial Exposition, bringing these southwestern images—and his own discovery experience—to popular attention for the first time.[5]

Several devices are worth noting in Holmes's account of his cliffdweller discovery. First and most apparent is the physical challenge, which involved daring, courage, and resourcefulness in attaining the heights of the cliffs.[6] The second is the sense of standing on undisturbed ground, of establishing virtual contact with the ancient inhabitants by finding their utensils, pots, and other artifacts exactly as they had left them on the ground—in effect, picking up where they had left off. This experiential connection is closely linked to imaginative scenarios in which the prehistoric people suddenly left, simply abandoning their homes in panicky flight, literally leaving their hearth fires burning.

The importance of this sense of immediacy—as if the intervening centuries had passed in a night—is evidenced by the frequency of its invocation over many decades. It is as common among the hypothetical accounts of the "Moundbuilders" between 1790 and 1870 as it is among cliffdweller accounts of the last quarter of the century.[7] Indeed, this is only one of several ways in which cliffdwellers succeeded moundbuilders in post–Civil War mythmaking. Comparison of the two is instructive. Both prehistoric peoples were imagined to be reluctant warriors who completely disappeared after taking a "last stand" against fierce, nomadic enemies. For earlier observers, the Ohio Valley landscape was an imaginative locus and a stage for prehistoric romance, valor, and tragic loss in this vein. Josiah Priest, for example, in his phenomenally popular *American Antiquities and Discoveries in the West* (1833) conjured up armies "equal to those of Cyrus, of Alexander the Great, or of Tamerlane the powerful," flourishing their trumpets and marching to battle on the shores of the Ohio River. He saw, too, "the remnant of a tribe or nation, acquainted with the arts of excavation and defense, making a last struggle against the invasion of an overwhelming foe; where, it is likely, they were reduced by famine, and perished amid the yells of their enemies."[8]

Sixty years later, Priest's site of conflict moved across the Mississippi, but his essential narrative of the destruction of peaceful, communal agriculturalists remained intact. Holmes simply repopulated the deserted and mysterious spaces of the canyon landscape and re-enacted the tragic drama. But there is another important continuity between the prehistoric imaginings that occurred on either side of the American continent and either side of the Civil War. Constructions of both the moundbuilders and the cliffdwellers suggest that the prehistory of America was inarticulately but intimately associated with the extension of national manhood: contact with the ancients' earthly ruins would serve as a medium of lineage from American fathers to sons. General (later President) William Henry Harrison, in his 1839 "Discourse on the Aborigines of the Valley of the Ohio," expressed the urgency of providing models of martial valor for American boys. His concern arose from a fear that, in contrast to the European and classical worlds, the pristine character of the American land—its historical and moral virginity—would deprive young men of the vital object lessons of history and would thereby prevent the development of manly virtues. James McCulloh, in his *Researches on America* of 1817, similarly bemoaned his country's ahistorical condition. While the politics and battles of the Old World, he wrote, yielded "incidents connected with their histories which we reflect on with enthusiasm," in America mnemonic monuments of heroism and patriotism were sadly lacking.[9]

Holmes, born in 1846, did not serve in the Civil War, and he shared the sensibility of the postwar generation, one even more deeply imbued with the prominence of military exploits and prowess but lacking a major war to fight. The Civil War cast a long shadow over that generation of young men. Almost without exception, their fathers and heroes were military figures and, as has often been noted, the territorial explorations in which Holmes and other early observers of the Southwest took part were thoroughly military in organization and inspiration. But the full implications of this environment have been underappreciated. Understandably, dichotomies revolving around peace and war formed an essential set of distinctions in their lives—in mimetic imagination if not in lived experience.

In the decade or so following Holmes's San Juan summers, many observers and travelers—including Cushing, Bandelier, and other anthropologists—encountered the cliffdwellings of the Southwest. None enjoyed as much immediate fame as Charles Lummis, however. In the famous set of picaresque letters of 1884 that he eventually (1891–92) transformed into *A Tramp across the Continent* and *Some Strange Corners of Our Country: The Wonderland of the Southwest,* Lummis recalled the first time he saw cliffhouses, immediately east of Flagstaff in Walnut Canyon. While he avoided speculation about extinct races (the cliff-dwellers, he said, were "only Pueblo Indians like those among whom I live to-day"), he was fascinated by "these long-forgotten ruins": "[I]n them I dug, from under the dust of centuries, dried and shrunken corn-cobs, bits of pottery, an ancient basket of woven yucca fibre exactly such as is made to-day by the Pueblos of remote, cliff-perched Moqui [Hopi], and a few arrow-heads."[10] In *Some Strange Corners* Lummis recounted his ascent of Montezuma Castle along Beaver Creek in the Verde Valley in Arizona in phrases reminiscent of Holmes (whose 1878 report he elsewhere cited):

> I had to climb to the castle by a crazy little frame of sycamore branches, dragging it after me from ledge to ledge, and sometimes lashing it to knobs of rock to keep it from tumbling backward down the cliff. It was a very ticklish ascent, and gave full understanding how able were the builders, and how secure they were when they had retreated to this high-perched fortress and pulled up their ladders—as they undoubtedly did every night. A monkey could not scale the rock; and the

> cliff perfectly protects the castle above and on each side. Nothing short of modern weapons could possibly affect this lofty citadel.
>
> Even in those far days the Pueblos were patient, industrious, home-loving farmers, but harassed eternally by wily and merciless savages—a fact which we have to thank for the noblest monuments in our new-old land.[11]

Lummis's account, enhanced by Thomas Moran's engraving of "An Ancient Cliff-Dwelling" and another by W. Taber entitled "A Night Attack of Apaches Upon the Cliff-Fortress," stressed the defensive nature of the dwellings and the pacific lives of their inhabitants. Lummis also reminded his readers that several canyons with dwellings were "easily accessible" from the railroad station in Flagstaff.[12] Ever with an eye on the touring public, Lummis pointed to the fascinating fact that within the boundaries of the most advanced nation on earth—this "new-old land"—were to be found the signs of a deep and savage history. By 1892 this was already a common theme in southwestern discourse. John Gregory Bourke, for instance, in *Snake-Dance of the Moquis* (1884), the first popular account of the Hopi ritual, had exclaimed his amazement that such savagery persisted "within our own boundaries, less than seventy miles from the Atlantic and Pacific Railroad in the year of our Lord 1881." Bourke, no less than Lummis, took pleasure in his work as *exposé*:

> The south-western part of our own country has been penetrated by the railroad and the telegraph since the years when Mr. [Hubert Howe] Bancroft completed his then monumental collection of data [in 1875]. Not a day passes that some new discovery is not made by the ubiquitous newspaper correspondents, untiring mining prospectors, tourists, or government scouts, who are poking about in all the bends and angles of what less than a decade ago was more of a *terra incognita* than Central Africa.[13]

Lummis adopted the same stance of the knowing guide in introducing his 1891 collection of essays, *A New Mexico David*: "These true pictures of the wonderful and almost unknown Southwest . . . are not the impressions of a random tourist across its bare, brown waste, but are drawn from intimacy with its quaint peoples, its weird customs, and its dangers."[14]

The early 1890s marked the peak of Lummis's enchantment with the Pueblo Southwest.[15] In the same years, too, appeared Frederick Chapin's *Land of the Cliff Dwellers* (1892), based on the mountain climber's explorations of the region of Mesa Verde in 1889 and 1890 under the direction and guidance of Richard,

Al, and John Wetherill. In Chapin's work, several familiar themes reappear: the history of Spanish settlement, Anglo-American explorations, the familiar division of Native Americans into warlike "wild tribes" and peaceful "Pueblo tribes" ("a very orderly and industrious people [who] live in harmony with each other"). On five occasions Chapin refers to Holmes's San Juan explorations, and his own efforts with the Wetherill brothers seem to derive much from that precedent. In Acowitz Canyon—"a strange, wild, lonely cañon"—they have a difficult climb to the dwellings, but once in the upper rooms Chapin reflects: "How long since human foot had trod those sandstone floors? Certainly not since the forgotten prehistoric race had deserted the caves. Certainly no white man had ever entered these walls before." [16] The men begin to dig in the dirt floors, and Chapin's words uncannily echo Holmes's of fifteen years before:

> The floor of the ledge was covered with fine dust; when disturbed by the spade it raised a choking cloud, and forced the would-be excavator to beat a retreat. . . . It was a fascinatingly queer place; but we must away, for time-consuming caution must be used in the retreat from our citadel. We were struck with the strength of the position, and believed that we could have kept in check a small army of primitive combatants, if they should have dared to storm our position, armed, like ourselves, only with stones.[17]

His imagination stirred, Chapin finds himself at sunset pondering past events: "There must have been a fearful struggle between a people who were emerging from barbarism, and more savage hordes, or some great catastrophe of Nature overwhelmed them." [18] With Chapin, though, a formulaic quality has already developed, and the sequence of his narrated events is no longer fresh: sight of the ruins, a strenuous climb, digging beneath the floors, meditative moments, imaginative reenactment, return, and writing of the events. Significantly, the experience closes with open questions (Who were these people? What happened to them?), inviting others (Lummis's railroad tourists?) to undertake the experience for themselves. By the 1890s, in other words, a quality of prescription has begun to mark the discursive pattern of the southwestern discovery narrative, one that anticipates the sequence of experience and directs the repertoire of emotion to be called forth at each point (wonder, excitement, curiosity, or pensiveness, for example).[19] Thus is established the expectation of connection between external and internal discovery.

This was not a novel development in the recent history of Euro-American landscape aesthetics. A century earlier, the cult of the sublime had reached such hackneyed precision that a clear sequence of response to natural wonders had already been determined for cultured travelers. "The description of an awesome, rugged, or astonishing natural object," Albert Furtwangler writes, "regularly fell into three stages: an exclamation of shock or awe, an appreciation of aesthetic fine points, and a scientific account of possible origins of this natural prodigy or of its outstanding possibilities or dimensions."[20] The contradiction in this development lay between the routine of prescription and the hoped-for freshness of discovery. By its very nature, discovery can be reported but cannot really be prescribed; the complex of emotional and aesthetic responses cannot be repeated without a sense of imitation, no matter how well established the traditions of instruction may be. The act of narrating discovery unavoidably influences the listeners or readers who choose to follow. Powell's 1875 account of his Colorado River exploits, however self-servingly constructed (and even false in places), to a degree determined the experiences of the thousands who have since traveled the Colorado, simply by creating language and images with which to confront the river and by inevitably instilling expectations.[21]

From Jefferson's famous descriptions of the Natural Bridge and the Blue Ridge Mountains in *Notes on the State of Virginia* (1784) through early-nineteenth-century descriptions of Niagara Falls and the Adirondacks to the first images of Yellowstone after the Civil War, providing *terms of sensibility* has been central to the processes of familiarization and domestication—loosely speaking, public appreciation—of the North American continent.[22] For most people, the American West was something altogether strange, a seemingly hostile place. Wallace Stegner, in his essay "Thoughts in a Dry Land," comments on the obvious but often forgotten fact that the West—especially the desert Southwest—has been visually unprecedented, even shocking, for most visitors. It calls for new aesthetic terms: "You have to get over the color green." Lummis wrote similarly of the unreliability of the easterner's untrained eye in viewing southwestern landscapes.[23] In recording their responses for others, writers of a century ago, such as Lummis and Chapin, were engaging in that strange fusion of styles and registers that has constituted American travel writing, "a practice," suggests Terry Caesar, "that writes across generic boundaries," one that is "most acutely performed with fluid transformations of and quick negotiations between the governing polarities of propriety and deviancy, fact and fiction."[24] They were acting, in effect, to bring the cliffdweller country within emotional and aesthetic range, providing terms of sensibility sufficiently familiar to open a psychically "safe" approach to strange places.[25] Whether intentionally or not, they were also preparing national public sentiment for legislation to preserve prehistoric sites (through, for example, the Antiquities Act of 1906).

There were other preparations as well. In 1893, H. Jay Smith & Company recreated Battle Rock Mountain in southwestern Colorado on the grounds of the World's Columbian Exposition in Chicago. "Inside," notes art historian Julie K. Brown, "were displays of original artifacts and reproductions of prehistoric Indian rock tombs and ceremonial and settlement complexes such as the Cliff Palace." The company charged an admission fee and sold photographs of the structure and exhibits and, for added authenticity, "even reproductions of the prints and drawings used to create them."[26] An American flag flew prominently atop the structure, and the surrounding grounds of neatly manicured grass were marked off with chains and benches—clear signs of taming and domestication. It was a popular exhibit, netting $87,000.

The popularity of the Smith & Company exhibit in Chicago reflected a new public fascination with the cliffdwellers. In mid-1891 Gustav Nordenskiöld, a young Swede suffering from the tuberculosis that would kill him only four years later, undertook travels that brought him to Denver, where he heard about the mysterious cliffdwellings at Mesa Verde. Planning a week's stay, he remained for two months, hiring the Wetherill brothers to dig for him, amassing a valuable collection of artifacts that eventually found their way to Finland, and producing *The Cliff Dwellers of the Mesa Verde* two years later. Published simultaneously in Swedish and English, Nordenskiöld's copiously illustrated volume was the first serious effort to describe the structures and remains of the cliff country of southern Colorado.[27] The sober, even mundane, quality of Nordenskiöld's account contrasts sharply with those of Holmes, Lummis, and Chapin: "From the bottom of the cañon we force our way through dense thickets some hundreds of feet up the steep slope. . . . The ruin lies upon one of the lowest ledges, and the climb, though troublesome, is attended with no serious difficulties."[28] To his parents he described a typical day of excavating:

> [After breakfast] we wash up, whereupon we saddle our horses, the water bottles are filled, and we set off along the narrow path to a place on the mesa above the ruin where we are working. We unsaddle our horses and tie their forelegs together. Then we climb a long, roundabout way down to the ruin. There we dig,

> sketch, photograph, label finds and so on till the sun is high in the sky. Then we have dinner, a tin of corned beef and a loaf of bread is all we get, for we cannot have much with us; then we resume work again until the sun begins to sink in the west and the shadows on the side of the canyon grow long. Then up in the saddle again and back to camp. Soon the campfire blazes up, the tea can is put on the flame, and supper, with about the same menu as breakfast, is eaten rather faster if possible.[29]

If Nordenskiöld brought sober intentions to the cliffdweller phenomenon, the ancient peoples of the mesa country were presented more excitingly to the public a few years later through the exploits of Frederick Hodge. When the Hemenway Expedition collapsed in 1889, Hodge found immediate employment at the Bureau of Ethnology (as previously arranged for him by Cushing).[30] Over the next several years, Hodge concentrated on editorial and office work, gradually gathering a reputation for his expertise in Pueblo cultures and languages.[31] He developed a close working relationship with Jesse Fewkes, who (after Mary Hemenway's death in 1894) continued his southwestern archaeology under the direct aegis of Samuel P. Langley, secretary of the Smithsonian Institution.[32]

In the summer of 1896 Hodge accompanied Fewkes on his fieldwork at the Hopi ruins of Sikyatki and Awatovi pueblos. During the season he visited Acoma pueblo and attempted, unsuccessfully, to ascend Katsímo, or "La Mesa Encantada" (Enchanted Mesa), the huge, striking red sandstone mesa three miles northeast of the village of Acoma. Hodge intended to test the truth of an Acoma legend, recounted variously by Lummis in his early publications,[33] which told of an ancient people who had lived on Katsímo. One day, according to the legend, when all the men of the village were at work below, a mass of rock fell into the narrow passage up the side of the mesa, closing it off completely. The women and children, left on the summit of a cliff 430 feet high, slowly starved to death, and the community disappeared. Hodge failed in his first attempt to reach the mesa top, but he did find in the detritus at the base of the mesa some shards of pottery, as well as indentations in the wall which he took to be possible hand- and footholds for climbing.

Doubting Lummis's account and possibly stimulated by Hodge's adventure, in the following July William Libbey, Jr., a professor of geology and natural history at Princeton University, took a small exploring party—including a journalist for the *Brooklyn Eagle*—to the mesa. "Equipped with the apparatus of the

Life Saving Service," Libbey shot a strong rope over the mesa and hauled himself up, seated on a plank from one of his packing crates.[34] After a two-hour reconnaissance of the 16-acre mesa summit, Libbey came down, claiming to have found no signs of a prehistoric community on Enchanted Mesa: "Not the slightest trace was found which would enable me to believe that a human foot had ever before passed over the top of this famous rock."[35] He immediately telegraphed his news to the world.

Lummis was furious at the easterner's presumption in contradicting both Indian legend and Lummis (with an anger that still burned thirty years later),[36] and Hodge found his own reputation potentially impugned by the Princeton professor.[37] Lummis urged his friend to act, and Hodge responded a few weeks later. Fully prepared this time with rope and extension ladder, and accompanied by photographer A. C. Vroman, Hodge scaled the cliff. In a stay of less than 48 hours he found several fragments of pottery, two stone ax-heads, a flint arrow-point, and part of a shell bracelet. When he descended he announced that the mesa had indeed been inhabited at some point in prehistory, which was a possible confirmation of the Acoma legend and certain vindication of both Lummis and himself. Hodge telegraphed Lummis from Laguna: "Just returned Enchanted Mesa; found evidence former occupancy," and Lummis went to work on Libbey.[38] Hodge's adventure story circulated widely—in *Century, Harper's* and Lummis's *Land of Sunshine*—complete with Vroman's photographs of the exploring party on the mesa and their small artifact assemblage. Both Hodge and the mysterious lost people of the Enchanted Mesa quickly entered southwestern folklore.[39] In 1903 the popular travel writer and lecturer John L. Stoddard included a lengthy account of the dispute and discovery in his published lecture on the Southwest (including a photograph of Libbey on his plank board that made him look ludicrous).[40] In addition, Willa Cather, as we have seen, adapted the legend a few years later in her short story "The Enchanted Bluff."

By the early years of the new century, the use of a narrative of cliffdweller discovery as an effective means of self-promotion was so well established that Edgar Lee Hewett could present the process on a single newspaper page. In this set of representations, Hewett appears in three roles: as explorer, as photographer, and as professorial lecturer. He first espies the dwellings from across the canyon, inspects and photographs them, and finally returns to civilization to conduct a lantern-slide talk on his finds. The formal portrait photograph at the

Edgar Lee Hewett tells the story of the cliffdwellers, 1906.

bottom confirms his urbane status. Hewett thus enacts a newspaper narrative of the heroic discovery, recovery, and control of the prehistoric past.

Although they began their anthropological careers in the Southwest of the late 1880s, Hodge and Fewkes (and later Hewett) already belonged to a generational consciousness distinct from that of Cushing, Bourke, and Matthews—a consciousness, it must be said, that was both determined and derivative, striving mightily to be authentic but already elaborating inherited experience and imagination.[41] At the same time, for these men drawing the line between scientific purpose and concern with the potential touring public was becoming less easy, and probably less desirable. Fewkes's self-conscious strivings and justifications were transparent in this respect, even to contemporary critics. Reporting from Casa Grande in 1906, he professed that he was "not looking primarily for specimens, but developing ruined buildings so that the visitor may see in them an object lesson in Southwestern archaeology. . . . If supported in this work, I can make a mecca of [for] American archaeologists in this desert. The mounds are here. All I need is money with which to excavate them. . . . It is not, of course, for myself, but for advancement of archaeological science in our country." A few weeks later he was predicting in a similar vein that under his archaeological supervision Casa Grande would become the "Pompeii of the Southwest."[42] At such moments the conflation of scientific archaeology, commercial tourism, and thinly veiled ambition becomes transparent.

In 1925 Willa Cather again conjured up the country of enchanted mesas with "Tom Outland's Story," a central flashback in *The Professor's House*. Working for a cattle company in New Mexico, the adolescent orphan Outland stumbles upon a canyon of cliffdwellings on mysterious Blue Mesa, unvisited and untouched by humans since the sudden departure of the inhabitants hundreds of years ago. To Outland the vision is sombre and awesome:

> I wish I could tell you what I saw there, just *as* I saw it, on that first morning, through a veil of lightly falling snow. Far up above me, a thousand feet or so, set in a great cavern in the face of the cliff, I saw a little city of stone, asleep. It was as still as sculpture—and something like that. It all hung together, seemed to have a kind of composition. . . .
>
> Such silence and stillness and repose—immortal repose. That village sat looking down into the canyon with the calmness of eternity. . . . I knew at once that I had come upon the city of some extinct civilization, hidden away in this inaccessible mesa for centuries, preserved in the dry air and almost perpetual sunlight like a fly in amber, guarded by the cliffs and the river and the desert.[43]

Outland and his partner, Roddy Blake, save sufficient money to spend most of a year exploring the ruins and amassing a large collection of artifacts in their cabin. As Outland's attachment to the site grows, he ponders its history:

> The town hung like a bird's nest in the cliff, looking off into the box canyon below, and beyond into the wide valley we called Cow Canyon, facing an ocean of clear air. A people who had the hardihood to build there, and who lived day

> after day looking down upon such grandeur, who came and went by those hazardous trails, must have been, as we often told each other, a fine people. But what had become of them? What catastrophe had overwhelmed them?[44]

Their love for the spot and its lost people grows. Father Duchene, Outland's mentor and priest, shares their reverence for a sacred spot where humans attempted to grow from "mere brutality" to community, order, and security: "They built themselves into this mesa and humanized it."[45] At his suggestion, Outland decides to offer their discovery and collection to the Smithsonian Institution and travels to Washington in a prolonged effort to interest the government anthropologists. But there is no interest in Washington—"They don't care much about dead and gone Indians"—and he returns to the mesa only to find that, in his absence, Blake has sold their collection for $4,000 to a visiting German collector. Horrified, Outland upbraids his friend: "But I never thought of selling them, because they weren't mine to sell—nor yours! They belonged to this country, to the State, and to all the people. They belonged to boys like you and me, that have no other ancestors to inherit from."[46]

Demoralized and alone, Outland decides to spend the summer on the mesa. Here he undergoes a conversion that turns his loss to gain and his adventure to a "religious emotion." For the first time he feels that he truly possesses the cliff-house country: "It was my high tide. Every morning, when the sun's rays first hit the mesa top, while the rest of the world was in shadow, I wakened with the feeling that I had found everything, instead of having lost everything. Nothing tired me."[47]

"Tom Outland's Story" represents a fictional culmination of the mesa-cliffdweller trope that we have been tracing from 1876. Youthful discovery of a timeless place set aside from history offers direct connection to a deep American past—and an inheritance to a nation with "no other ancestors to inherit from." The indifference of government bureaucrats leads to the loss of the artifacts, but Outland learns through the loss that the true aboriginal inheritance is spiritual, not tangible, and that it involves a nonmaterial relationship, a stewardship of the land.

The larger narrative of *The Professor's House* places the Outland story within the familiar post–World War I climate of decline and disillusionment with the direction of American economics and morality.[48] Outland dies heroically in the war, but not before he has invented a vital airplane part. The patent yields a fortune for the professor's daughter, Rosamund—Outland's betrothed. After his death, Rosamund marries Louis Marsellus, an unimaginative electrical engineer, and they name their new country mansion Outland. Cather's lesson is clear: something has gone terribly wrong during the nation's coming of age; something fresh and hopeful has been tragically, irretrievably lost. The once-possible prospect of a melding of people with landscape—Father Duchene's "humanizing" of cliff and mesa—has been superseded by a need for domination and a sense of greed. The youthful spiritual legacy of Tom Outland (and the early American republic) has been inherited by a jaded American *nouveau riche* of boorishness and Babbitry.

Adobe Walls and Corn Grinding: Stasis as Aesthetic Therapy

The evolution of the mesa-cliffdweller trope had many parallels in the imaginative development of the Southwest between 1875 and 1925. Through these constructions, visitors made a region that, while undeniably the locus of momentous past events, remained somehow *essentially* unchanged—a fly in amber. Writing from Mexico City in 1887, Sylvester Baxter's close friend and fellow journalist Frederic R. Guernsey reminded readers of the *Boston Herald* that the Indian, "unlike the white man, does not change. He may seem to, but he is still an Indian. As he was at the time of the conquest, so, substantially, he is now."[49] In *Children of the Sun,* his 1883 account of the Cushings' life at Zuñi pueblo, Chicago journalist William E. Curtis described the aridity and stillness of "desolate, mystic" New Mexico:

> One can scarcely find a more remarkable country; remarkable in landscape and in history. Barren hills of clay and sandstone, flung up at random out of the earth; strange jagged peaks and grotesque cliffs, yellow banks serrated by floods, and shells glistening in the billows of sand, scattered by the sea when it receded, all overhung by a rich, glowing, dreamy atmosphere, with glimpses of haze far off in the horizon, inspire a feeling of awe and wonder that a fertile country can not produce. Here is a desolate, mystic land, nothing but sunshine, burning sands, and legends, where human enterprise, in centuries that are forgotten, battled with hunger and thirst and barbarity, and where, before and since the wind swept away their trails, the silence of desolation has reigned. Everything dries here. The earth dries, the grass dries, the river dries, the wagons dry and fall to pieces.

> There is no juice in anything, animate or inanimate, and one listens to hear if the men and mules can walk without creaking.[50]

A few years later Charles Lummis, in *Land of Poco Tiempo* (1893), a book dominated by images of drowsiness and sleep, conveyed a region subjected to repeated invasions and depredations yet of such self-healing powers that it remained ultimately untouched: "The most superhuman marches, the most awful privations, the most devoted heroism, the most unsleeping vigilance wrested this bare, brown land to the world; and having wrested it, went to sleep."[51] For Lummis, the actions of human history are finally erased, baked out of earth and consciousness by the shimmering noonday heat of New Mexico. Susan Wallace, writing from Santa Fe in a similar fashion for *Harper's,* saw vigilance among the pueblos; she portrayed the remnant tribe of ancient Pecos as waiting through the centuries, with sentinels preserving the eternal fire, on the watch for the second coming of Montezuma: "The eternal fire flickered, smoldered in embers, but endured through all change and chance, like a potent will; . . . they would rest on the promise till sun and earth should die."[52] "Bounded by religious conservatism as a wall," Wallace added, "in all these ages they have slight change by contact with the white race."[53]

The sense of an immutable landscape resistant to human alteration came out most strikingly in the fascination with adobe architecture. Pueblo architecture provided an irresistible example of authentic life, an act of direct transformation (as with pottery) of the very mud underfoot into the essentials of domestic life. In Southwest commentary, pueblo/cliffdweller architecture really *became* landscape, and vice versa. The works of nature and those of Native Americans (prehistoric or historic) seemed to dissolve into one another through the eyes of the Anglo. Cushing described Zuñi as "a little island of mesas . . . reared from a sea of sand," standing in seemingly mock rivalry with Nature. John Wesley Powell, approaching Hopi through Moenkopi Wash in 1875, turned around the equation and the *tromp l'oeil:* he saw cliffs "of bright colors, golden, vermilion, purple and azure hues, and so storm-carved as to imitate Gothic and Grecian architecture on a vast scale. Outlying buttes were castles, with minaret and spire; the cliffs, on either side, were cities looking down into the valley, with castles standing between; the inhabitants of these cities and castles are a million lizards: great red and black lizards, the kings [and] nobles; little gray lizards, the common people, and here and there a priestly rattlesnake."[54] Baxter rhapsodized on the trail to Zuñi:

> The most wonderful and majestically beautiful of architectural forms are here, carven in the rich sandstone which ranges through all the warm hues from brown to red and yellow, with gray and black for sober relief. Castles, halls, temples, with grand gables, terraces, gateways, and porches, turrets and pinnacles, lofty towers and graceful spires, form vast titanic cities. Though only the theatre of the dusk of a race of man, here well might be the scene of the *Götterdämmerung*. . . .
>
> And here the earth's ruins only are foliage-garbed and tree-crowned. Nature has kept her funeral wreaths for her own remains alone. Forests deck the roofs of this natural architecture, and their fringes drape the sides, flank the towers, adorn the buttresses, and fill the crevices of the magnificent masonry. . . . Meanwhile the ruins of man's buildings crouch pitiably bare at the feet of the mighty structures.[55]

According to these representations, while the age-old, steady processes of nature—forest growth and decay, erosion, canyon cutting—continued unabated, within the warm adobe walls of the pueblo there went forward, as it had for ages, a rhythmic, harmonious daily and seasonal life. The construction of an Apollonian Southwest began in these accounts. Baxter, one of the first to contribute to the myth, attributed Pueblo harmony in life and religion to "an innate gentleness of spirit."[56] Anthill, beehive, mud-sparrows—the favored metaphors of these early accounts—stressed natural, unquestioned activity, a steadiness of communal purpose largely devoid of deviance and disruption. Early morning and sunset scenes further accentuated diurnal rhythms, often with strong biblical referents: women at the spring, men bringing in the flocks, women preparing the evening meal.[57] Through views of unchanging tradition and rhythmic regularity, this discursive formation presented southwestern Indian life and history as a series of cyclical events.

Domestic scenes—especially those displaying communal labor, social harmony, and artistic or spiritual life—became central to the Pueblo Southwest of the Anglo imagination. For middle-class Americans of the last quarter of the nineteenth century, the home, specifically the front parlor, was the locus of civilized life. It seemed a bastion against the emotional and economic uncertainties of the factory, the marketplace, and a largely unregulated public life, and it

Returning from the field.

provided both a haven of moral stability and a field for social display. The Victorian parlor, Karen Halttunen has recently argued, didactically announced the moral stature of its inhabitants. Accordingly, a moral aesthetic determined its interiors, including the placement of wall decorations and furniture.[58] Here one could rely on finding a "standardized air of propriety"—orderly, predictable, respectable. Not surprisingly, it was through the parlor that the photograph was first employed in the American household, as personal portraits or as informative and uplifting stereographic entertainment. Stereographs, Louise Stevenson has observed, "permitted viewers to take visual excursions at bargain prices to see people and places near and far from their parlors." And among the favorite, non-threatening scenes were those of Native Americans. Americans collected and viewed them by the thousands.[59]

Visitors found various ways to represent pueblo domesticity. In 1875 one of Powell's favorite artists, H. H. Nichols, sketched "A Tusayan Interior," which featured corn-grinding troughs, flagstone flooring, and blankets hanging along one wall. Twenty years later, A. C. Vroman photographed a remarkably similar "Zuni Interior"—a spacious, day-lighted room with blankets to one side and pottery along the back wall. In 1882 Cushing verbally scanned the inside of a Zuñi household:

> Between the fire-place and the end of the room, eight or ten *metates* were slantingly set side by side in a trough of stone,—the mills, coarse and fine, of the household. Along the opposite side of the room was suspended from the rafters a smooth pole, upon which hung blankets, articles of clothing, and various other family belongings. More of the like, including quivers and bows, war-clubs, and boomerangs or "rabbit-sticks," disks of haliotis shell, and other ornaments, depended from pegs, and deer or antelope-horns on the walls. Some large, finely decorated water-jars, and a black earthen cooking-pot by the fire-place, two or three four-pronged stools of wood, sundry blanket rugs and robes, made up the furniture of the apartment. Furnishings and all, it differed not from hundreds of its kind throughout the pueblo.[60]

These interior landscapes are marked by the absence of active individuals—or rather, the presence of an invisible population. (Cushing's use of the passive voice is especially effective in this respect.) As in an untouched cliffdwelling, there are all the material signs of an ordered domestic life, but the interiors appear almost as timeless stage-sets, inviting imaginative peopling of the scene by the observer.

In other scenes, however, people are actively engaged in either group labor or individually creative work. A favorite scene was corn grinding, a communal woman's activity. An early engraving appeared in Powell's 1875 Hopi series in *Scribner's;* Metcalf pictured it in Cushing's "My Adventures in Zuni." The scene was described repeatedly by writers, journalists, and anthropologists. While living with Frank and Emily at the pueblo in 1883–84, Emily's sister Margaret drew Zuni women at the mealing-trough for Cushing's *Zuñi Breadstuff* series and privately recorded the women's experience on which her sketch was based:

> This evening in our walk we were attracted by singing into a little by-way where we stopped to listen in front of a house. The door suddenly opened and a woman came out and seeing us insisted upon our going in to visit. When the darkness caused by our entrance cleared away and the light from the small [door] again shone into the room, I saw eight women kneeling behind eight little flat troughs in the floor, each of which was paired with a large, slanting, flat stone, upon which they rubbed up and down in perfect time as to movement & song, a long flat

Zuñi women at the mealing-trough.

stone corresponding in texture with the first. While in rapid motion, without any pause, they would slip one hand to the middle of the long stone to balance it, and with the other dexterously toss the meal in proper place. Their corn meal is as fine as our softest flour & it is not considered by them in proper condition till it has passed successively through all the eight mills. The first stone is very rough to break the whole grains of corn, the next a little smoother & so on till both wheat & corn are ground as fine as it is possible to make them. The flour is ground three times in each mill & then passed on to the next until it reaches the last who puts it into a large tray which is immediately borne off (by someone waiting) to be tasted. Their shining black hair, which is cut evenly round the face, falls down in front & flips up & down, all at the same time looking very curious. To day only the women sang. They have queer shrill piping little voices which are very attractive to me on account of the novelty. I think it a very wise

> place to make a frolic of work, as they do. All their friends are invited to a grinding bee, (as we call them) & there is a grand merrymaking.[61]

Such representations of pueblo life were contributions to an ongoing but muted dialogue about labor, leisure, and creativity, because there was certainly not much "frolic" in the factories and sweatshops of the United States in 1883. On the contrary, between 1873 and 1917 the United States experienced chronic economic depression and incessant, costly labor-management violence. Between the severe depressions of 1873–77 and 1893–97, the mill towns of America were transformed into manufacturing metropolises—with ugly results.[62] "Riots, strikes, lockouts, assassinations, brutalities, exploitations, marked the economic life of this period," wrote Lewis Mumford sixty years ago. "At no period in American history has the working class in America been more desperately enslaved."[63] By 1886, the year of Chicago's Haymarket bombing, American labor resistance to government and employer repression had reached unprecedented heights. Nor did the next quarter-century bring any fundamental changes in this pattern.[64]

In contrast to the industrial violence of modern America, labor and the processes of production in pueblo life seemed models of strenuous but rewarding toil—for the individual and community alike. While the Arts and Crafts movement did not emerge with vigor in the United States until almost the turn of the century, the influences of John Ruskin and William Morris—at least in the form of unease with the processes and results of modern factory production—were already being felt by the 1880s, and certainly the poetics of Walt Whitman and the socialist politics that often inspired and undergirded the Arts and Crafts aesthetic were visible well before the end of the century.[65]

The signs of unease and complaint can be found in odd corners and at stray moments, and, as always, language is telling. In the fall of 1882 that meticulous transatlantic arbiter and critic of taste Henry James, visiting the domestic workplace of Monsieur Ulysse, a French potter located on a sidestreet in Blois, indulged himself in relevant reflections:

> As we all know, this is an age of prose, of machinery, of wholesale production, of coarse and hasty processes. But one brings away from the establishment of the very intelligent M. Ulysse the sense of a less eager activity and a greater search for perfection. He has but a few workmen and he gives them plenty of time. The

> place makes a little vignette, leaves an impression—the quiet white house in its garden on the road by the wide, clear river, without the smoke, the bustle, the ugliness, of so much of our modern industry. It struck me as an effort Mr. Ruskin might have inspired and Mr. William Morris—though that be much to say—have forgiven.[66]

It is worth pausing over James's description of the pottery shop in Blois. The language (allowing for the substitution of an adobe house) transfers well to the contemporaneous American Southwest in its emphasis on quiet, small-scale production. But what is it that makes for James's "greater perfection," for a work of art? He offers a clue in the contrast he draws between "haste" and "greater time." Artistic creativity, he is suggesting, requires *reflective time,* a measured pace of life and work that includes leisure in its regular rhythm. The industrial epoch, William Morris argued, had turned men into "an enormous stock of human machines, who had little chance of earning a bare livelihood if they lingered over their toil to think of what they were doing." For Morris and his followers, the dilemma of the modern age lay precisely in the disassociation between work and the time to think creatively.[67]

In the themes we have been examining—a denial of historical change, an emphasis on temporal stasis, an appeal to natural rhythms—the early shapers of southwestern imagery were variously expressing their sense of recovering this vital aesthetic time. Again and again, in encountering early representations of the Southwest one is struck with the appeal of an unhurried life—in James's words, "the sense of a less eager activity."[68] In the hands of the artist, the aesthetic confrontation, whether in Blois or at Zuñi, itself becomes a subject for wonder and reflection, and an opportunity for reflexive art. Thus James records *his* response to the village scene: it "makes a little vignette, leaves an impression." So, too, Lummis is the hero of his own narratives, and Cushing tells of "My Adventures in Zuñi." In these constructions the man of sensibility stands noticeably at the center, engaging his artistry in still unspoiled places.[69]

Garry Wills has recently suggested that for nineteenth-century Americans "liminal experiences—twilight, dreams, daydreaming, melancholy, premonitions—were not fuzzings but intensifications of knowledge." They presented opportunities for threshold experiences, "an opening onto other worlds."[70] The Southwest, with its pastel colors and deceptive vistas, provided many such openings. Susan Wallace, writing from Santa Fe in 1880, recalled that Nathaniel

Hawthorne had complained of the lack of "the poetic element" in modern American life, which possessed "no shadow, no mystery, no antiquity . . . nor anything but commonplace prosperity in broad and simple daylight." But in the Southwest life was muted and mysterious, and there was rich material for the poet. Here, she advised, "imagination may flower out in fancies rich and strange."[71] Bright daylight, prosperity, prosaic life—such was the condition of industrial America in contrast to the hazy world of mesa, canyon, and pueblo. Lummis caught the sense, calling the Southwest "impressionist": the lack of precise vision, as at dusk, was a particular invitation to poetic insight. The region, in other words, provided a field for imaginative play, room to react and record oneself reacting, watching scenes and experiences reemerge as if on photographic plates when they are being developed.

Viewed from this perspective, Cushing's insistence that Indian myths and folklore constituted a valid starting point for scientific archaeology in the region—which was his methodological premise for the Hemenway work—reached well beyond anthropology as an implicit critique of the cultural patterns of Victorian America. Cushing sought a different epistemology: the poetic knowledge that the Southwest—as he, Baxter, and others experienced and imagined it—appeared to promise. It would serve as an antidote to prosaic industrial daylight, to the militant time-clock world their fathers had made. It would serve as a way to reclaim the land through experiential connection—digging in the dirt—and to blur the painfully sharp grids and boundaries of the world from which they came.

They all had their reasons to escape that world. Bandelier trudged through the Southwest to forget a massive family bank failure back in Illinois, while Fred Chapin turned to the canyon country as respite from financial success in an inherited drugstore business. Lummis fled marital complications and fragile health in various places. In the Southwest they all sought license to imagine; they all claimed the right, as Cushing plaintively wrote in his 1882 account of the "Nation of the Willows" (Havasupai), to poetically believe:

> A fairy story is this of the Nation of the Willows; *and while science teaches us another tale, may we not poetically believe, with these simple natives,* that they have always lived here, apart from the world of nations; that ever since they wandered forth from the four fertile wombs of mother earth, this little strip of land and river and willow, and the great rock-walls, so near together, yet so sublime and

impassable, have bounded their generations of life, have had shadows cast on them by the smoke-clouds of the numberless funeral pyres of all their unnamed dead? (Emphasis added)[72]

Conclusion

Within such personal and cultural parameters, the Hemenway Southwestern Archaeological Expedition of the late 1880s contributed to the regional identity construction of the Southwest. By unearthing prehistory and ethnohistory from the Salt River Valley to northwestern New Mexico, Cushing and his colleagues focused attention on the human depth of superficially barren landscapes.[73] By demonstrating the extent and complexity of previous habitation, the expedition promised to give new cultural meaning to arid and forbidding space, linking visions of past civilizations with projections of future development. In this context, certain acts of discovery—for example, Cushing's seemingly intuitive locating of prehistoric irrigation canals—had profound resonance at the time. They seemed to suggest that the desert Southwest would again become what it had once been: a habitable place, Father Duchene's "humanized landscape." In April 1887, when Cushing's crew was busily digging at Los Muertos, the editor of the *Phoenix Daily Herald* predicted that the prospect of "pleasure, health and wealth" would "lead Phoenix on to a position that will rival the numbers of the natives whose ashes are mixed with almost every acre of our soil and ruined canals."[74] In such terms did the rhetoric of civic promotion link aboriginal culture to future growth.

Cushing had always worked to join Indian peoples, past or present, to the landscape in a mutually authenticating relationship. He taught that neither a people nor a landscape is truly understandable except in terms of the other. But his more challenging lesson was that the non-Indian settler can only establish a legitimate, meaningful relationship to this land and its history—can only truly belong in it—to the extent that he or she engages its aesthetic and mythoreligious dimensions. That is to say, the Southwest invites and demands a personal commitment beyond military conquest, political sovereignty, or legal ownership. Belonging must be dirt-deep, with the bones of the dead—Los Muertos.[75]

This was Tom Outland's lesson, and it was Thea Kronborg's revelation in

Cather's *The Song of the Lark* as well. In the stream that flows through "Panther Cañon" Thea feels "a continuity of life that reached back into the old time," and her daily bath in the water becomes "ritualistic." The restoration and new determination Cather's operatic heroine finds in the cliffdweller canyon comes from a new sense of deep connection and sustained purpose: "All these things made one feel that one ought to do one's best, and help to fulfill some desire of the dust that slept there. . . . These potsherds were like fetters that bound one to a long chain of human endeavor." Shattered and defeated on her arrival, Thea leaves the canyon country "united and strong."[76]

"Desire of the dust"—through its haze we can glimpse the intimacy between archaeology and the process of culturally defining the Southwest in the closing years of the nineteenth century and the first decades of the twentieth. By the late 1920s, the period that Walter W. Taylor once labeled the "Cushing-Fewkes Period" of southwestern archaeology was clearly over. The transition to a new sobriety and a new set of analytical tools was marked by A. V. Kidder's 1924 *Introduction to the Study of Southwestern Archaeology* and the Pecos classification he proposed three years later.[77] But just as southwestern archaeology took on new scientific rigor, the Southwest of fictive imagination adopted the romance of archaeological discovery as a central trope in exploring larger issues of national youth and aging, of America's history and purpose.[78]

In that process, what did archaeology teach? What kind of human society had grown and might arise again in this landscape? Here the lessons of Mary Hemenway's expedition promised to reach well beyond archaeology. They pointed toward a future social order, one that would resemble and to a degree resurrect the prehistoric communities then being discovered. It would be a human world premised on cooperation rather than destructive competition, mutual tolerance and interdependence rather than divisive greed, peaceful commonwealth rather than warlike imperium.[79] After all, "they weren't fighters, anyhow"—this much was known of the mysterious cliffdwellers, Tip told his boyhood chums.[80] And those boys had all promised that whoever got there first would "tell the rest of us exactly what he finds." It was a fraternal bond Cushing and Baxter would certainly have understood and—having gotten there first—one they tried to honor.

Notes

Introduction to the Multivolume Work

1. Obituary of Mary Tileston Hemenway, *Boston Transcript,* 10 March 1894.

2. Fewkes's career as director of the "Second" Hemenway Expedition is the subject of Edwin L. Wade and Lea S. McChesney's *America's Great Lost Expedition: The Thomas Keam Collection of Hopi Pottery from the Second Hemenway Expedition, 1890–1894.*

3. Emil W. Haury, *The Excavations of Los Muertos and Neighboring Ruins in the Salt River Valley, Southern Arizona.*

4. Hodge to Haury, 5 October 1931, Frederick Webb Hodge Collection, Southwest Museum, Los Angeles (hereafter FWHC), no. 138.

5. Foreword to Haury, *Excavations,* vii–ix.

6. Handwritten notes from Hodge to Haury, 30 March 1934, X-file 94-36, H-2, Peabody Museum Archives.

7. Ira Jacknis, "The Stewart Culin Papers," MS, Brooklyn Museum.

8. Culin to Hodge, 28 February 1921, FWHC.

9. Neil Judd et al., "Frederick Webb Hodge, 1864–1956." The Southwest Museum recently completed a computerized inventory of the Hodge and Cushing Collections.

10. Raymond Stewart Brandes, "Frank Hamilton Cushing: Pioneer Americanist"; Adolph Bandelier, *The Southwest Journals of Adolph F. Bandelier, 1880–1882.*

11. Joan Mark, "Frank Hamilton Cushing and an American Science of Anthropology," 484; Green, *Zuni: Selected Writings of Frank Hamilton Cushing;* Green, *Cushing at Zuni: The Correspondence and Journals of Frank Hamilton Cushing, 1879–1884.*

12. See also Hinsley, *The Smithsonian and the American Indian;* Hinsley, "'I Command I Shall Be Believed': Cushing, the Hemenway, and Scientific Poetics"; Hinsley and Lea S. McChesney, "Anthropology as Cultural Exchange: The Shared Vision of Mary Hemenway and Frank Cushing"; McChesney, "The Vision of Mary Hemenway"; and David R. Wilcox and Charles Sternberg, *Additional Studies of the Architecture of the Casa Grande and Its Interpretation.*

13. Frederic A. Eustis, *Augustus Hemenway, 1805–1876: Builder of the United States Trade with the West Coast of South America.*

14. Cushing's personal diaries were given to Jesse Green by Anne E. Smullen, a grandniece of Cushing's wife, Emily Magill Cushing; see Green, *Cushing at Zuni,* 348.

15. Wilcox et al., *One Hundred Years of Archaeology at La Ciudad de los Hornos.*

16. The installments of Cushing's itinerary constitute the second volume of this work.

17. Wade and McChesney's exhibit catalogue, *America's Great Lost Expedition* (see note 2 above) appeared in 1980. See also Curtis Hinsley, *The Smithsonian and the American Indian;* "Ethnographic Charisma and Scientific Routine: Cushing and Fewkes in the American Southwest, 1879–1893"; "From Shell-Heaps to Stelae: Early Anthropology at the Peabody Museum"; and "Wanted: One Good Man to Discover Central American History."

18. David R. Wilcox and Jerry B. Howard, "The Contribution of the Hemenway Expedition to Hohokam Archaeology"; Wilcox et al., *One Hundred Years of Archaeology;* Wilcox, "Pueblo Grande in the Nineteenth Century."

19. See, e.g., Rina Swentzell, "Levels of Truth: Southwest Archaeologists and Anasazi/Pueblo People."

PART 1. Introduction: Boston Meets the Southwest

1. Cushing to Baxter, 5 March 1887, Frank H. Cushing Letterbooks, Huntington Free Library, Bronx, New York (hereafter FHCLB), 1:205–14.

2. Bandelier to Norton, 27 December 1889, Papers of the Archaeological Institute of America, box 4.

3. Charles Lummis, "The White Indian," 11–12.

4. Hodge to Haury, 5 October 1931, FWHC no. 138.

5. Washington Matthews, "The Cities of the Dead," 213 (editor's note).

6. Baxter, letter to the *Boston Herald,* 7 June 1925.

7. Sylvester Baxter, "Descendants of Thomas Baxter," in James Phinney Baxter, "Baxter Family: A Collection of Genealogies" (typescript). The younger Baxter himself eventually belonged to the Masonic Order, as well as to the Society of Mayflower Descendants, the Puddingstone Club, the New England Poetry Club, and the Boston Authors' Club; obituary of Sylvester Baxter, *Boston Herald,* 29 January 1927.

8. Yarmouth Vital Records, Sturgis Library, Sturgis, Massachusetts; Sylvester Baxter, "A Reporter's Memories of Boston's Great Fire"; Baxter, "Descendants."

9. Yarmouth Vital Records, Sturgis Library. The name of Rosella's mother, Ford's first wife, is not recorded.

10. "Honors 100th Birthday of Mother, Now Dead," *Boston Herald,* 29 January 1915.

11. Baxter, Last Will and Testament, para. 11, Middlesex County Courthouse, Cambridge, Massachusetts.

12. Sylvester Baxter, "Descendants of Thomas Baxter," in James Phinney Baxter, "Baxter Family," 94–95.

13. Baxter, "A Reporter's Memories."

14. Lewis Mumford, *The Brown Decades: A Study of the Arts in America, 1865–1895,* 2. "The laval flow of industrialism after the war had swept over all the cities of the spirit, leaving here and there only an ashen ruin, standing erect in the crumbled landscape" (p. 23). Following Henry Adams, George Santayana had set the tone of this interpretation in 1921, calling New England's intellectual products of the late nineteenth century a mere "harvest of leaves" (quoted in Edward Lurie, *Nature and the American Mind: Louis Agassiz and the Culture of Science,* 18–19). In his influential literary history, *New England: Indian Summer, 1865–1915,* Van Wyck Brooks further elaborated Santayana's notion of a loss of passion and consequence in New England's intellectual life, a failure to grapple directly with social change.

15. Edwin D. Mead, *Boston Memories of Fifty Years,* 11.

16. Edward Page Mitchell, *Memoirs of an Editor: Fifty Years of American Journalism,* 78–79.

17. Baxter, "Baxter Family," 96. On the importance of Delano Goddard and his wife, Martha LeBaron Goddard, in "this brilliant *Advertiser* group," see Mead, *Memories,* 15–16. Martha Goddard was a confidante of Mary Hemenway and a member of the board of directors of the Hemenway Expedition.

18. Van Wyck Brooks, *New England: Indian Summer,* 231.

19. Baxter, "Baxter Family," 96.

20. Mead, *Memories,* 22–24; Mead, "The Old South Work."

21. Baxter, "Baxter Family," 96.

22. Baxter, "A Plea for Mercy"; see also Baxter, "Mr. Baxter at Conclusion."

23. On this point, see Martin Green, *The Problem of Boston: Some Readings in Cultural History;* and Stow Persons, *The Decline of American Gentility.*

24. Lyman to Agassiz, 4 May 1873, Alexander Agassiz Papers. Lyman's tone well represents the group of Gilded Age Bostonians who saw themselves, in David Shi's terms, as a "saving remnant, imbued with an abiding sense of public duty and a presumptive sense of moral and intellectual superiority"; *The Simple Life,* 157.

25. Neil Harris, "The Gilded Age Revisited: Boston and the Museum Movement," 551.

26. Norton to Charles W. Eliot, 15 January 1874, C. W. Eliot Papers.

27. Lyman to Eliot, 8 June 1871, C. W. Eliot Papers.

28. Mead, *Memories,* 28. Hale was, according to Mead, "the incarnation of the Boston spirit," a powerful leader for whom "the United States itself was only prophecy and program for a united world, and the earth itself was but a precinct of the kingdom of heaven in the making" (p. 21). The words with which Julia Ward Howe described Mary Hemenway's and her minister, James Freeman Clarke, could as easily have applied to his close friend Hale: "His ardent temperament and sanguine disposition bred in him that natural hopefulness which is so important an element in all attempted reform. . . . There ran through the whole course of his ministrations an exquisite tone of charity and good-will" (Burton Raffel, *Politicians, Poets and Con Men,* 68).

29. Mitchell, *Memoirs,* 75.

30. J. R. Adams, *Edward Everett Hale;* J. Holloway, *Edward Everett Hale: A Biography.* See also Curtis M. Hinsley, "Zunis and Brahmins: Cultural Ambivalence in the Gilded Age."

31. H. M. Winslow, *Literary Boston of Today.*

32. On the patterns of Boston-based railroad investment after the Civil War, see Arthur M. Johnson and Barry E. Supple, *Boston Capitalists and Western Railroads: A Study in the Nineteenth-Century Railroad Investment Process,* esp. chaps. 14 and 15, on the Atchison, Topeka and Santa Fe and its subsidiaries. For contemporary representations of Mexico, see, e.g., Frederick A. Ober, *Travels in Mexico and Life among the Mexicans;* José Margati, *A Trip to the City of Mexico;* and W. H. Bishop, *Old Mexico and Her Lost Provinces: A Journey in Mexico, Southern California, and Arizona, by Way of Cuba.* All provide examples of the Mexico travel-investment prospectus genre that began to proliferate at this time and to which Baxter contributed for twenty years. An anonymous *Harper's* reviewer of Bishop's book described the Euro-American population of contemporary Mexico: "bands of prospectors, speculators in real estate, agents for the introduction of novel manufactures, venders

of new methods of ore reduction, searchers for mines, civil engineers surveying or track-laying, newspaper correspondents, scientific explorers, archaeologists, tourists . . . a foray of enterprise and industry into the heart of the indolent, fête-loving, conservative republic" (*Harper's* 52 [1883]: 833–34). For a contrasting note of caution intended for potential investors, see John Bigelow, "The Railway Invasion of Mexico."

33. E. H. Hale, "Report of the Council," in *Proceedings of the American Antiquarian Society for 1878,* 23–24, 31. See also Hale, "The Colonization of the Desert," a sermon he originally preached in 1891. In 1886 Hale rejoiced that "the railroad lines spreading over the country [of Mexico], bringing it nearer the United States, and promoting traffic, intercourse, and intelligent travelling, are helping the energetic efforts of wise and liberal statesmen of Mexico to put their country on a level with the most prosperous and civilized nations in the world." Besides, as he commented at another point in the same work, Mexico was becoming "a lovely playground for tired Americans" (*A Family Flight through Mexico,* 263, 291). Hale was giving genial expression to what Ronald E. Robinson has recently and aptly called the "imperial propensities of locomotion"—that is, the seemingly ineluctable historical connection between railroad development and imperial appetites ("the locomotive as the main engine of imperialism"); see Robinson, "Railway Imperialism," 2, 3. For the global economic and political context of foreign railroad investment in Mexico during the Porfiriato and its connection to the domestic reform visions of President Porfirio Díaz and the Científicos, see William E. French, "In the Path of Progress: Railroads and Moral Reform in Porfirian Mexico."

34. Baxter, "Baxter Family," 96–97. Baxter's fictional account of a journey by rail from Boston to Mexico City, *The Cruise of a Land-Yacht,* makes frequent reference to this and Baxter's subsequent visits of the early 1880s through Baxter's self-character, Eliot Sampson.

35. Elizabeth de Veer, *Sunlight and Shadow: The Life and Art of Willard Leroy Metcalf,* 23. Baxter's review of the new edition of *Leaves of Grass* appeared in the *Boston Herald* on 30 October 1881 under the name "Sylvan." Whitman found it "live" and "affectionate" (Whitman, *Walt Whitman: Notebooks and Unpublished Prose Manuscripts,* 3:1133). In Whitman's last years, after he returned to Camden, New Jersey, Baxter was instrumental in raising funds to support the aging poet and build him a home (funds that Whitman expended for other purposes); see Justin Kaplan, *Walt Whitman: A Life,* 25. For a touching tribute, see Baxter, "Walt Whitman in Boston": "Walt Whitman, in his journeyings, wove himself pretty thoroughly into the texture of the land that formed the grand theme of his verse" (p. 5). Baxter recalled vividly his first contact with Whitman: "His hand, which was rather small,

but relieved from any effect of daintiness by an unusual hairiness, had a warm, magnetic touch, like that of a man of strong physical nature. . . . [His attire] clothed Walt Whitman as a tree is clothed by its bark, or an animal by its fur" (pp. 6–7).

36. Frederick Ober, who traveled widely and wrote voluminously and enthusiastically of Mexico in this period, described the *Mexican Financier* as "a weekly bilingual journal, founded by a New York gentleman, and conducted by young Boston journalists of great promise and ability" (*Travels in Mexico,* 304).

37. The full title of the journal was *Outing and the Wheelman: An Illustrated Monthly of Recreation*. It moved to New York in 1886. Baxter's article "A Winter in Sonora" appeared in the March 1885 issue.

38. F. H. Cushing, "Preliminary Notes on the Origin, Working Hypothesis and Primary Researches of the Hemenway Southwestern Archaeological Expedition." Morse and Baxter were the first Americans to attend a meeting of the Congress of Americanists in Europe (ibid., 194). They did not actually present Cushing's paper, since it was not prepared in time for the conference; instead, Baxter presented a copy of his pamphlet *The Old New World*.

Edward Sylvester Morse (1838–1925), a student of Louis Agassiz and an internationally recognized expert on brachiopods, was (with his protégé Ernest F. Fenollosa and close friend William Sturgis Bigelow) instrumental in introducing Japanese art and culture to the United States. For years he directed the Peabody Museum of Salem (now the Peabody/Essex Museum)—it was, in effect, his private museum. His priceless collection of Japanese potteries came to the Boston Museum of Fine Arts in 1890 (*Dictionary of American Biography,* 7:242–43). See Dorothy Godfrey Wayman, *Edward Sylvester Morse: A Biography;* Morse's autobiographical *Japan Day by Day;* and Money Hickman and Peter Fetchko, *Japan Day by Day: An Exhibition in Honor of Edward Sylvester Morse*.

39. Baxter, "Baxter Family," 98–99.

40. Mumford, *The Brown Decades,* 22–23 (including the quoted passage from Bellamy). For a useful comparison of late-nineteenth-century utopian schemes, see John L. Thomas, "Utopia for an Urban Age: Henry George, Henry Demarest Lloyd, Edward Bellamy."

41. Baxter's letters to Bellamy from 1889 to 1897 were in fact somewhat sychophantic (Bellamy Papers, Houghton Library, Harvard). Bellamy's ideas were considered dangerously radical by the "proper folk" of Boston (Mead, *Memories,* 28). To his friend Walt Whitman, Baxter earnestly recommended Bellamy's book as "a noble work, and delightful as well. It has made a profound impression and will do much towards realizing a grander future for our land" (Whitman, *Walt Whitman: The Correspondence,* 4:256). According to his most recent biographer, Whitman was not impressed with either Bellamy's treatise or Baxter's political radicalism:

"'[Baxter] is very radical-progressive, he is enthusiastic over Bellamy's book. . . . But no—no—no—we are not going to be reformed in this way, by parcels—not by Henry Georgian Socialism, anarchism, Schools—any one agency'" (David S. Reynolds, *Walt Whitman's America: A Cultural Biography,* 559).

42. Whitman to Horace Traubel, 24 August 1888, as quoted in Traubel, *With Walt Whitman in Camden,* 2:192. "He is one of my cordial, truest friends—an out and out assenter to the Leaves [of Grass]: radical, progressive, with lots of look ahead" (8 May 1888, 1:121). In their conversations, Traubel recorded several descriptions of Baxter by Whitman, who was struck by Baxter's Germanic, professorial look. During his years in Europe, Whitman observed, Baxter had "got greatly Germanized" (5 January 1889, 3:464).

43. On Olmsted's career in Boston, see Cynthia Zaitzevsky, *Frederick Law Olmsted and the Boston Park System.* She outlines Baxter's central role in the development of the park system on pp. 122–23. On Olmsted's landscape architecture as social reform, see Geoffrey Blodgett, "Frederick Law Olmsted: Landscape Architecture as Conservative Reform"; C. B. Sutton, "Frederick Law Olmsted, 1822–1903"; Roger Starr, "The Motive Behind Olmsted's Park"; and Paul S. Boyer, *Urban Masses and American Moral Order.*

44. Mumford, *The Brown Decades,* 27. For wider perspectives on Baxter's years in the movement for civic improvement, see John W. Reps, *The Making of Urban America: A History of City Planning in the United States;* M. Christine Boyer, *Dreaming the Rational City: The Myth of American City Planning;* and William H. Wilson, *The City Beautiful Movement.* For comparative metropolitan studies, see Francis G. Couvares, *The Remaking of Pittsburgh: Class and Culture in an Industrializing City, 1877–1919;* Sam Bass Warner, *Streetcar Suburbs: The Process of Growth in Boston, 1870–1900;* and Stanley Schultz and Clay McShane, "To Engineer the Metropolis: Sewers, Sanitation, and City Planning in Late Nineteenth Century America."

45. See, e.g., Baxter, "How the Bills of Socialism Will Be Paid"; "The Beautifying of Village and Town"; "Art in Public Places: Aqueducts, Water-Towers, Power-Houses, Reservoirs, Bridges"; "The Metropolitan Park System"; (with William H. Downes), "Greater Boston"; and "Hotel Cluny of a New England Village."

46. "In Memoriam: Lucia Allen Millet Baxter, January 1, 1917, Homeward Laden."

47. Baxter seems never to have made the transition from journalist to man of letters that he, like many others who began in post–Civil War newspaper work, so desired. The line between them was never clearly drawn, but it was nonetheless real. On this point, Van Wyck Brooks explains William Dean Howells' attitude toward

newspapermen as they had emerged by the turn of the century: "Like Henry James and Henry Adams, he detested these glib young journalists who represented the new publicity. As an old newspaperman, he disliked to see this new type pushing aside the journalist with a feeling for letters" (*New England: Indian Summer,* 217). For a telling instance of Baxter's marginality in this respect—despite his obvious "feel for letters"—see the local flap of 1895, in which he was centrally involved, regarding Edward Eggleston, Howells, and Robert Louis Stevenson, as recounted in Howells, *Selected Letters,* 4:96–97. It is perhaps indicative, too, that in his study of Howells' literary career, *Howells: His Life and World,* Brooks does not mention Baxter.

48. Baxter, "The New B. and M." His "Cutting Cape Cod" was a curious combination of a history of the Cape and a celebration of canal technology.

49. See Baxter, *Spanish-Colonial Architecture in Mexico.*

50. Ibid., 1:4–5, 20; cf. *The Old New World* (this vol.). There is rich irony in Baxter's romantic conjuring of a pre-industrial Mexican workforce at the very time that President Profirio Díaz and his elite group of Científicos were attempting to parley foreign railroad and mineral investment into the development of a "peaceful, hard-working, and suitably motivated" industrial labor force (William E. French, "In the Path of Progress: Railroads and Moral Reform in Porfirian Mexico," 94).

51. Baxter, *Spanish-Colonial Architecture in Mexico,* 1:28.

52. He did return to Mexico, passionately, in his memories and his poetry. In "Blue Waters," published posthumously, he wrote movingly of "those days of young manhood, days steeped in sunlight" in Mexico, and of the connectedness of words, music, and landscape: "the music of Spanish speech weaves itself throughout the scenes I knew: music as from brooks unseen in a woodland—rivulets of words in a golden flow, words whose very sounds convey the essence of their sense; sonorous words, meltingly rounded and melody bearing" (*The Tree and the Ring,* 59–62).

53. Raymond Stewart Brandes, "Frank Hamilton Cushing: Pioneer Americanist." Brandes states that there is confusion about the number of Cushing's sisters (p. 4).

54. E. Anthony Rotundo, *American Manhood: Transformations in Masculinity from the Revolution to the Modern Era,* 90. The discussion here is particularly indebted to chapter 4, "Youth and Male Intimacy," but Rotundo's analysis of the generation born between 1840 and 1860 (the generation of Cushing and Baxter) and the emergence of "feminine" tendencies in the last decades of the century is remarkable (see pp. 264ff.).

55. *Tenatsali* means medicine flower. In "An Aboriginal Pilgrimage," (p. 533) Baxter tells of receiving his name, Thli a kwa (blue medicine stone, or turquoise), on the 1882 trip of the Zuñi chiefs to Boston. Zuñi ethnographer Edmund Ladd, in "Cushing among the Zuñi: A Zuñi Perspective", suggests that Cushing's name

came from an ear-piercing ceremony, not from initiation; that Cushing designed the "Zuñi" symbol for his name "in a very un-Zuñi-like fashion"; and that no one actually knows the symbol for his name (p. 31).

56. Cushing to Baxter, 30 November 1886, FHCLB, 1:14; Cushing to Baxter, 29 January 1887 FHCLB, 1:48.

57. Rotundo, *American Manhood,* 187.

58. Cushing once wrote: "Thank you, my dear boy, for your often-repeated and kind letters. They are rest to me when I am weary, and good to me when I am hungered or athirst" (Cushing to Baxter, 10 January 1887, FHCLB, 1:113).

59. Cushing to Baxter, 23 March 1894, FHCLB.

60. See, e.g., Baxter to Morse, 26 October 1895, Edward S. Morse Collection, Phillips Library, Peabody/Essex Museum, Salem, Massachusetts (hereafter ESMC), 828; Baxter to Cushing, 6 and 7 June 1891, Frank Hamilton Cushing Collection, Southwest Museum, Los Angeles (hereafter FHCC), MS 6, 97; Baxter to Cushing, 19 March 1894, FHCC, MS 6, 101. Bandelier concurred in the negative judgment of Fewkes and also re-established his friendship with Cushing in the nineties partly on this basis. See Paul Radin, ed., *The Unpublished Letters of Adolphe F. Bandelier,* 30.

61. Baxter to Morse, 19 June 1923, ESMC, 846.

62. As cited in Cushing, *Cushing at Zuñi,* 155. Baxter provided the song in full in "Solved at Last" (this vol.). Cushing offered a somewhat different rendition and translation a few years later in "How He Learned to Hunt," pt. 14 of "Zuñi Breadstuff."

63. Baxter, "Solved at Last."

64. Ibid.

65. In his insightful study *American Technological Sublime,* David E. Nye concludes: "For nineteenth-century Americans . . . the rugged western landscape and the transcontinental railroad were complementary forms of the sublime that dramatized an unfolding national destiny" (p. 76). But it was not always so. The first generation of transcontinental rail passengers could suffer a sense of deflation. Almon Gunnison, recording his 1883 travels, apologized that "in most aggravating security we make our journey, and return home in a state of mortifying safety" (*Rambles Overland: A Trip across the Continent,* 229). Twenty years later, the Englishman Richard Townshend, revisiting scenes of his youth, saw through his touring car (unlike Baxter) only a human landscape at risk: "How much longer can they last? For our devouring civilization presses hard upon their heels. Looking back from the Painted Desert beyond the green ribbon of the Little Colorado far on the horizon, I saw a dark streak that lay across the sky, and I knew it for the smoke of a passing train upon the line of the Atchison, Topeka, and Santa Fé Railway. The iron monster has gotten as far as the edge of the Painted Desert and the Grand

Cañon, though he has not yet invaded their recesses; but he brings you to the very borders of the Navajo country, and as you look out from the windows of your Pullman car you see particoloured flocks of spotted sheep grazing, and, beside them, standing in the sage brush, the picturesque figures of their nomad shepherds" (*Last Memories of a Tenderfoot,* 196–97).

66. For a fine discussion of the frequency and symbolic functions of such figures, and their biblical referents, in early representations of the American Southwest, see Barbara A. Babcock, "'A New Mexican Rebecca': Imaging Pueblo Women," and Babcock, "Bearers of Value, Vessels of Desire: The Reproduction of the Reproduction of Pueblo Culture."

67. "Along the Rio Grande," 687–88. Culinary improvement as a measure of civilization is a striking trope in early southwestern literature. Indeed, matters of food are obsessively discussed. John G. Bourke, in his *Snake-Dance of the Moquis* (1884), remarks frequently on filth, foul odors, and noxious food. "The sight of a neatly-arranged supper or dinner" seemed to him "a gratifying demonstration of the rapid approach of railroad connections, of increasing wealth and commerce, and consequent refinement of manners and sentiment." Bourke considered a well-laid table and a well-stocked larder "the best index" of civilized progress (p. 89). For an hilarious account of cooking at Camp Hemenway, see Baxter's "Archaeological Camping in Arizona—III" (this vol.).

68. "Along the Rio Grande," 691–93.

69. The discussion here draws on Barbara Kirshenblatt-Gimblett, "Objects of Ethnography," especially her employment of the work of John MacAloon and Dean MacCannell (pp. 406–16).

70. In his striking book *The Railway Journey: The Industrialization of Time and Space in the Nineteenth Century,* Wolfgang Schivelbusch demonstrates the many ways in which this new technology of transportation altered temporal and spatial consciousness. The railroad, ubiquitous and inescapable, emerges as an axial element in Baxter's southwestern landscapes: trestles, bridges, Pullman cars, and stations all serve as vantage points and markers, bounding and incessantly redefining through their rapid appearance the deserts and mountains of the region. For example, in the following passage from a report for the *Boston Herald* of 17 July 1881, not only the spatial vistas but also the temporal rhythms of the day (sunset, sleep, sunrise) appear as the functions and terms of railway travel—the literary imposition of industrial over natural time: "The approach to El Paso over the new branch of the Atchison, Topeka & Santa Fe from Rincon, in New Mexico, is full of picturesque interest. In these midsummer days night has quite fully fallen by the time the train has reached Albuquerque, and, when we are awakened from our comfortable sleep in the Pullman to change cars for El Paso, the dawn is just glimmering over the eastern

mountains. As we stand on the platform at Rincon junction waiting for our train to come up, the night air is laden with a strange herbish odor like witch hazel mingled with a suggestion of peppermint and sage."

71. Baxter, "Father of the Pueblos," 78–79.

72. Ibid., 79–80. After Cushing's return to the pueblo in the fall of 1882 with his wife, Emily, her sister Margaret Whitehead Magill, and a personal cook, the Cushing household at Zuñi received further attention as an interior of Victorian domesticity and exotica. See, e.g., William E. Curtis's description in his 1883 popularization of Cushing's life at Zuñi, *Children of the Sun,* which concludes: "The Cushing residence is a dirty mud hut without, but within a bower of beauty" (p. 42). For Baxter's appreciative description on his return in late 1882, see "Zuñi Revisited" (this vol.).

73. Karen Halttunen, "From Parlor to Living Room: Domestic Space, Interior Decoration, and the Culture of Personality," 164–65.

74. Molly Lee, "Appropriating the Primitive: Turn-of-the-Century Collection and Display of Native Alaskan Art," 12.

75. Quoted in Lee, "Appropriating the Primitive," 12.

76. E. Anthony Rotundo, *American Manhood,* 262–63; Margaret Marsh, "Suburban Men and Masculine Domesticity, 1870–1915."

77. On the freedom offered by a state of nature, Baxter wrote: "Nature, though impassive, and unresponsive and overwhelmingly vast, suggests an unrestrained freedom to her children in a spaciousness where they can be themselves if they will, with the gladness that is born of ample room for the feet to rove and the thoughts to roam" ("Archaeological Camping—IV," this vol.).

78. See Mark C. Carnes, *Secret Ritual and Manhood in Victorian America.* Cushing and Baxter were hardly alone in comparing ancient orders with contemporary fraternal organizations. Augustus Le Plongeon, for example, argued that there were direct historical connections between the Mayan world and Freemasonry. See Lawrence G. Desmond and Phyllis M. Messenger, *A Dream of Maya: Augustus and Alice Le Plongeon in Nineteenth-Century Yucatan.*

79. T. J. Jackson Lears, *No Place of Grace: Antimodernism and the Transformation of American Culture, 1880–1920.* Paula Blanchard's enlightening biography *Sarah Orne Jewett: Her World and Her Work* argues strongly for the widespread post–Civil War sensibility of Emersonian connectedness between past and present, human and natural, and its rupture by the dislocations of industrial life. Casey Nelson Blake suggests, in *Beloved Community,* that the quest by some cultural critics of late Victorian America for meaning in what they experienced as a decaying bourgeois culture of vacuous women and absent or mercenary men led to visions of "a return to the mother, of merging souls, of mystical unity with the physical environment

and ultimately the cosmos, and of the dissolution of the self into a loving community of friends" (p. 24). While Baxter hardly viewed his culture with such a critical eye, as suggested elsewhere he did evince a desire to find a meaning beneath or beyond the quotidian.

80. Baxter, "The Tenacity of Indian Customs."

81. Among students of the Navajos, the equivalent locus was the medicine lodge: "Got into the medicine-lodge and saw things I never dreamt of," Matthews reported excitedly and proudly to Cushing in 1884 (quoted in Hinsley, *The Smithsonian and the American Indian,* 199). The prototype experience and description, however, was John Wesley Powell's *The Hopi Villages: The Ancient Province of Tusayan,* which first appeared in *Scribner's Monthly* in 1875.

82. In 1883, Willard Metcalf wrote to Cushing after their memorable trip to Oraibi: "My life shall be to follow those teachings that you so generously set forth to me in our quiet talks snowed up in Moqui [Hopi]—those talks which have become as sacred to me as the rituals of the Zunis" (FHCC, 368, as quoted in Green, *Cushing at Zuni,* 403).

83. In the history of southwestern anthropology, the role of campfire intimacy and associated rituals of initiation and knowledge exchange in the form of, for example, stories and anecdotes has yet to be examined by scholars. On the creation of "little circles" of intimacy during the Cushing and Zuñi visit to the East in 1882, see Hinsley, "Zunis and Brahmins," 180–88.

84. Mary Dewey, "Visit of the Zuni Indians to the Summer House of Mrs. Mary Hemenway in 1886."

85. Baxter, "Archaeological Camping in Arizona—III" (this vol.).

86. The phrase is borrowed from critic John Lahr, *The New Yorker,* 14 November 1994, p. 124.

87. Ann Douglas, *The Feminization of American Culture,* 12–13.

88. Baxter's strategy of resolution was not universally shared, however, even by those on the Hemenway Expedition. Herman F. C. ten Kate, the world-traveling physical anthropologist who served with Cushing on the expedition, could not make a similar accommodation with the changes in the Southwest he knew in the 1880s. After traversing much of the globe, he returned in 1906 for one last look, from Tempe Butte, at the scene he recalled so fondly:

> At the foot of the hill lies the Salado [River], dusty as ever, and the little town [Tempe], now remarkably larger, changed beyond recognition. Around me, solitude and silence. Only the rustling of the bushes and a roadrunner searching for food.
>
> I look far and wide across the land. That has also changed beyond recognition, except for the mountains. The white man has turned the sandy desert plain into green

fields, many with alfalfa, and orchards with orange trees. A new life has developed on the ruins of the gray past. In the distance I search for the location where Los Muertos, the City of the Dead, was situated and where we were camped, but I only see an ocean of green. . . .

Dusk falls and forces me to leave the hilltop. I wished I was able to flee the present and to roam solitarily in the silence of the old City of the Dead. (Herman F. C. ten Kate, diary entry for 31 March 1906; from ten Kate, *Over Land en Zee: Schetsen en Stemmingen van een Wereldreisiger,* translation courtesy of Pieter Hovens)

PART II. Visiting and Revisiting Zuñi, 1881–1883

1. See Green, *Cushing at Zuni,* introduction and first three chapters; and Hinsley, *The Smithsonian and the American Indian,* 195–96.

2. E. E. Hale to Emily Hale, 24 March 1882, Hale Papers, New York State Historical Society, Albany.

3. Although the irony escaped notice two hundred years later, Deer Island had been the site of imprisonment in the fall of 1675 for the Christian ("praying") Indians of Massachusetts during King Philip's War. They were released the following spring. See Patrick M. Malone, *The Skulking Way of War: Technology and Tactics among the New England Indians,* 85–87.

4. For a fuller interpretive account of this trip, see Hinsley, "Zunis and Brahmins: Cultural Ambivalence in the Gilded Age."

5. Baxter, "Father of the Pueblos," 81. According to Mary Louise Pratt, "First, and most obvious, the landscape is estheticized. The sight is seen as a painting and the description is ordered in terms of background, foreground, . . . and so forth. . . . It is important to note that within the text's own terms the esthetic *pleasure* of the sight singlehandedly constitutes the value and significance of the journey" (Pratt, *Imperial Eyes: Travel Writing and Transculturation,* 204).

6. Jesse Green demonstrates that Cushing had begun seriously studying the Seven Cities question in the second half of 1880; Green, *Cushing at Zuni,* chap. 3.

7. Regarding the "Logan affair," see Jesse Green's review in Green, *Cushing at Zuni,* 261ff. Justus D. Doenecke, *The Presidencies of James A. Garfield & Chester A. Arthur,* 13. Baxter's exposure of "corruption" in Indian affairs was typical of the Mugwump reformers of his day; see, e.g., his "Indian Questions: Some More Facts about Agency Corruptions," written for the *Boston Herald* when he had been in the Southwest less than a month (26 June 1881).

8. *New Mexican Review* (Albuquerque), 18 July 1883.

9. Baxter had returned only three years previously from Germany, where he had attended performances of Richard Wagner's operatic works. More generally,

Baxter's initial attempts to portray western America in the familiar aesthetic terms of European travel conformed to a common pattern. See Anne Farrar Hyde, *An American Vision: Far Western Landscape and National Culture, 1820–1920,* esp. chaps. 3 and 4.

10. General Luther P. Bradley, commandant of Fort Wingate.

11. Dr. Washington Matthews (1843–1905) became a lifelong friend of Cushing (Hinsley, *The Smithsonian Institution and the American Indian,* 197–99, 210). He was the chief author (along with Jacob Wortman and John S. Billings) of the first monograph from the Hemenway Expedition: "Human Bones in the Hemenway Collection in the U. S. Army Medical Museum." See Robert M. Poor, "Washington Matthews: An Intellectual Biography."

12. One of Cushing's closest friends, John G. Bourke, also published extensively on southwestern ethnography, notably on the Hopi Snake Dance (1884); see Joseph C. Porter, *Paper Medicine Man: John Gregory Bourke and His American West.*

13. General George Crook had arrived in the Southwest in 1871 as a veteran of wars against Native Americans in Oregon, Idaho, and California. During the 1870s he pursued a relentless campaign against the Apache peoples.

14. The people of Taos pueblo speak northern Tiwa, and the Isletans speak southern Tiwa; see Edward H. Spicer, *Cycles of Conquest.*

15. On Zuñi language and culture, see Dorothea C. Leighton and John Adair, *People of the Middle Place;* Dennis Tedlock, trans., *Finding the Center: Narrative Poetry of the Zuni Indians;* and Ruth Bunzel, *Zuni Ceremonialism.*

16. On the extent of Zuñi territory, see T. J. Ferguson and E. Richard Hart, *A Zuni Atlas.*

17. Both Bandelier (in his "Outline of the Documentary History of the Zuni Tribe" [1892]) and Hodge (in "The Six Cities of Cibola in 1581–1680" [1926]) extensively discuss the identification of the Seven Cities of Cibola. For a modern discussion, see Keith W. Kintigh, *Settlement, Subsistence and Society in Late Zuni Prehistory.*

18. For a recent discussion of where Estevan was killed at Zuñi, see Madeline Turrell Rodack, "Cibola Revisited."

19. Spencer Fullerton Baird, assistant secretary (1850–1878) and secretary (1878–1887) of the Smithsonian Institution, first hired Cushing in 1875 and remained his mentor for many years; see Edward F. Rivinus and Elizabeth M. Youssef, *Spencer Baird of the Smithsonian.*

20. For the results of this trip, see Cushing, "The Nation of the Willows."

21. As the problem of deciphering the Mayan inscriptions emerged in the late nineteenth century, acquiring a linguistic and ethnographic base through fieldwork among living Maya was frequently urged as the necessary approach to Mayan

epigraphy. The assumptions expressed here by Cushing guided the training of Alfred Tozzer and Sylvanus G. Morley at Harvard after the turn of the century. See Hinsley, "Wanted: One Good Man to Discover Central American History."

22. For the Bow Priesthood, or cult of the Gods of War ('a pi'la 'a siwani), see Edmund Ladd, "Zuni Social and Political Organization," 485.

23. As far as we can determine, this story, a central part of Cushing's explanation of the origin of the Zuñi quest for ocean water, has not been substantiated. However, about two hundred years previously, in 1680, the Pueblo Revolt forced the Spaniards to withdraw temporarily from New Mexico, taking various Pueblo people with them. Thus there is some plausibility to the tale.

24. Neither Baxter nor Cushing was consistent at this point on the Aztec-Toltec distinction, but they were hardly alone in their confusion. On the origin and persistence of the "ancient Toltecs" in nineteenth-century visions of New World prehistory, see Robert Silverberg, *Moundbuilders of Ancient America: The Archaeology of a Myth,* 156–57. According to some accounts, these predecessors of the Aztecs had an empire that stretched from Mexico up through the Mississippi Valley. However, by the 1880s the century-old notion of a separate, mysterious "Moundbuilder race" was under direct attack by the Bureau of Ethnology's Mounds Survey (begun in 1882). Cyrus Thomas directed the survey for a decade and in 1894 wrote its compendious final report, which authoritatively pronounced historical links between living tribes and makers of the North American mounds.

25. John Wesley Powell, *Introduction to the Study of Indian Languages with Words, Phrases and Sentences to be Collected.*

26. Grant Allen (1848–1899), was an English author who wrote on the history of art and the psychology of aesthetics. He was also a novelist and a biographer of Darwin. Oskar Ferdinand Peschel (1826–1875), was the author of *The Races of Man, and Their Geographical Distribution.* On Powell's low opinion of Spencer, see Hinsley, *The Smithsonian and the American Indian,* 126–33.

27. The Cushing-Putnam collaboration never took place. The hemispheric unity of New World aboriginal peoples was a recurrent idea in nineteenth-century anthropology, especially in the first half of the century; but it was championed as well by Daniel G. Brinton, for example. Cushing returned to the idea during the Hemenway Expedition, arguing mistakenly that he had found figurines of guanacos in his excavations.

28. This mountain was also called Corn Mountain. See T. J. Ferguson's unpublished dissertation (1993) for its occupation by the Zuñi during the period of the Pueblo Revolt.

29. Powell, "Sketch of the Mythology of the North American Indians."

30. See Cushing, "Oraibi in 1883"; and Cushing, "Monthly Report for December

1882 and January 1883" and "Annual Report on Field Work for Year Ending June 30, 1883." For a summary of the trip, see Green, *Cushing at Zuni,* 255–60.

31. Emily Magill Cushing and her sister, Margaret Whitehead Magill, were inseparable until October 1888, when Cushing and Emily went east but Margaret stayed with her fiancé, Fred Hodge, at Zuñi.

32. Douglas D. Graham opened a trading store south of Zuñi pueblo in 1879 and served in various federal government capacities in the region over the next twenty years.

33. James H. Willson arrived in Zuñi in October 1882 and stayed about six years; Green, *Cushing at Zuni,* 402 n.25.

34. Cushing's older brother, Enos, a dentist in Albion, New York, was visiting Zuñi with his wife.

35. The family cook's name was Abram. Hodge recalled, many years later, that the Zuñis, who had rarely if ever seen a black man, were so curious about Abram and his cooking that "they used to gather around the kitchen door, and made it so dark in there that poor Abram could hardly see to do anything" (from a transcription of the tape recording "Frederick Webb Hodge's Anecdotes and Reminiscences," made on 9 September 1955 in Santa Fe, New Mexico, p. 10; in author's possession, courtesy of Genevieve Pease).

36. Cf. Baxter's 1881 description of Cushing's Zuñi room in "Solved at Last" (this vol.). William E. Curtis, in *Children of the Sun* (1883) and Herman ten Kate, in his memoirs published in 1925, also described warmly the tasteful mixture of southwestern and Oriental aesthetics in the Cushings' Zuñi home.

37. Baxter and his friend arrived during the season of the Shalako ceremony.

38. Baxter, "Father of the Pueblos" (this vol.).

PART III. Reporting from Camp Hemenway, 1888–1889

1. *Dictionary of America Biography,* 5:236–37. The 1880s saw renewed interest, in some New England circles, in the supposed landing of the Norseman Leif Ericson in North America prior to Columbus; see, e.g., Thomas Wentworth Higginson's 1882 article "The Visit of the Vikings." Eben Horsford was especially active in this movement—to the gentle amusement of his friends. Edward Everett Hale, commenting in 1886 on the depth of southwestern history, played with Horsford's obsession: "You have to turn an old windmill at Newport into a Norseman's watchtower, if you want to have anything legendary at hand [in New England], while you had all the time waiting for you here [in Arizona Territory] an architecture and a civilization primeval as far as you know, and certainly individual and national" (Hale, *A Family Flight through Mexico,* 273).

2. Cushing to Powell, 31 October 1885, Smithsonian Instituion Archives, 4024-C.

3. Cushing to Powell, 16 November 1885, Smithsonian Instituion Archives, 4024-C.

4. Cushing to Harris, n.d., but probably postscript to letter of 26 June 1891, FHCC, MS 6, no. 116.

5. The Hemenway estate was named in honor of the popular romantic novel *Ramona* (1884), by Helen Hunt Jackson, which concerned the plight of the mission Indians of California and encroachment on their lands.

6. Mary E. Dewey, "Visit of the Zuni Indians to the Summer House of Mrs. Mary Hemenway in 1886," Peabody Museum Archives, Peabody Museum of Archaeology and Ethnology, Harvard University, Acc. 980-2. The amanuensis referred to was Rufus B. Leighton, who served for a time as an accountant for the expedition and briefly as Cushing's stenographer.

7. William Torrey Harris (1835–1909)—educator, author, philosopher, and first U.S. commissioner of education (1889–1906)—was the leader of the St. Louis Hegelians and the superintendent of schools in St. Louis from 1868 to 1880; see William H. Goetzmann, ed., *The St. Louis Hegelians*. In 1880 he helped to found the Concord (Massachusetts) School of Philosophy, and through these activities he came to the attention of Mary Hemenway. He became her trusted adviser on issues of educational reform, in which she took a deep interest. On Martha LeBaron Goddard, see Edwin D. Mead, "Boston Memories of Fifty Years." Mead notes that Harriet Preston's popular novel *Love in the Nineteenth Century* was based on the courtship and marriage of the Goddards (p. 15).

8. Dr. Jacob L. Wortman, a comparative anatomist and colleague of Washington Matthews in the Army Medical Museum in Washington, had been associated with paleontologist Edward Drinker Cope for many years. At the suggestion of Matthews, Dr. John Shaw Billings, the director of the museum, assigned him to the Hemenway Expedition for six months. He arrived at Camp Hemenway on 25 November 1887 and departed on 10 May 1888. Though there was some confusion about his instructions, during most of that period he served as an assistant to Herman ten Kate in the field. He later contributed to two publications concerning excavated skeletal material.

9. Baxter to Mary Hemenway, 21 February 1888. FHCLB, 3:333–36. Ray Brandes, one of the first to notice Baxter's importance to the emergence of the archaeological Southwest, justifiably called Baxter's report "priceless"; Brandes, "Archaeological Awareness of the Southwest," 23.

10. Ten Kate's father, H.F.C. ten Kate, Sr. (1822–1891), generously supported his son's travel and scientific work. On ten Kate's career in anthropology, see Pieter Hovens, *Herman F. C. ten Kate, Jr. (1858–1931) en de Antropologie der Noord-*

Amerikaanse Indianen; and Hovens, *Odagot: Photographs of American Indians (1860–1920),* 7–15.

11. The "irresponsible journalist" theme ran throughout Cushing's career, as Green, *Cushing at Zuñi,* amply illustrates. Cushing's stance was disingenuous, to say the least, since he also relied on journalists (notably Baxter) to spread his reputation. In the face of negative reactions, he could disavow responsibility for false or exagerrated claims. Archaeologists of the period generally shied away from on-site publicity for fear of attracting competitors or looters to their sites, or simply to avoid arousing local opposition to the removal of artifacts.

12. Powell, "The Ancient Province of Tusayan." Population estimates by archaeologists today are much smaller. At Los Muertos, for example, with 35 "blocks" (now called compounds) Wilcox estimates 20 people per compound, or a total of about 700 (assuming absolute contemporaneity of the compounds). Pueblo Grande may have had as many as 1,500 people. The total population of the 40 or more "platform mound" communities in the "Phoenix Basin" (comprising the lower Salt [Salado] and middle Gila Rivers) is estimated at about 24,000; see Wilcox, "Hohokam Social Complexity." The recent demonstration that there were numerous settlements lacking platform mounds in the Phoenix Basin during the same period would raise this estimate somewhat; David A. Gregory and Gary Huckleberry, *An Archaeological Survey of the Blackwater Area,* vol. 1: *The History of Human Settlement in the Blackwater Area.* Other archaeologists estimate fewer people; William H. Doelle, Douglas B. Craig, and Henry D. Wallace, "Measuring Prehistoric Demographic Trends." These settlements were not "cities," as Cushing inferred.

13. For a modern discussion of Hohokam irrigation, see Jerry B. Howard, "A Paleohydraulic Approach to Examining Agricultural Intensification in Hohokam Irrigation Systems." The story of the Mormons restoring Hohokam canals is also told by Omar Turney in *Prehistoric Irrigation in Arizona.*

14. Turney shows this feature on his map of the irrigation systems of the Salt River Valley; see *Prehistoric Irrigation in Arizona.*

15. Bandelier, *Final Report of Investigations among the Indians of the Southwestern United States,* pt. 2.

16. Recent studies of petroglyphs in the Picacho Mountains, south of the Phoenix Basin, found that two earthquakes had disturbed them: (1) the great Sonoran earthquake of 1887, and (2) an earlier one that may date to the Classic period of the Hohokam sequence, or about the time Cushing postulated that an earthquake destroyed Los Muertos; see Henry D. Wallace and James P. Holmlund, *Petroglyphs of the Picacho Mountains, South Central Arizona.*

17. For his health, Cushing, his wife, and her sister, Margaret Magill, went to San Diego on 26 September 1887. In late October they moved to San Francisco, where they stayed until 16 December.

18. Many years later, in his foreword to Emil Haury's *Excavations of Los Muertos,* Hodge offered a version of this story, but he cited it to illustrate Cushing's "visionary" nature. That there were also sound observations involved (as Baxter shows) he ignored. Hodge was not present on the occasion in question.

19. The historical accounts of Casa Grande and an analysis of its architecture are presented by Fewkes in "Casa Grande, Arizona" and by David R. Wilcox and Lynette O. Shenk in *The Architecture of the Casa Grande and Its Interpretation.*

20. The Hohokam ceramic sequence did begin about 2,000 years ago. Both Los Muertos and Casa Grande are now thought to date between A.D. 1300 and 1450; see Wilcox and Shenk, *The Architecture of the Casa Grande;* and Wilcox, "Hohokam Social Complexity."

21. Cushing had been unstinting in his praise of Frederick Ward Putnam's archaeological methods in the Ohio Valley. On Putnam's work there, see Hinsley, "Frederick Ward Putnam, 1839–1915"; and Dexter, "The Putnam-Metz Correspondence on Mound Explorations in Ohio."

22. Cushing, "A Study of Pueblo Pottery, as Illustrative of Zuñi Culture Growth."

23. The reference is to the turquoise-encrusted toad that Cushing was later accused of "faking. Of the documentation surrounding this still-debated episode, Cushing's letter of 4 January 1898 to Frederick Ward Putnam (a copy of a letter originally dated June 1897), in the Peabody Museum Archives, contains his most complete statement of what he was trying to do with the specimen. While admitting that "it was a mistake, but a conscientious mistake," Cushing also insisted that "you may without hesitation exhibit this example not only as the first type specimen, but also, as accurate and authentic." The affair of the jewelled frog/toad, a very complex matter that began in early August 1887 and deeply colored Cushing's reputation subsequently, will be discussed in detail in a forthcoming volume in this work.

24. Baxter is referring here to the "hyoid bone" discovery. See Wortman and ten Kate, "On an Anatomical Characteristic of the Hyoid Bone of the Pre-Columbian Pueblo Indians of Arizona"; and Wortman, "The Hyoid Bone."

25. Cushing's suggestion that his discovery of llama- or alpaca-like figurines (guanacos) indicates a connection between the prehistoric Southwest and ancient Peruvian peoples was greeted with some skepticism; see, e.g., Washington Matthews, "The Cities of the Dead," 218, 221. To date, no camelid bones have been found in Hohokam sites.

26. Cushing's hypothesis of copper working in the Salt River Valley was published in the *American Anthropologist* in 1894. A critical review of the data today indicates that the closest place to the Southwest where copper working occurred was in western Mexico. See David M. Pendergast, "Metal Artifacts in Prehispanic Mesoamerica"; and Roderick Sprague and Aldo Signori, "Inventory of Copper Bells."

27. Here Baxter cited "The Old New World," *Boston Herald,* April 15, 1888, reprinted in pamphlet form by the Salem Press.

28. "Sonora" was also known as San Pablo. For a recent anthropological study of this community, see Scott W. Solliday, "The Journey to Rio Salado: Hispanic Migrations to Tempe, Arizona."

29. Baxter first met ten Kate when ten Kate visited Cushing at Mary Hemenway's Old Farm home in June 1886.

30. The Peabody Museum of Harvard University retains a drawing of this Gila Polychrome jar and a statement of the context in which it was found (Acc. No. 94-36, box 8, field catalogue #585a).

31. A stripe down the back is an unusual feature in this class of artifacts. However, the Brooklyn Museum possesses a sketch of an incomplete specimen which shows this feature. It may be a drawing of the specimen before Cushing restored it.

32. According to Thomas Wilhelm's *Military Dictionary and Gazetteer,* "The Sibley tent (invented by Maj. Sibley, 2nd Dragoons) is conical, light, easily pitched, erected on a tripod holding a single pole, and will comfortably accommodate 12 soldiers with their accoutrements. A fire can be made in the centre of this tent, and all soldiers sleep with their feet to the fire" (p. 578).

33. The method described is borne out for the Los Muertos platform mound but is not the one used to build Casa Grande; see Wilcox and Shenk, *The Architecture of the Casa Grande;* and Wilcox and Charles Sternberg, *Additional Studies of the Architecture of the Casa Grande and Its Interpretation.*

34. For detailed analyses of the mortuary remains from Los Muertos, see Emil W. Haury, *The Excavations of Los Muertos and Neighboring Ruins in the Salt River Valley, Southern Arizona,* and the recent reanalysis by Judy L. Brunson, "The Social Organization of the Los Muertos Hohokam: A Reanalysis of Cushing's Hemenway Expedition Data."

35. See note 22 above. Baxter reviewed Cushing's "A Study of Pueblo Pottery, as Illustrative of Zuñi Culture Growth" at length in the *American Architect and Building News* 23 (11 February 1888): 66–68.

PART IV. Conclusion: The Promise of the Southwest

1. Herbert J. Spinden, "Fine Art and the First Americans," 8.

2. Willa Cather, "The Enchanted Bluff," reprinted in *Willa Cather's Collected Short Fiction, 1892–1912,* 69–77; quoted passages are from pp. 74 and 76.

3. William Henry Holmes, "Random Records of a Lifetime Devoted to Science and Art, 1846–1931," 4:30.

4. William Henry Holmes, "Report on the Ancient Ruins of Southwestern Colorado, Examined during the Summers of 1875 and 1876," 390.

5. Peter B. Hales, *William Henry Jackson and the Transformation of the American Landscape;* Beaumont Newhall and Diana E. Edkins, *William H. Jackson.*

6. In an analysis of William Henry Jackson's 1874 photograph "Ancient Ruins in the Cañon of the Mancos," Susan Hegeman observes: "it might be argued that the story of this photograph is not about the Indian ruins but rather about the brave uncovering of the hidden and ancient resources of the West, its conquest through observation" (Hegeman, "Landscapes, Indians, and Photography in the Age of Scientific Exploration," 57).

7. For an analysis of the Moundbuilder genre, see Curtis M. Hinsley, "Digging for Identity: Reflections on the American Cultural Background of Repatriation."

8. Quoted in Robert Silverberg, *Mound Builders of Ancient America: The Archaeology of a Myth,* 83–84.

9. William Henry Harrison, "A Discourse on the Aborigines of the Valley of the Ohio"; James H. McCulloh, *Researches on America; Being an Attempt to Settle Some Points Relative to the Aborigines of America &c.,* 209–10.

10. Charles Lummis, *A Tramp across the Continent,* 240.

11. Charles Lummis, *Some Strange Corners of Our Country: The Wonderland of the Southwest,* 138, 141.

12. Ibid., 107.

13. John Gregory Bourke, *The Snake-Dance of the Moquis,* 169, 224–25.

14. Lummis, Prefatory Note for *A New Mexico David.*

15. On the trajectory of the influences of Lummis, see Richard H. Frost, "The Romantic Inflation of Pueblo Culture."

16. Frederick Chapin, *The Land of the Cliff-Dwellers,* 115, 131.

17. Ibid., 132–33.

18. Ibid., 155.

19. In her recent doctoral dissertation, "Imagining the Primitive," Leah Dilworth suggests that accounts of the Hopi Snake Dance show a shift in language from the first generation of writers, such as Bourke and Fewkes (ca. 1884–1895), to

a second generation, represented by Walter Hough and George Wharton James (ca. 1895–1905), who were characterized by expectation rather than discovery. A tourist rhetoric appears in the decade surrounding the turn of the century.

20. Albert Furtwangler, *Acts of Discovery: Visions of America in the Lewis and Clark Journals,* 29.

21. Richard B. Townshend, a visiting Englishman, camped at the bottom of the Grand Canyon in the summer of 1903, a year after Powell's death, and ruminated: "It was sunset now and we were already in twilight. I hurried back over that waste ground in this most desolate spot and reached camp before dark. And always the roaring, roaring of the water in our ears. I thought of the first explorer, Powell, and his men and their life in that perpetual roar, and their wonder whether some Niagara might not wait for them round the next bend." *Last Memories of a Tenderfoot,* 188–89. On Powell's construction of the narrative, see Martin T. Anderson, "John Wesley Powell's *Explorations of the Colorado River* . . . Fact, Fiction, or Fantasy?"

22. For a brilliant account of this process, see Furtwangler, *Acts of Discovery,* esp. chaps. 1, 3, and 8.

23. Wallace Stegner, "Thoughts in a Dry Land," 54. On Lummis, see Curtis M. Hinsley, "Authoring Authenticity," 467–68.

24. Terry Caesar, "Romancing the Facts in American Travel Writing," 123.

25. Because the creation of the Southwest occurred across all media of representation, these remarks apply as well to painting, photography, and engraving. For an insightful and in some respects parallel analysis of photographic representations in the period, see Susan Hegeman, "Landscape, Indians, and Photography in the Age of Scientific Exploration." Drawing on Michel deCerteau, Hegeman analyzes photographic techniques used by Jackson and Hillers that tended to transform the West's impersonal space into potentially habitable (and personally meaningful) places. Part of the self-conscious heroism and the cultural status of the exploring photographer lay in this function, which bears close resemblance to the "humanizing" of the landscape discussed below.

26. Julie K. Brown, *Contesting Images: Photography and the World's Columbian Exposition,* 84; cf. Curtis M. Hinsley, "The World as Marketplace: Commodification of the Exotic at the World's Columbian Exposition."

27. Gustav Nordenskiöld, *The Cliff Dwellers of the Mesa Verde, Southwestern Colorado: Their Pottery and Implements,* with introductions by Ron Switzer, Charlie Steen, and Robert Lister.

28. Ibid., 14.

29. Ibid., from the introduction by Charlie Steen, p. 24.

30. Cushing himself did not return to active employment in the Bureau of

Ethnology until February 1892. By 1895 both men were listed as ethnologists, and Cushing was earning only four dollars a month more than his former secretary. Langley to Cushing, 22 November 1894, and Langley to Hodge, 22 November 1894, in Group 34: Secretary's Correspondence, 1891-1907, Outgoing Correspondence: ethnology box 23, folder 4.1, Smithsonian Institution Archives.

31. See, e.g., Hodge to Matilda Coxe Stevenson, 18 January 1893, Stevenson Papers, National Anthropological Archives. Hodge's activities in these years can be traced in the annual reports of the Smithsonian Institution and the Bureau of Ethnology.

32. "Expedition Hemenwayamus mortius est sed non ethnologia Fewkesiania spero" (The Hemenway Expedition is dead but not, I hope, Fewkes's ethnology). Fewkes to Hodge, 19 May 1895, FWHC.

33. According to one of Lummis's versions, "The pueblo was once situated on top of the Mesa Encantada (Enchanted Table-land), which rises seven hundred [*sic*] feet in air near the mesa now occupied. Four hundred years ago or so, a frightful storm swept away the enormous leaning rock which served as a ladder, and the patient people—who were away at the time—had to build a new city" (*Some Strange Corners of Our Country,* 263). He presented a more detailed version, "The Enchanted Mesa: A Legend of New Mexico in the Fifteenth Century," in *A New Mexico David* (1891): 39–53, concluding: "Scientific expeditions have exhausted the ingenuity of civilization to scale the Rock of Katzimo, and recover its archaeological treasures, but all in vain. The natives shun it, believing it accursed" (p. 53).

34. "Professor Libbey's Own Story of His Perilous Ascent to its Top." Unidentified newspaper article of 31 July 1897 in Princeton Scientific Expeditions: Ethnographic and Geographic Expeditions, box 2, folder 23 (Enchanted Mesa Expedition 1897), Mudd Manuscript Library, Princeton University. The same folder contains Libbey's considerably longer account, "A Disenchanted Mesa," published on 21 August 1897 in an unidentified newspaper.

35. Libbey, "How He Climbed the Mesa Rock."

36. Henry Fairfield Osborn, "A Thrilling Life Story: The Travels and Adventures of William Libbey '77." Osborn maintained that Lummis "claimed sole rights to the mesa and made a defamatory attack upon William Libbey's integrity, knowledge and personal characteristics." In another version of this article, Osborn added: "but Libbey was quite capable of routing him, if so inclined" (Osborn, *Fifty Years of Princeton '77: A Fifty-Four Year Record of the Class of 1877 of Princeton College and University,* 213).

37. It should be noted that Libbey had been undertaking expeditionary work in various parts of the world for many years and continued to do so, including participating in the Peary Relief Expeditions to Greenland of 1894 and 1899. He

was, among other things, an accomplished field photographer and a formidable figure in explorers' circles. See N. H. Darnton, "Memorial of William Libbey." He was also well installed at Princeton: his father was a trustee, and his wife's family numbered in its ancestry no less than ten trustees of the university, including President Jonathan Dickinson (Libbey Faculty/Research Staff File, Mudd Library).

38. "Frederick Webb Hodge, Ethnologist: A Tape-Recorded Interview," 5 and 26 April 1956, typescript in author's possession. Hodge recalled: "Lummis must have hit the skies when he got [the telegraph message]. He started in. And if he didn't play Libbey to the queen's taste, you know!" (p. 126).

39. Lawrence Clark Powell, "Sky, Sun, and Water: The Southwest of Frederick Webb Hodge." Powell ends his reflections by recounting his own attempt to follow Hodge's footsteps up the mesa. While Powell unquestioningly admires Hodge, current archaeological evidence has not confirmed prehistoric habitation on Enchanted Mesa. Hodge found a small number of artifacts, but the much ridiculed Professor Libbey was, in all likelihood, ultimately correct.

40. John L. Stoddard, *Lectures,* 10:129–34.

41. For a comparable and contemporaneous case of derivative forms, see my discussion of WJ McGee's Seri expeditions of 1894 and 1895 in *The Smithsonian and the American Indian,* 238–40.

42. Fewkes to Hodge, 12 and 28 November 1906, FWHC.

43. Willa Cather, *The Professor's House,* 201–2.

44. Ibid., 213.

45. Ibid., 221.

46. Ibid., 242.

47. Ibid., 251.

48. Publishing in the same year as Cather, Zane Grey gave fuller vent to the sense of revulsion: "The world of man, race against race, the world of men and women, of strife and greed, of hate and lust, of injustice and sordidness, the materialism of the Great War and its horrible aftermath, the rush and fever and ferocity of the modern day with its jazz and license and drink and blindness—with its paganism,—these were not here in the grand shadow of Naza. No sharp wolfish faces of men limned against this silence! No beautiful painted faces of women! . . . The white man had not yet made Naza an object of his destructiveness. Nothing of the diseased in mind and body, the distorted images of mankind, the incomprehensible stupidity, the stony indifference to nature and beauty and ideals and good—nothing of these here in this moon-blanched canyon" (*The Vanishing American,* 301).

For evidence and an analysis of the impact of these postwar attitudes in anthropology, see George W. Stocking, "The Ethnographic Sensibility of the 1920s and the Dualism of the Anthropological Tradition;" and Stocking, "Ideas and Institutions in American Anthropology: Thoughts Toward a History of the Interwar Years."

49. Frederic R. Guernsey, "Boston in the Southwest," *Boston Herald,* 22 May 1887.

50. William E. Curtis, *Children of the Sun,* 95.

51. Charles F. Lummis, *The Land of Poco Tiempo,* 2.

52. Susan Wallace, "Among the Pueblos," 225.

53. Ibid., 215.

54. Cushing, "My Adventures in Zuni, I," 191; John Wesley Powell, "The Ancient Province of Tusayan," *Scribner's Monthly* 11 (1875): 15.

55. Sylvester Baxter, "The Father of the Pueblos," 73.

56. Baxter, "Zuñi Revisited," 124.

57. According to Earl Pomeroy, "Travelers passing the Pueblo villages of the Southwest in the eighties were invited to recall the villages of ancient Egypt and Nubia, Nineveh and Babylon, rather than to study the remnants of American aboriginal life" (*In Search of the Golden West: The Tourist in Western America,* 39). Baxter frequently invoked biblical imagery in describing the American Southwest and Mexico: "A New England lady stopping in Cuautla for the winter with her artist son, when out for a stroll one evening, and seeing one of these family groups with the mother and infant on donkey-back drawing up at a *meson* [inn], the great door swinging back to receive them, and revealing the numerous animals huddled in the great square interior court, exclaimed, "'Oh, Palestine!' " ("An Indian Fair in the Mexican Hot Country," 760).

58. Karen Halttunen, "From Parlor to Living Room: Domestic Space, Interior Decoration, and the Culture of Personality," 161.

59. Louise Stevenson, *The Victorian Homefront: American Thought and Culture 1860–1880,* 13, 15; Thomas J. Schlereth, *Victorian America: Transformations in Everyday Life, 1876–1915,* 195–97.

60. As cited in Cushing, *Zuñi: Selected Writings of Frank Hamilton Cushing,* 62.

61. Margaret W. Magill, letter to "Uncle Ferd" (including 1883 journal excerpts), 31 January 1884, pp. 21–23, FWHC.

62. Herbert G. Gutman, *Work, Culture, and Society in Industrializing America: Essays in Working Class and Social History,* 3–78, 234–59.

63. Lewis Mumford, *The Brown Decades: A Study of the Arts in America, 1865–1895,* 22.

64. S. Akerman and H. Norman, "Political Mobilization of the Workers:

The Case of the Worcester Swedes," 236; Sheila Slaughter and Edward T. Silva, "Looking Backwards: How Foundations Formulated Ideology in the Progressive Period," 66.

65. See T. J. Jackson Lears, *No Place of Grace: Antimodernism and the Transformation of American Culture, 1880–1920.*

66. Henry James, *A Little Tour in France,* 38.

67. Stuart Ewen, *All Consuming Images: The Politics of Style in Contemporary Culture,* 123.

68. As Willa Cather's Thea Kronberg reflects at the bottom of Panther Canyon in *The Song of the Lark,* "All her life she had been hurrying and sputtering, as if she had been born behind time and had been trying to catch up. Now . . . she had got to a place where she was out of the stream of meaningless activity and undirected effort" (p. 236).

69. As Wolfgang Schivelbusch notes in *The Railway Journey,* by the 1840s leisurely experience was already under widespread threat, whether in the United States or James's France: "[Walter] Benjamin mentions the Parisian fad of the 1840s that involved walking turtles on a leash in these arcades; he conjectures that this was the *flaneur*'s way of asserting his eccentrically unhurried way of life, but it is, more likely, a sign of the general alienation from slow speeds" (p. 189).

70. Garry Wills, *Lincoln at Gettysburg: The Words that Remade America,* 73.

71. Susan Wallace, "Among the Pueblos," 215.

72. F. H. Cushing, "The Nation of the Willows," 559.

73. In 1889 Richard J. Hinton observed: "As the bird flies it is about fifty miles north by west to that portion of the secondary table-land that rises from the Salt River Valley and flows southward to the Gila, on which are located the mounds that the [Hemenway] exploring party have been working at. No one riding over that desolate *mesa* on horseback and by stage, as I have done, would without previous information ever imagine it to have been the seat of thriving human life. Yet the evidence thereof is cumulative" ("The Great House of Montezuma," 398).

74. *Phoenix Daily Herald,* 6 April 1887.

75. The ironies of southwestern longing and belonging continue to compound. The *New York Times* recently featured an exclusive new subdivision in Cortez, Colorado. Advertised as "Indian Camp," its main attraction was "its own Anasazi ruin" in the owners' backyards. Prospective owners at Indian Camp must agree to preserve the integrity of the ruins, and upon an owner's death any excavated artifacts must go to a museum. Having "fallen in love with the Southwest," the developers explained, they felt compelled "to develop along archaeological lines, because there [the ruins] were." As one new homeowner who had had her house blessed by a Navajo chanter remarked, it is fortunate that all who build in this unique spot are

"into preservation." ("For Sale: Homes amid Prehistory in the American Southwest," *New York Times,* 13 November 1994, p. 36.)

76. Willa Cather, *The Song of the Lark,* 239–41.

77. Walter W. Taylor, "Southwestern Archeology: Its History and Theory"; Alfred V. Kidder, *An Introduction to the Study of Southwestern Archaeology with a Preliminary Account of the Excavation at Pecos.*

78. In some cases the romance was quite literal. In his popular book of 1906, *On the Great American Plateau,* T. Mitchell Prudden pictured a form of love in the ruins, where "the rustic swain is wont to signalise his regard for his Dulcinea by digging for her out of the desolate graves what articles the chances of the hour may bring. She, cosily seated amid piles of broken pottery, darting lizards and dead men's bones, smiles complacently the while upon the dusty delver from the chaste recesses of a sun-umbrella" (103–4). Prudden presented this odd contemporary mating ritual with apparent seriousness.

79. The stirring phrases with which Lewis Henry Morgan closed *Ancient Society* (1877) expressed well the reformist vision that also inspired the Hemenway enterprise: "The dissolution of society bids fair to become the termination of a career of which property is the end and aim; because such a career contains the elements of self-destruction. Democracy in government, brotherhood in society, equality in rights and privileges, and universal education, foreshadow the next higher plane of society to which experience, intelligence and knowledge are steadily tending. It will be a revival, in a higher form, of the liberty, equality, and fraternity of the ancient gentes" (p. 561–62).

80. The cliffdwellers must have been "a timid, nest-building folk, like the swallows" (Cather, *The Song of the Lark,* 238).

References Cited

Abbreviations

FHCC Frank Hamilton Cushing Collection, Southwest Museum, Los Angeles

FHCLB Frank H. Cushing Letterbooks, Huntington Free Library, Bronx, New York

FWHC Frederick Webb Hodge Collection, Southwest Museum, Los Angeles

ESMC Edward S. Morse Collection, Phillips Library, Peabody/Essex Museum, Salem, Massachusetts

Manuscript Collections

Agassiz, Alexander. Papers. Museum of Comparative Zoology, Harvard University.

Bellamy, Edward. Papers. Houghton Library, Harvard University.

Cushing, Frank H. Collection. Southwest Museum, Los Angeles.

Cushing, Frank H. Letterbooks. Huntington Free Library, Bronx, New York.

Eliot, Charles W. Papers. Harvard University Archives, Pusey Library, Harvard University.

Hale, Edward Everett. Papers. New York State Historical Society, Albany.

Hodge, Frederick W. Collection. Southwest Museum, Los Angeles.

Holmes, William Henry. "Random Records of a Lifetime Devoted to Science and

Art, 1846–1931." Scrapbook, 1931, 20 vols. Archives of American Art, Smithsonian Institution, Washington, D.C.

Libbey, William. Faculty Research/Staff File. Mudd Manuscript Library, Princeton University.

Metcalf, Willard L. File. Archives of American Art, Smithsonian Institution, Washington, D.C.

Morse, Edward S. Papers. Phillips Library, Peabody/Essex Museum, Salem, Massachusetts.

Princeton Scientific Expeditions. Collection. Mudd Manuscript Library, Princeton University.

Smithsonian Institution. Correspondence of the Secretary (Samuel P. Langley, 1887–1909). Smithsonian Institution, Washington, D.C.

Stevenson, Matilda Coxe. Papers. National Anthropological Archives, Smithsonian Institution, Washington, D.C.

Newspapers

Boston Advertiser, 1880–1885.

Boston Herald, 1878–1927.

Phoenix Herald, 1887–1889.

Published Works and Individual Manuscripts

Adams, J. R. *Edward Everett Hale*. Boston: Twayne Publishers, 1977.

Akerman, S., and H. Norman. "Political Mobilization of the Workers: The Case of the Worcester Swedes." In *American Labor and Immigration History, 1877–1920s: Recent European Research,* edited by D. Hoerder, 235–58. Urbana: University of Illinois Press, 1983.

Anderson, Martin J. "John Wesley Powell's *Explorations of the Colorado River* . . . Fact, Fiction, or Fantasy?" *Journal of Arizona History* 24 (December 1983): 363–80.

Babcock, Barbara A. "Bearers of Value, Vessels of Desire: The Reproduction of the Reproduction of Pueblo Culture." *Museum Anthropology* 17 (1993): 43–57.

———. "'A New Mexican Rebecca': Imaging Pueblo Women." *Journal of the Southwest* 32 (1990): 400–437.

Bandelier, Adolf F. *Final Report of Investigations among the Indians of the South-*

western United States. 2 pts. Papers of the Archaeological Institute of America. American Series 3 and 4. Cambridge, Mass., 1890–92.

———. "An Outline of the Documentary History of the Zuni Tribe." In *A Journal of American Ethnology and Archaeology,* edited by Jesse Walter Fewkes, 1–115. Salem, Mass., 1892.

———. *The Southwest Journals of Adolph F. Bandelier, 1880–1882*. Edited by Charles H. Lange and Carroll L. Riley. Albuquerque: University of New Mexico Press, 1966.

Bartlett, John Russell. *Personal Narrative of Explorations & Incidents in Texas, New Mexico, California, Sonora, and Chihuahua: Connected with the United States and Mexican Boundary Commission, during the Years 1850, '51, '52, and '53*. New York: Appleton, 1854.

Baxter, James Phinney. "Descendants of Thomas Baxter." In "Baxter Family: A Collection of Genealogies." 1920. Typescript at the New England Historical and Genealogical Society, Boston.

Baxter, Sylvester. "An Aboriginal Pilgrimage." *Century Magazine* 24, n.s. 2 (August 1882): 526–36.

———. "Along the Rio Grande." *Harper's New Monthly Magazine* 70 (April 1885): 687–700.

———. "Art in Public Places: Aqueducts, Water-Towers, Power-Houses, Reservoirs, Bridges." *Century Magazine* 64 (1902): 912–21.

———. "The Beautifying of Village and Town." *Century Magazine* 63 (1902): 844–51.

———. *The Cruise of a Land-Yacht*. Boston: Authors' Mutual Publishing Co., 1891.

———. "Cutting Cape Cod." *Outlook* 96 (1910): 932–42.

———. "The Father of the Pueblos." *Harper's New Monthly Magazine* 65 (June 1882): 72–91.

———. "Hotel Cluny of a New England Village." *Publications of the Ipswich Historical Society* 10 (1901): 1–11.

———. "Howells's Boston." *New England Magazine* 9 (1892): 129–52.

———. "How the Bills of Socialism Will Be Paid." *Forum* 17 (1894): 699–709.

———. "An Indian Fair in the Mexican Hot Country." *Harper's New Monthly Magazine* 84 (1891): 757–71.

———. "In Memoriam: Lucia Allen Millet Baxter, January 1, 1917." In *Homeward Laden*. Boston: Privately printed, 1917.

———. Letter to the *Boston Herald,* 7 June 1925.

———. "The Metropolitan Park System." In *Proceedings of the Massachusetts Horticultural Society for 1894*, 152–74. Boston, 1894.

———. "Mr. Baxter at Conclusion." *Boston Herald,* 26 November 1918.

———. "The New B. and M." *Boston Herald,* 21 November 1910.

———. "New England's New Poet." *American Review of Reviews* (1915): 432–34.

———. *The Old New World: An Account of the Explorations of the Hemenway Southwestern Archaeological Expedition in 1887–88, under the Direction of Frank Hamilton Cushing*. Salem, Mass: Salem Press. Reprinted from the *Boston Herald,* April 15, 1888.

———. "A Plea for Mercy." *Boston Herald,* 23 November 1918.

———. "A Reporter's Memories of Boston's Great Fire." *Boston Herald,* 23 October 1922.

———. Review of *Fourth Annual Report of the Bureau of Ethnology.—III: Frank Hamilton Cushing on Pueblo Pottery and Zuni Culture Growth. American Architect and Building News* 23 (7 January 1888): 66–68.

———. *The Ring and the Tree and Other Poems*. Boston: Bruce Humphries, 1938.

———. "Solved at Last: Mysteries of Ancient Aztec History Unveiled by an Explorer from the Smithsonian Institution; Wonderful Achievements of Frank H. Cushing." *Boston Herald,* 16 June 1881.

———. *Spanish-Colonial Architecture in Mexico*. 10 vols. Boston: J. B. Millett, 1901.

———. "The Tenacity of Indian Customs." *American Architect and Building News* 12 (21 October 1882): 195–97.

———. *The Unseen House and Other Poems*. Boston, 1917.

———. "Walt Whitman in Boston." *New England Magazine,* August 1892. Reprinted in *On Walt Whitman,* Folcroft Library Editions, 1973, pp. 5–12.

———. "A Winter in Sonora." *Outing and the Wheelman: An Illustrated Monthly of Recreation* 5 (March 1885): 403–13.

———. "Zuñi Revisited." *American Architect and Building News* 13 (17 March 1883): 124–26.

Baxter, Sylvester, and William H. Downes. "Greater Boston." *Leslie's Weekly* 80 (1895): 347–66.

Bigelow, John. "The Railway Invasion of Mexico." *Harper's New Monthly Magazine* 65 (October 1882): 745–57.

Bishop, W. H. *Old Mexico and Her Lost Provinces: A Journey in Mexico, Southern California, and Arizona, by Way of Cuba*. New York: Harper & Bros., 1883.

Blake, Casey Nelson. *Beloved Community: The Cultural Criticism of Randolph*

Bourne, Van Wyck Brooks, Waldo Frank, & Lewis Mumford. Chapel Hill: University of North Carolina Press, 1990.

Blanchard, Paula. *Sarah Orne Jewett: Her World and Her Work*. Reading, Mass.: Addison Wesley, 1994.

Blodgett, Geoffrey. "Frederick Law Olmsted: Landscape Architecture as Conservative Reform." *Journal of American History* 62 (1976): 869–89.

Bourke, John G. *The Snake-Dance of the Moquis*. 1884. Reprint. Tucson: University of Arizona Press, 1984.

Boyer, M. Christine. *Dreaming the Rational City: The Myth of American City Planning*. Cambridge, Mass.: MIT Press, 1983.

Boyer, Paul S. *Urban Masses and American Moral Order*. Cambridge, Mass.: Harvard University Press, 1978.

Brandes, Raymond Stewart. "Archaeological Awareness of the Southwest." *Arizona and the West* 2 (January 1960): 6–25.

———. "Frank Hamilton Cushing: Pioneer Americanist." Ph.D. diss., University of Arizona, 1965.

Brooks, Van Wyck. *Howells: His Life and World*. New York: E. P. Dutton, 1959.

———. *New England: Indian Summer, 1865–1915*. New York: E. P. Dutton, 1940.

Brown, Julie K. *Contesting Images: Photography and the World's Columbian Exposition*. Tucson: University of Arizona Press, 1994.

Brunson, Judy L. "The Social Organization of the Los Muertos Hohokam: A Reanalysis of Cushing's Hemenway Expedition Data." Ph.D. diss., Arizona State University, 1989.

Bunzel, Ruth. *Zuni Ceremonialism*. Albuquerque: University of New Mexico Press, 1992.

Burrus, Ernest J. *Kino and Manje: Explorers of Sonora and Arizona*. Rome: Jesuit Historical Institute, 1971.

Caesar, Terry. "Romancing the Facts in American Travel Writing." In *Temperamental Journeys: Essays on the Modern Literature of Travel,* edited by Michael Kowalewski, 109–25. Athens: University of Georgia Press, 1992.

Carnes, Mark C. *Secret Ritual and Manhood in Victorian America*. New Haven, Conn.: Yale University Press, 1989.

Cather, Willa. "The Enchanted Bluff." *Harper's Magazine* 118 (April 1909): 3–15. Reprinted in *Willa Cather's Collected Short Fiction, 1892–1912,* edited by Virginia Faulkner, 69–77. Lincoln: University of Nebraska Press, 1965.

———. *The Professor's House*. 1925. Reprint. New York: Vintage, 1973.

———. *The Song of the Lark*. 1915. Reprint. New York: Bantam, 1991.

Chapin, Frederick. *The Land of the Cliff-Dwellers*. 1892. Reprint. Tucson: University of Arizona Press, 1988.

Chenault, Mark L., Richard V. N. Ahlstrom, and Thomas N. Motsinger. *In the Shadow of South Mountain: The Pre-Classic Hohokam of La Ciudad de los Hornos; 1991–1992 Excavations*. 2 vols. SWCA Environmental Consultants Archaeological Report No. 93-30. Tucson, 1993.

Cook, Mabel Collins. *Through the Gates of Gold: A Fragment of Thought*. 1887. Reprinted in Olive Schreiner, *Dreams*, 1–109. New York: H. M. Caldwell, n.d.

Couvares, Francis G. *The Remaking of Pittsburgh: Class and Culture in an Industrializing City, 1877–1919*. Albany: State University of New York Press, 1984.

Cranston, Sylvia. *The Extraordinary Life and Influence of Helena Blavatsky, Founder of the Modern Theosophical Movement*. New York: G. P. Putnam's Sons, 1993.

Curtis, William E. *Children of the Sun*. Chicago: Inter-Ocean Publishing, 1883.

Cushing, Frank Hamilton. Annual Report on Field Work for Year Ending June 30, 1883. National Anthropological Archives, Washington, D.C.

———. Monthly Report for December 1882 and January 1883. National Anthropological Archives, Washington, D.C.

———. "My Adventures in Zuñi, I," *Century Magazine* 25 (December 1882): 191–207.

———. "My Adventures in Zuñi, II," *Century Magazine* 25 (February 1883): 500–511.

———. "The Nation of the Willows." *Harper's New Monthly Magazine* 50 (September, October 1882): 362–74, 541–59. Reprint. Flagstaff, Ariz.: Northland Press, 1966.

———. "Outlines of Zuñi Creation Myths." In *Thirteenth Annual Report of the Bureau of Ethnology, 1891–1892*, 321–447. Washington, D.C.: GPO, 1896.

———. "Preliminary Notes on the Origin, Working Hypothesis and Primary Researches of the Hemenway Southwestern Archaeological Expedition." In *Congrès International des Américanistes, Berlin, 1888*, 151–94. Berlin: W. H. Kühl, 1890.

———. "A Study of Pueblo Pottery, as Illustrative of Zuñi Culture Growth." In *Fourth Annual Report of the Bureau of Ethnology for 1882–83*: 467–521. Washington, D.C.: GPO, 1886.

———. "Zuñi Breadstuff." *The Millstone: An Illustrated Monthly Journal, Devoted to the Advancement of Milling and Mechanical Interests* 9–10 (January 1884–July 1885). Reprint. *Zuñi Breadstuff,* Indian Notes and Monographs, vol. 8. Edited by F. W. Hodge. New York: Museum of the American Indian, Heye Foundation, 1920.

———. "Zuñi Fetishes." In *Second Annual Report of the Bureau of Ethnology for 1880–81,* 3–45. Washington, D.C.: GPO, 1883.

Darnton, N. H. "Memorial of William Libbey." *Bulletin of the Geological Society of America* 39 (1927): 35–40.

Davis, Clarence B., and Kenneth E. Wilburn, Jr., eds. *Railway Imperialism.* New York: Greenwood Press, 1991.

Desmond, Lawrence G., and Phyllis M. Messenger. *A Dream of Maya: Augustus and Alice Le Plongeon in Nineteenth-Century Yucatan.* Albuquerque: University of New Mexico Press, 1988.

De Veer, Elizabeth. *Sunlight and Shadow: The Life and Art of Willard Leroy Metcalf.* New York: Abbeville Press, 1987.

Dewey, Mary. "Visit of the Zuni Indians to the Summer House of Mrs. Mary Hemenway in 1886." 1886. Ms. in the Peabody Museum, Harvard University.

Dexter, Ralph W. "The Putnam-Metz Correspondence on Mound Explorations in Ohio." *Ohio Archaeologist* 32, no. 4 (April 1982): 24–28.

Dilworth, Leah. "Imagining the Primitive: Representations of Native Americans in the Southwest, 1880–1930." Ph.D. diss., Yale University, 1992.

Doelle, William H., Douglas B. Craig, and Henry D. Wallace. "Measuring Prehistoric Demographic Trends." Paper presented at the 57th Annual Meeting of the Society for American Archaeology, 1992.

Doenecke, Justus D. *The Presidencies of James A. Garfield & Chester A. Arthur.* Lawrence: Regents Press of Kansas, 1981.

Douglas, Ann. *The Feminization of American Culture.* New York: Alfred A. Knopf, 1977.

Effland, Richard W., Jr., comp. "Archaeological Investigations at La Ciudad de los Hornos: Lassen Substation Parcel." *Arizona Archaeologist,* no. 24. Phoenix: Arizona Archaeological Society, 1990.

Eustis, Frederic A. *Augustus Hemenway, 1805–1876: Builder of the United States Trade with the West Coast of South America.* Salem, Mass.: Peabody Museum, 1955.

Ewen, Stuart. *All Consuming Images: The Politics of Style in Contemporary Culture.* New York: Basic Books, 1988.

Ferguson, T. J. "Historic Zuñi Architecture and Society: A Structural Analysis." Ph.D. diss., University of New Mexico, 1993.

Ferguson, T. J., and E. Richard Hart. *A Zuni Atlas*. Norman: University of Oklahoma Press, 1985.

Fewkes, Jesse Walter. "Casa Grande, Arizona." In *Twenty-eighth Annual Report of the Bureau of American Ethnology,* 25–180. Washington, D.C.: GPO, 1912.

Fewkes, Jesse Walter, and Elsie Clews Parsons. "Contributions to Hopi History." *American Anthropologist* 24 (1923): 253–68.

Fowler, Don D., ed. *"Photographed All the Best Scenery": Jack Hillers' Diary of the Powell Expeditions, 1871–1875*. Salt Lake City: University of Utah Press, 1972.

French, William E. "In the Path of Progress: Railroads and Moral Reform in Porfirian Mexico." In *Railway Imperialism,* edited by Clarence B. Davis and Kenneth E. Wilburn, Jr., 85–102. New York: Greenwood Press, 1991.

Frost, Richard H. "The Romantic Inflation of Pueblo Culture." *American West* 17, no. 1 (1980): 5–9, 56–60.

Fuller, Clarissa Parsons. "Frank Hamilton Cushing's Relations to Zuni and the Hemenway Southwestern Expedition, 1879–1889." M.A. thesis, University of New Mexico, 1943.

Furtwangler, Albert. *Acts of Discovery: Visions of America in the Lewis and Clark Journals*. Urbana: University of Illinois Press, 1993.

Goetzmann, William H., ed. *The St. Louis Hegelians: An Intellectual Episode in the History of Western America*. New York: Alfred A. Knopf, 1973.

Gomes, Michael. *Theosophy in the Nineteenth Century: An Annotated Bibliography*. New York: Garland Publishing, 1994.

Green, Jesse, ed. *Cushing at Zuni: The Correspondence and Journals of Frank Hamilton Cushing, 1879–1884*. Albuquerque: University of New Mexico Press, 1990.

———. *Zuni: Selected Writings of Frank Hamilton Cushing*. Lincoln: University of Nebraska Press, 1979.

Green, Martin. *The Problem of Boston: Some Readings in Cultural History*. New York: W. W. Norton, 1966.

Gregory, David A., and Gary Huckleberry. *An Archaeological Survey of the Blackwater Area*. Volume 1: *The History of Human Settlement in the Blackwater Area*. Archaeological Consulting Services Cultural Resources Report No. 86. Tempe, 1994.

Grey, Zane. *The Vanishing American*. New York: Grosset and Dunlap, 1925.

Gunnison, Almon. *Rambles Overland: A Trip across the Continent*. Boston: Universalist Publishing House, 1884.

Gutman, Herbert G. *Work, Culture, and Society in Industrializing America: Essays in Working Class and Social History*. Urbana: University of Illinois Press, 1976.

Hale, Edward Everett. "The Colonization of the Desert." In *Life and Letters of Edward Everett Hale,* 8:355–70. Boston: Little, Brown, 1917.

———. *A Family Flight through Mexico*. Boston: D. Lothrop and Co., 1886.

———. "Report of the Council." In *Proceedings of the American Antiquarian Society for 1878,* 23–31. Worcester, Mass., 1878.

Hales, Peter B. *William Henry Jackson and the Transformation of the American Landscape*. Philadelphia: Temple University Press, 1988.

Halttunen, Karen. "From Parlor to Living Room: Domestic Space, Interior Decoration, and the Culture of Personality." In *Consuming Visions: Accumulation and Display of Goods in America, 1880–1920,* edited by Simon J. Bronner, 157–89. New York: W. W. Norton, 1989.

Harris, Neil. "The Gilded Age Revisited: Boston and the Museum Movement." *American Quarterly* 14 (1962): 546–66.

Harrison, William Henry. "A Discourse on the Aborigines of the Valley of the Ohio." *Transactions of the Historical and Philosophical Society of Ohio* 1, pt. 2 (1834): 217–67.

Haury, Emil W. "Ball Courts." In *Excavations at Snaketown: Material Culture,* by Harold S. Gladwin, Emil W. Haury, E. B. Sayles, and Nora Gladwin, 36–49. 1937. Reprint. Tucson: University of Arizona Press, 1965.

———. *The Excavations of Los Muertos and Neighboring Ruins in the Salt River Valley, Southern Arizona*. Papers of the Peabody Museum of American Archaeology and Ethnology 24, no. 1. Cambridge, Mass.: Peabody Museum, 1945.

Hegeman, Susan. "Landscapes, Indians, and Photography in the Age of Scientific Exploration." In *The Big Empty: Essays on the Land as Narrative,* edited by Leonard Engel, 49–74. Albuquerque: University of New Mexico Press, 1994.

Hickman, Money, and Peter Fetchko. *Japan Day by Day: An Exhibition in Honor of Edward Sylvester Morse*. Salem, Mass.: Peabody Museum of Salem, 1977.

Higginson, Thomas Wentworth. "The Visit of the Vikings." *Harper's New Monthly Magazine* 65 (1882): 515–27.

Hinsley, Curtis M. "Authoring Authenticity." *Journal of the Southwest* 32 (Winter 1991): 462–78.

———. "Digging for Identity: Reflections on the American Cultural Background of Repatriation." In *The Repatriation of American Indian Remains and Sacred Objects,* edited by Devon A. Mihesuah. Urbana: University of Illinois Press, 1996.

———. "Ethnographic Charisma and Scientific Routine: Cushing and Fewkes in the American Southwest, 1879–1893." In *History of Anthropology,* edited by George W. Stocking, 1:53–69. Madison: University of Wisconsin Press, 1983.

———. "Frederick Ward Putnum, 1839–1915." *Encyclopedia of the History of Archaeology*. New York: Garland Publishing, 1996.

———. "From Shell-Heaps to Stelae: Early Anthropology at the Peabody Museum." In *History of Anthropology,* edited by George W. Stocking, 3:49–74. Madison: University of Wisconsin Press, 1985.

———. "'I Command I Shall Be Believed': Cushing, the Hemenway, and Scientific Poetics." Paper presented at the 87th Annual Meeting of the American Anthropological Association, 1988.

———. *The Smithsonian and the American Indian: Making a Moral Anthropology in Victorian America*. Washington, D.C.: Smithsonian Institution Press, 1994.

———. "Wanted: One Good Man to Discover Central American History." *Harvard Magazine,* November–December 1984, pp. 64A–64H.

———. "The World as Marketplace: Commodification of the Exotic at the World's Columbian Exposition." In *Exhibiting Cultures: The Poetics and Politics of Museum Display,* edited by Ivan Karp and Steven D. Lavine, 344–65. Washington, D.C.: Smithsonian Institution Press, 1991.

———. "Zunis and Brahmins: Cultural Ambivalence in the Gilded Age." In *History of Anthropology,* edited by George W. Stocking, 6:169–207. Madison: University of Wisconsin Press, 1989.

Hinsley, Curtis M., and Lea S. McChesney. "Anthropology as Cultural Exchange: The Shared Vision of Mary Hemenway and Frank Cushing." Paper presented at the joint meeting of the American Ethnological Society and the Southwestern Anthropological Association, 1984.

Hinton, Richard J. "The Great House of Montezuma." *Harper's Weekly,* 18 May 1889 (Supplement), 398–401.

Hodge, Frederick Webb. Foreword to *The Excavations of Los Muertos and Neighbor-*

ing Ruins in the Salt River Valley, Southern Arizona, by Emil Haury, vii–ix. Papers of the Peabody Museum of American Archaeology and Ethnology 24, no. 1. Cambridge, Mass.: Peabody Museum, 1945.

———. Frederick Webb Hodge: A Tape-Recorded Interview. 1956. Typescript copies on deposit at the Southwest Museum and the Bancroft Library, and in possession of Curtis M. Hinsley.

———. "The Six Cities of Cibola in 1581–1680." *New Mexico Historical Review* 1 (1926): 478–88.

———. Transcription of Tape Recordings: Frederick Webb Hodge's Anecdotes and Reminiscences. 1955. Transcribed by Genevieve Pease. Typescript in possession of C. M. Hinsley.

Holloway, J. *Edward Everett Hale: A Biography*. Austin: University of Texas Press, 1956.

Holmes, William Henry. "Report on the Ancient Ruins of Southwestern Colorado, Examined during the Summers of 1875 and 1876." In *Tenth Annual Report of the United States Geological and Geographical Survey of the Territories,* 381–408. Washington, D.C.: GPO, 1878.

Horowitz, Helen Lefkowitz. *Culture & the City: Cultural Philanthropy in Chicago from the 1880s to 1917*. Lexington: University Press of Kentucky, 1976.

Hovens, Pieter. *Herman F. C. ten Kate, Jr. (1858–1931) en de Antropologie der Noord-Amerikaanse Indianen*. Meppel, Netherlands: Krips Repro, 1990.

———. *Odagot: Photographs of American Indians, 1860–1920*. Amsterdam: Fragment Uitgeverij, 1992.

Howard, Jerry B. "The Casa Buena Hornos: A Study in Morphology, Typology, Function, and Formation Processes." In *Excavations at Casa Buena: Changing Hohokam Land Use along the Squaw Peak Parkway,* edited by Jerry B. Howard, 1:145–200. Soil Systems Publications in Archaeology No. 11. Phoenix, 1988.

———. "A Paleohydraulic Approach to Examining Agricultural Intensification in Hohokam Irrigation Systems." In *Economic Aspects of Water Management in the Prehispanic New World,* edited by Vernon L. Scarborough and Barry L. Issac, 263–324. Research in Economic Anthropology, Supplement No. 7. Cincinnati: JAI Press, 1993.

Howells, William Dean. *Selected Letters*. Edited by George W. Arms et al. 6 vols. Boston: Twayne Publishers, 1979–83.

Hoyle, Pamela. *The Boston Ambience: An Exhibition of Nineteenth-Century Photographs*. Boston: Boston Athenaeum, 1981.

———. *The Development of Photography in Boston, 1840–1875*. Boston: Boston Athenaeum, 1979.

Hyde, Anne Farrar. *An American Vision: Far Western Landscape and National Culture, 1820–1920*. New York: NYU Press, 1990.

Jacknis, Ira. Inventory of the Stewart Culin Papers. 1985. Ms., Brooklyn Museum.

Jackson, Helen Hunt. *Ramona*. 1884. Reprint. New York: Penguin Books, 1988.

James, Henry. *A Little Tour in France*. 1884. Reprint. New York: Weidenfeld & Nicolson, 1987.

Johnson, Arthur M., and Barry E. Supple. *Boston Capitalists and Western Railroads: A Study in the Nineteenth-Century Railroad Investment Process*. Cambridge, Mass.: Harvard University Press, 1967.

Judd, Neil, M. R. Harrington, and S. K. Lothrop. "Frederick Webb Hodge, 1864–1956." *American Antiquity* 22 (1957): 401–4.

Kaplan, Justin. *Walt Whitman: A Life*. New York: Simon and Schuster, 1980.

Kennan, George. *Tent-Life in Siberia; And Adventures among the Koraks and Other Tribes in Kamchatka and Northern Asia*. New York: G. P. Putnam's Sons, 1872.

Kidder, Alfred Vincent. *An Introduction to the Study of Southwestern Archaeology with a Preliminary Account of the Excavation at Pecos*. New Haven, Conn.: Yale University Press, 1924.

Kintigh, Keith W. *Settlement, Subsistence, and Society in Late Zuni Prehistory*. Anthropological Papers of the University of Arizona No. 44. Tucson: University of Arizona Press, 1985.

Kirshenblatt-Gimblett, Barbara. "Objects of Ethnography." In *Exhibiting Cultures: The Poetics and Politics of Museum Display,* edited by Ivan Karp and Steven D. Lavine, 386–443. Washington, D.C.: Smithsonian Institution Press, 1992.

Ladd, Edmund. "Cushing among the Zuñi: A Zuñi Perspective." *Gilcrease Journal* 2, no. 2 (Autumn 1994): 20–35.

———. "Zuni Social and Political Organization." In *Handbook of North American Indians,* vol. 9: *Southwest,* edited by Alfonso Ortiz, 482–91. Washington, D.C.: Smithsonian Institution Press, 1979.

Lears, T. J. Jackson. *No Place of Grace: Antimodernism and the Transformation of American Culture, 1880–1920*. New York: Pantheon, 1981.

Lee, Molly. "Appropriating the Primitive: Turn-of-the-Century Collection and Display of Native Alaskan Art." *Arctic Anthropology* 28 (1991): 6–15.

Leighton, Dorothea C., and John Adair. *People of the Middle Place*. Behavior Science Monographs. New Haven, Conn.: Human Relations Area Files, 1966.

Lummis, Charles. *The Land of Poco Tiempo*. 1893. Reprint. Albuquerque: University of New Mexico Press, 1952.

———. *A New Mexico David, and Other Stories and Sketches of the Southwest*. 1891. Reprint, 1969.

———. *Some Strange Corners of Our Country: The Wonderland of the Southwest*. 1891–92. Reprint. Tucson: University of Arizona Press, 1989.

———. *A Tramp across the Continent*. 1892. Reprint. Lincoln: University of Nebraska Press, 1982.

———. "The White Indian." *Land of Sunshine* 13 (1900): 8–17.

Lurie, Edward. *Nature and the American Mind: Louis Agassiz and the Culture of Science*. New York: Science History Publications, 1974.

Malone, Patrick M. *The Skulking Way of War: Technology and Tactics among the New England Indians*. Lanham, N.Y.: Madison Books, 1991.

Margati, José. *A Trip to the City of Mexico*. Boston: Putnam, Messervy & Co., 1885.

Mark, Joan. "Frank Hamilton Cushing and an American Science of Anthropology." *Perspectives in American History* 10 (1976): 449–86.

Marsh, Margaret. "Suburban Men and Masculine Domesticity, 1870–1915." In *Meanings for Manhood: Reconstructions of Masculinity in Victorian America,* edited by Mark C. Carnes and Clyde Griffen, 111–27. Chicago: University of Chicago Press, 1990.

Matthews, Washington. "The Cities of the Dead." *Land of Sunshine* 12 (1900): 213–21.

Matthews, Washington, Jacob L. Wortman, and John S. Billings. "Human Bones in the Hemenway Collection in the U.S. Army Medical Museum." *Memoirs of the National Academy of Sciences* 6 (1893): 139–286.

McChesney, Lea S. "The Vision of Mary Hemenway." Paper presented at the 87th Annual Meeting of the American Anthropological Association, 1988.

McCulloh, James H. *Researches on America; Being an Attempt to Settle Some Points Relative to the Aborigines of America &c*. Baltimore: Joseph Robinson, 1817.

McLuhan, T. C. *Dream Tracks: The Railroad and the American Indian, 1890–1930*. New York: Abrams, 1985.

Mead, Edwin D. *Boston Memories of Fifty Years*. Boston, 1932.

———. "The Old South Work." *New England Magazine,* October 1892. Reprinted as pamphlet, *The Old South Work*. Boston: Old South Meeting House, 1892.

Mitchell, Edward Page. *Memoirs of an Editor: Fifty Years of American Journalism*. New York: Charles Scribner's Sons, 1924.

Morgan, Lewis Henry. *Ancient Society: Or, Researches in the Lines of Human Progress from Savagery through Barbarism to Civilization*. Edited by Eleanor Burke Leacock. 1877. Reprint. Cleveland: World, 1963.

Morse, Edward Sylvester. *Japan Day by Day*. 2 vols. Boston: Houghton Mifflin, 1917.

Mumford, Lewis. *The Brown Decades: A Study of the Arts in America, 1865–1895*. New York: Harcourt, Brace and Co., 1931.

Newhall, Beaumont, and Diana E. Edkins. *William H. Jackson*. Dobbs Ferry, N.Y.: Morgan & Morgan, 1974.

Nordenskiöld, Gustav. *The Cliff Dwellers of the Mesa Verde, Southwestern Colorado: Their Pottery and Implements*. 1893. Reprint, with introductions by Ron Switzer, Charlie Steen, and Robert Lister. Glorieta, N.M.: Rio Grande Press, 1979.

Nye, David E. *American Technological Sublime*. Cambridge, Mass.: MIT Press, 1994.

Ober, Frederick A. "How a White Man Became War Chief of the Zuñis." *Wide Awake* 14 (June 1882): 382–88.

———. *Travels in Mexico and Life among the Mexicans*. London: Frederick Warne and Co., 1887.

Osborn, Henry Fairfield. *Fifty Years of Princeton '77: A Fifty-Four Year Record of the Class of 1877 of Princeton College and University*. Princeton, N.J.: Princeton University Press, 1927.

———. "A Thrilling Life Story: The Travels and Adventures of William Libbey '77." *Princeton Alumni Weekly* 28, no. 5 (28 October 1927): 129.

Patrick, Herbert R. *The Ancient Canal Systems and Pueblos of the Salt River Valley, Arizona*. Phoenix Free Museum Bulletin No. 1. Phoenix, 1903.

Pendergast, David M. "Metal Artifacts in Prehispanic Mesoamerica." *American Antiquity* 27 (1962): 520–45.

Persons, Stow. *The Decline of American Gentility*. New York: Columbia University Press, 1973.

Peschel, Oskar Ferdinand. *The Races of Man, and Their Geographical Distribution*. 1874. Reprint. New York: Appleton & Co., 1900.

Pinart, Alphonse. *Journey to Arizona in 1876*. Los Angeles: Zamorano Club, 1962.

Pomeroy, Earl. *In Search of the Golden West: The Tourist in Western America*. Lincoln: University of Nebraska Press, 1957.

Poor, Robert M. "Washington Matthews: An Intellectual Biography." Master's thesis, University of Nevada, Reno, 1975.

Porter, Joseph C. *Paper Medicine Man: John Gregory Bourke and His American West*. Norman: University of Oklahoma Press, 1986.

Powell, John Wesley. "The Ancient Province of Tusayan." *Scribner's Monthly* 11 (December 1875): 193–213.

———. *The Hopi Villages: The Ancient Province of Tusayan*. 1875. Reprint. Palmer Lake, Colo.: Filter Press, 1972.

———. *Introduction to the Study of Indian Languages with Words, Phrases and Sentences to be Collected*. Washington, D.C.: GPO, 1877.

———. "On Limitations to the Use of Some Anthropologic Data." In *First Annual Report of the Bureau of Ethnology for 1879–80,* 71–86. Washington, D.C.: GPO, 1881.

———. "Sketch of the Mythology of the North American Indians." In *First Annual Report of the Bureau of Ethnology for 1879–80,* 17–56. Washington, D.C.: GPO, 1881.

Powell, Lawrence Clark. "Sky, Sun, and Water: The Southwest of Frederick Webb Hodge." *Southwest Review* 39 (1954): 157–65.

Pratt, Mary Louise. *Imperial Eyes: Travel Writing and Transculturation*. London and New York: Routledge, 1992.

Prudden, T. Mitchell. *On the Great American Plateau: Wanderings among Canyons and Buttes, in the Land of the Cliff-Dweller, and the Indian of Today*. New York: G. P. Putnam's Sons, 1906.

Radin, Paul. *The Unpublished Letters of Adolphe F. Bandelier*. El Paso, Tex.: Carl Hertzog, 1942.

Raffel, Burton. *Politicians, Poets and Con Men*. Hamden, Conn.: Archon Books, 1986.

Reynolds, David S. *Walt Whitman's America: A Cultural Biography*. New York: Alfred A. Knopf, 1995.

Reps, John W. *The Making of Urban America: A History of City Planning in the United States*. Princeton, N.J.: Princeton University Press, 1965.

Rivinus, Edward F., and Elizabeth M. Youssef. *Spencer Baird of the Smithsonian*. Washington, D.C.: Smithsonian Institution Press, 1992.

Robinson, Ronald E. Introduction to *Railway Imperialism,* edited by Clarence B. Davis and Kenneth E. Wilburn, Jr., 1–6. New York: Greenwood Press, 1991.

Rodack, Madeline Turrell. "Cibola Revisited." In *Southwestern Culture History: Collected Papers in Honor of Albert H. Schroeder,* edited by Charles H. Lange, 163–82. Papers of the Archaeological Society of New Mexico No. 10. Santa Fe, 1985.

Rotundo, Anthony. *American Manhood: Transformations in Masculinity from the Revolution to the Modern Era*. New York: Basic Books, 1993.

Schivelbusch, Wolfgang. *The Railway Journey: The Industrialization of Time and*

Space in the Nineteenth Century. Berkeley: University of California Press, 1986.

Schlereth, Thomas J. *Victorian America: Transformations in Everyday Life, 1876–1915*. New York: Harper Collins, 1991.

Schultz, Stanley, and Clay McShane. "To Engineer the Metropolis: Sewers, Sanitation, and City Planning in Late Nineteenth Century America." *Journal of American History* 65 (December 1978): 389–411.

Shi, David. *The Simple Life: Plain Living and High Thinking in American Culture*. New York: Oxford University Press, 1985.

Silverberg, Robert. *Mound Builders of Ancient America: The Archaeology of a Myth*. Greenwich, Conn.: New York Graphic Society, 1968.

Slaughter, Sheila, and Edward T. Silva. "Looking Backwards: How Foundations Formulated Ideology in the Progressive Period." In *Philanthropy and Cultural Imperialism: The Foundations at Home and Abroad,* edited by Robert F. Arnove, 55–86. Boston: G. K. Hall, 1980.

Solliday, Scott W. "The Journey to Rio Salado: Hispanic Migrations to Tempe, Arizona." Master's thesis, Arizona State University, 1993.

Spicer, Edward H. *Cycles of Conquest: The Impact of Spain, Mexico, and the United States on Indians of the Southwest, 1533–1960*. Tucson: University of Arizona Press, 1962.

Spinden, Herbert J. "Fine Art and the First Americans." In *Introduction to American Indian Art*. New York: Exposition of Indian Tribal Arts, 1931.

Sprague, Roderick, and Aldo Signori. "Inventory of Prehistoric Copper Bells." *Kiva* 28, no. 4 (1963): 1–20.

Starr, Roger. "The Motive behind Olmsted's Park." *Public Interest* 74 (1974): 66–69.

Stegner, Wallace. "Thoughts in a Dry Land." In *Where the Bluebird Sings to the Lemonade Springs: Living and Writing in the West*. New York: Random House, 1992.

Stevenson, Louise. *The Victorian Homefront: American Thought and Culture, 1860–1880*. New York: Twayne Publishers, 1991.

Stocking, George W. "The Ethnographic Sensibility of the 1920s and the Dualism of the Anthropological Tradition." In *History of Anthropology,* edited by George W. Stocking, 6:208–76. Madison: University of Wisconsin Press, 1989.

———. "Ideas and Institutions in American Anthropology: Thoughts toward a History of the Interwar Years." In *Selected Papers from the* American Anthropologist, *1921–1945,* edited by George W. Stocking, 1–53. Washington, D.C.: American Anthropological Association, 1976.

Stoddard, John L. *Lectures*. Volume 10: *Southern California, the Grand Cañon, and Yellowstone Park*. Boston: Balch Brothers, 1903.

Sutton, C. B. "Frederick Law Olmsted, 1822–1903." In *Civilizing American Cities,* edited by C. B. Sutton, 1–20. Cambridge, Mass.: MIT Press, 1971.

Swentzell, Rina. "Levels of Truth: Southwest Archaeologists and Anasazi/Pueblo People." In *Pueblo Past and Present: Papers in Honor of Stewart Peckham,* edited by Meliha S. Duran and David T. Kirkpatrick, 177–81. Albuquerque: Archaeological Society of New Mexico, 1991.

Taylor, Walter W. "Southwestern Archaeology: Its History and Theory." *American Anthropologist* 56 (1954): 561–75.

Tedlock, Dennis, trans. *Finding the Center: Narrative Poetry of the Zuni Indians*. New York: Dial Press, 1972.

———. "Zuni Religion and World View." In *Handbook of North American Indians,* vol. 9: *Southwest,* edited by Alfonso Ortiz, 499–508. Washington, D.C.: Smithsonian Institution Press, 1979.

Ten Kate, Herman F. C. *Over Land en Zee: Schetsen en Stemmingen van een Wereldreiziger*. Zutphen, Netherlands, 1925.

Thomas, John L. "Utopia for an Urban Age: Henry George, Henry Demarest Lloyd, Edward Bellamy." *Perspectives in American History* 6 (1972): 135–63.

Thompson, Lawrance. *Robert Frost: The Early Years*. New York: Holt, Rinehart and Winston, 1970.

Townshend, Richard B. *Last Memories of a Tenderfoot*. London: Bodley Head, 1926.

Traubel, Horace. *With Walt Whitman in Camden*. 3 vols. 1905–6. Reprint. New York: Rowman and Littlefield, 1961.

Turney, Omar. *Prehistoric Irrigation in Arizona*. Phoenix: Arizona Historian, 1929.

Wade, Edwin L., and Lea S. McChesney. *America's Great Lost Expedition: The Thomas Keam Collection of Hopi Pottery from the Second Hemenway Expedition, 1890–1894*. Phoenix: Heard Museum, 1980.

Wallace, Henry D., and James P. Holmlund. *Petroglyphs of the Picacho Mountains, South Central Arizona*. Institute for American Research Anthropological Papers No. 6. Tucson, 1986.

Wallace, Susan. "Among the Pueblos." *Harper's New Monthly Magazine* 46 (1880): 215–25.

Warner, Sam Bass. *Streetcar Suburbs: The Process of Growth in Boston, 1870–1900.* Cambridge, Mass.: Harvard University Press, 1962.

Wayman, Dorothy G. *Edward Sylvester Morse: A Biography*. Cambridge, Mass.: Harvard University Press, 1942.

White, G. Edward. *The Eastern Establishment and the Western Experience: The West of Frederic Remington, Theodore Roosevelt, and Owen Wister*. New Haven, Conn.: Yale University Press, 1968.

Whitman, Walt. *Walt Whitman: Notebooks and Unpublished Prose Manuscripts*. 6 vols. Edited by Edward F. Grier. New York: NYU Press, 1984.

———. *Walt Whitman: The Correspondence*. Edited by Edwin Haviland Miller. Vol. 4: *1886–1889*. New York: NYU Press, 1969.

Wilcox, David R. *Frank Midvale's Investigations of the Site of La Ciudad*. Arizona State University Anthropological Field Studies No. 19. Tempe, 1987.

———. "Hohokam Social Complexity." In *Chaco & Hohokam: Prehistoric Regional Systems in the American Southwest,* edited by Patricia L. Crown and W. James Judge, 253–76. Santa Fe: School of American Research, 1991.

———. "Pueblo Grande in the Nineteenth Century." In *Archaeology of the Pueblo Grande Platform Mound and Surrounding Features,* vol. 1: *Introduction to the Archival Project and History of Research,* edited by Christian E. Downum and Todd W. Bostwick, 43–72. Pueblo Grande Museum Anthropological Papers No. 1. Phoenix, 1993.

Wilcox, David R., and Jerry B. Howard. "The Contribution of the Hemenway Expedition to Hohokam Archaeology." Paper presented at the 87th Annual Meeting of the American Anthropological Association, 1988.

Wilcox, David R., Jerry B. Howard, and Rueben Nelson. *One Hundred Years of Archaeology at La Ciudad de los Hornos*. Soil Systems Publications in Archaeology No. 16. Phoenix: Soil Systems, 1990.

Wilcox, David R., and Lynette O. Shenk. *The Architecture of the Casa Grande and Its Interpretation*. Arizona State Museum Archaeological Series No. 115. Tucson: University of Arizona, 1977.

Wilcox, David R., and Charles Sternberg. *Additional Studies of the Architecture of the Casa Grande and Its Interpretation*. Arizona State Museum Archaeological Series No. 146. Tucson: University of Arizona, 1981.

———. *Hohokam Ballcourts and Their Interpretation*. Arizona State Museum Archaeological Series No. 160. Tucson: University of Arizona, 1983.

Wilhelm, Thomas, comp. *Wilhelm's Military Dictionary and Gazetteer*. Rev. ed. Philadelphia: L. R. Hamersley & Co., 1881.

Wills, Gary. *Lincoln at Gettysburg: The Words That Remade America*. New York: Simon & Schuster, 1992.

Wilson, William H. *The City Beautiful Movement*. Baltimore: Johns Hopkins University Press, 1989.

Winslow, H. M. *Literary Boston of Today*. Boston: L. C. Page & Co., 1902.

Wortman, Jacob. "The Hyoid Bone." *Memoirs of the National Academy of Sciences* 7 (1893): 203–11.

Wortman, Jacob, and Herman F. C. ten Kate. "On an Anatomical Characteristic of the Hyoid Bone of the Pre-Columbian Pueblo Indians of Arizona." *Compte-rendu du Quatrième Congrés des Américanistes,* 263–70. Berlin: W. H. Kühl, 1890.

Zaitzevsky, Cynthia. *Frederick Law Olmsted and the Boston Park System*. Cambridge, Mass.: Harvard University Press, 1982.

Figure Credits

From Frank Hamilton Cushing, "My Adventures in Zuñi, I," *Century Magazine* 25 (December 1882): 191–207.

General view of Zuni (Willard L. Metcalf, 1882, p. 193)
Indian water-carriers (Willard L. Metcalf, 1881, p. 194)
Returning from the field (Willard L. Metcalf, 1882, p. 196)

From Frank Hamilton Cushing, "My Adventures in Zuñi, II," *Century Magazine* 25 (February 1883): 500–511.

A bivouac in the valley of the pines (Willard L. Metcalf, 1882; p. 511)

From Sylvester Baxter, "An Aboriginal Pilgrimage." *Century Magazine* 24, n.s. 2 (August 1882): 526–36.

Portrait and autograph of Pa-lo-wah-ti-wa (p. 534)
Portrait and autograph of Nai-iu-tchi (p. 529)
The reception at Wellesley College (p. 533)
Zuñi autograph of F. H. Cushing (p. 528)
National seal of the Zuñis (p. 536)

From Frederick A. Ober, "How a White Man Became War Chief of the Zuñis." *Wide Awake* 14 (June 1882): 382–88.

At the "Ocean of Sunrise" (Artist unknown; p. 388)

From Sylvester Baxter, "The Father of the Pueblos." *Harper's New Monthly Magazine* 65 (June 1882): 72–91.

Frank H. Cushing (p. 74)
Portal and plume of the Goddess of Salt (p. 78)
Tá-ai-tä-lo-ne, or Thunder Mountain (p. 80)
Making pottery (p. 83)
A Zuñi chief (p. 85)
The herald (p. 86)
Around the council fire (p. 72)
Chief on horseback (p. 87)
Baking Hé-per-lo-ki on the house-tops (p. 89)

From Sylvester Baxter, *The Old New World: An Account of the Explorations of the Hemenway Southwestern Archaeological Expedition in 1887–88, under the Direction of Frank Hamilton Cushing*. Salem, Mass: Salem Press. Reprinted from the *Boston Herald,* April 15, 1888.

A double burial; male and female (p. 17)
Excavated cemetery at base of pyral mound (p. 18)
Skeleton of man crushed by wall probably overthrown by earthquake (p. 25)
Skeleton of maiden sacrificed to prevent earthquakes (p. 31)
Examples of decorated pottery excavated at Los Muertos (p. 1)
Excavated house-ruins (p. 33)

From the *Daily News* (Denver), April 1906.

Edgar Lee Hewett tells the story of the cliffdwellers, 1906

From Frank Hamilton Cushing, "Zuñi Breadstuff," *The Millstone: An Illustrated Monthly Journal, Devoted to the Advancement of Milling and Mechanical Interests* 9–10 (January 1884–July 1885); reprinted in *Zuñi Breadstuff,* Indian Notes and Monographs, vol. 8, edited by F. W. Hodge (New York: Museum of the American Indian, Heye Foundation, 1920).

Zuñi women at the mealing-trough (Margaret Magill, 1883–84; p. 391)

Index

About the Editors

CURTIS M. HINSLEY is a professor of history at Northern Arizona University. He has written widely on American cultural history and the history of anthropology and archaeology. Among his most recent publications are *A Matter of Vision: A Century of Science in Flagstaff, 1894–1994* and *The Smithsonian and the American Indian: Making a Moral Anthropology in Victorian America*. He lives in Flagstaff, Arizona, with his wife, historian Victoria L. Enders.

DAVID R. WILCOX is senior research archaeologist and special assistant to the deputy director at the Museum of Northern Arizona. He has written numerous monographs and articles on many aspects of southwestern archaeology and its history. Books and monographs he has co-edited, written, or co-written include *The Mesoamerican Ballgame* (University of Arizona Press, 1991), *The Architecture of the Casa Grande and Its Interpretation, Frank Midvale's Investigation of the Site of La Ciudad, One Hundred Years of Archaeology at La Ciudad de los Hornos,* and *The Protohistoric Period in the North American Southwest, A.D. 1450–1700*. He lives in Flagstaff, Arizona, with his wife, historical museum curator Susan L. Wilcox.

Baxter, Sylvester, 1850–1927.

The Southwest in the American imagination : the writings of Sylvester Baxter, 1881–1889 / edited by Curtis M. Hinsley and David R. Wilcox.

p. cm.—(Frank Hamilton Cushing and the Hemenway Southwestern Archaeological Expedition, 1886–1889 ; v. 1) (The Southwest Center series)

Includes bibliographical references and index.

ISBN 0-8165-1533-6 (cloth).–ISBN 0-8165-1618-9 (paper)

1. Indians of North America—Southwest, New. 2. Cushing, Frank Hamilton, 1857–1900. 3. Zuni Indians. 4. Southwest, New—Description and travel. 5. Hemenway Southwestern Archaeological Expedition (1886–1894) I. Hinsley, Curtis M. II. Wilcox, David R., 1944– . III. Title. IV. Series. V. Series: The Southwest Center series.

E78.S7F725 1996 vol. 1

979'.00497—dc20 95-41818